The Muvipix.com Guide to
# Adobe
# Premiere Elements 10
(Color version)
Steve Grisetti

The tools, and how to use them, to make movies
on your personal computer using the best-selling
video editing software program.

## Dedication

I continually look to my friends and colleagues at Muvipix.com for inspiration, challenge and, more often than not, help. To you, dear friends, I dedicate this book.

Thank you, Jeanne, for once again giving me the time, support and occasional neck massages that enabled me to complete this major project

Thank you, dear daughter Sarah, for blessing my heart by finding the inspiration in my work to take your own video work to the next level.

And thank you, Danielle, for jumping on board and helping me refine my text and chase down those stubborn typos.

And a special thanks to my Muvipix.com co-founders, Ron and Chuck, whose friendship and support for over half a decade have meant more to me than they can know.

## About Muvipix.com

Muvipix.com was created to offer support and community to amateur and semi-professional videomakers. Registration is free, and that gets you access to the world's friendliest, most helpful forum and lots of ad-free space for displaying your work. On the products page, you'll find dozens of free tips, tutorials, motion backgrounds, DVD templates, sound effects, royalty-free music and stock video clips. For a small annual subscription fee that we use to keep the site running, you'll have unlimited downloads
from the ever-growing library of support materials and media.

We invite you to drop by and visit our thriving community. It costs absolutely nothing – and we'd love to have you join the neighborhood!

http://Muvipix.com

## About the author

Steve Grisetti holds a master's degree in Telecommunications from Ohio University and spent several years working in the motion picture and television industry in Los Angeles. A veteran user of several video editing programs and systems, Steve is the co-founder of Muvipix.com, a help and support site for amateur and semi-professional videomakers. A professional graphic designer and video freelancer, he has taught classes in Photoshop and lectured on design. He lives in suburban Milwaukee.

## Other books by Steve Grisetti

*Adobe Premiere Elements 2.0 In a Snap* (with Chuck Engels)
*The Muvipix.com Guides to Adobe Premiere Elements 7, 8 and 9*
*The Muvipix.com Guides to Photoshop Elements & Premiere Elements*
  *versions 7, 8 , 9 and 10*
*Cool Tricks & Hot Tips for Adobe Premiere Elements*
*The Muvipix.com Guide to DVD Architect Studio 5*
*The Muvipix.com Guides to Vegas Movie Studio HD 10 and 11*

# An Introduction

Adobe continues to focus on improving performance as well as adding new features in Premiere Elements 10. Particularly when working with AVCHD and high-definition video, you should see significant improvements and much smoother operation.

Project files open more quickly, media files load more efficiently and timeline performance overall is much snappier.

And, in perhaps it's biggest development, Adobe has even released a version of the program that runs on Windows 7 64-bit, taking greater advantage of the more efficient 64-bit architecture and increased ability to store data in your RAM, as well as a version for Mac OSX Lion.

Additionally, you'll find a couple of terrific new features.

The new Pan and Crop tool, for instance, makes creating motion paths over your photos and video easier and more intuitive than ever.

New, professional-style color correction tools add pro-level power to this increasingly powerful consumer-level program.

And new Share tools add the option to output AVC video as both a file format and a disc burning option to the program.

Adobe has also cleaned up the interface – removing at long last the confusing Organize panel, and replacing it with a Media panel that displays only the media that is actually in your Premiere Elements project.

We discuss these new features in detail in Chapter 1. And, of course, we show you step-by-step how to use them throughout the book.

In all, the program is feature-packed, but efficient and snappy. Whether you're running Premiere Elements 10 on a Mac or a PC, on a 32-bit system or on Windows 7 64-bit, you should see a program that runs better than it has in several generations and provides a relatively easty-to-use video editing environment no matter what level of editing skills you bring to it.

**Muvipix.com** was created in 2006 as a community and a learning center for videomakers at a variety of levels. Our community includes everyone from amateurs and hobbyists to semi-pros, professionals and even people with broadcast experience. You won't find more knowledgeable, helpful people anywhere else on the Web. I very much encourage you to drop by our forums and say hello. At the very least, you'll make some new friends. And it's rare that there's a question posted there that isn't quickly, and enthusiastically, answered.

Our learning center consists of video tutorials, tips and, of course, books. But we also offer a wealth of support in the form of custom-created DVD and BluRay disc menus, motion background videos, licensed music and even stock footage. Much of it is absolutely free – and there's even more available for those who purchase one of our affordable site subscriptions.

Our goal has always been to help people get up to speed making great videos and, once they're there, provide them with the inspiration and means to get better and better at doing so.

Why? Because we know making movies is a heck of a lot of fun – and we want to share that fun with everyone!

Our books, then, are a manifestation of that goal. And my hope for you is that this book helps *you* get up to speed. I think you'll find, once you get over the surprisingly small learning curve, making movies on your home computer is a lot more fun than you ever imagined! And you may even amaze yourself with the results in the process.

Thanks for supporting Muvipix.com, and happy moviemaking!

Steve
http://Muvipix.com

# What do you want to do?

**Table of Contents**

# Table of Contents

**Chapter 17**

## Create Disc Menus ..................................... 195

*Authoring your DVDs and BluRay discs*

**Chapter 18**

## Share Your Movie ................................... 205

*Outputting from Premiere Elements 10*

**Table of Contents**

**Get to Know the Workspace**

**Basic Editing Moves**

**What's New in Version 10?**

Chapter 1

# Get to Know Premiere Elements 10

## What's what and what it does

The interface for Premiere Elements has been designed by Adobe to be as simple and as intuitive as possible. It is also remarkably customizable, with a wealth of powerful tools in obvious and, once in a while, not so obvious places.

There are few major changes to the interface since the last edition of the program. But you'll quickly find that Premiere Elements has been designed to be as simple and as intuitive as possible to use – and yet easily customizable.

The Monitor Panel

Docking
Headers

The multi-purpose
Tasks panel

The Sceneline

The Timeline

## Panels and tabs

There are three major panels that are visible by default when you open your Premiere Elements project. They are the **Monitor** panel, the **My Project** panel (aka the **Timeline/Sceneline**) and the **Tasks** panel.

We'll discuss each of these in greater detail as we explore the program's tools in upcoming chapters – and we'll recommend a few other panels (many available under the **Window** drop-down menu and some launched from buttons on other panels).

### The Monitor panel

As illustrated at the top of the facing page, the **Monitor** panel displays the video that you've assembled on your timeline or sceneline. The buttons along the bottom of the **Monitor** control your timeline's playback, while the tools in the lower right can be used for splitting clips, creating titles and grabbing a **Freeze Frame** from your video. We discuss the **Monitor** panel and these tools in detail in **Chapter 8, Edit with Monitor Panel Tools**.

### The Multi-Function Tasks Panel

The Premiere Elements **Tasks** panel is your multi-function access point for the vast majority of Premiere Elements' workspaces and tools.

The Monitor panel includes a toolbar for the playback of your video on the timeline and sceneline, access to the Titles workspace and some valuable editing functions.

Adobe has tried to make getting to each of the **Tasks** panel's workspaces and tools as intuitive as possible by making the paths to them task-oriented.

To gather your media, for instance, you click on the **Project** tab and select **Get Media**. Your video editing tools are accessible under the **Edit** tab. You select and customize your DVD and BluRay disc menus under the **Disc Menus** tab and you output to various media or devices by way of the **Share** tab.

Workspaces in the multi-purpose Tasks panel are accessed by following intuitive, task-oriented tabs and buttons.

Timeline editing mode

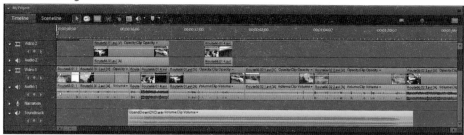

Sceneline editing mode

The 'My Project Panel' (or, as we call it, the Timeline/Sceneline Panel)

### The Timeline/Sceneline "My Project" Panel

The **My Project** panel (which, most of the time, we'll refer to as the **Timeline** or the **Sceneline panel**) is where the actual assembly of your movies will take place.

In **Sceneline** mode, you can quickly and easily assemble your movie's clips and add audio, effects and transitions between them. The focus here is on content more than how the elements in your video interact. Most veteran editors consider **Sceneline** the more elementary workspace for creating videos.

In **Timeline** mode, the emphasis is on time – not just what elements are included in your movie, but how and when they interact with each other. This mode is the much more traditional video editing workspace, giving you much greater access to Premiere Elements' true power.

In **Timeline** mode, you have a virtually unlimited number of audio and video tracks (officially up to 99 of each) as well as the ability to control effects, audio volume and the positions of your clips (such as titles) that may appear on top of or share screen space with your main video clips.

In short, if you have any interest at all in doing any *really cool* video editing, **Timeline** mode is where you'll likely spend most of your time.

In **Chapter 5**, we'll show you how to work in **Sceneline** mode. In **Chapter 6**, we'll show you how to assemble your movie in **Timeline** mode. And, in **Chapter 7**, we'll show you how to work with your timeline's audio tracks.

## Show Docking Headers

At Muvipix.com, we recommend that, as soon as you start up the program, you select the option to **Show Docking Headers**. This option is available under the **Window** drop-down on the Menu Bar.

These **Docking Headers** (gray bars along the tops of each panel that display the panel's name) serve a couple important functions.

The primary function of these headers is to allow you to "undock" the various panels in the interface. In other words, if you want to spread out your workspace or change their arrangement in the interface, you can do so by dragging a panel around your desktop by its **Docking Header**. This separates the panel from the rest of the interface so that you can place it anywhere you'd like on your computer's desktop.

The >> menus offer quick access to tools and features

This is particularly useful if you're using a very large monitor or even a two-monitor computer system. Spreading these panels out makes it much easier to see and to get to all of the tools on each.

But there's another reason for revealing the **Docking Headers**.

Do you see the black **>>** buttons in the upper right of many of the panels (as illustrated above)? These buttons open pop-up menus that allow you to turn off or on a number of very important features and functions for that particular work panel. In some cases, they also give you easy access to some great tools!

But, unless you **Show Docking Headers,** you won't even *see* these buttons on many of the panels! (In fact, until you reveal the **Docking Headers**, you won't even be able to see the *names* of the panels!)

So, whether you intend to undock your panels from the rest of the interface or not, activate the **Show Docking Headers** feature. You might well need access to what's otherwise hidden with them**.**

## Customize your workspace

The sizes and the arrangements of the various panels in the interface are easily customizable. Panels can be resized by dragging on the seams between them. They can also be "undocked" from the interface and moved to more convenient or efficient areas on your desktop.

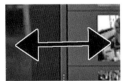

To resize your panels, hover your mouse over the seams between the panels until you see the double arrows – then click and drag.

Feel free to experiment and resize the panels by dragging on the borders between them. Or, if you've got a large computer monitor or, even better, a dual-monitor set-up, and you've activated **Show Docking Headers** (above) undock the panels by dragging them by their headers and position them to best take advantage of your computer's desktop.

As you move your panels around, you'll note that there is one panel you can not undock from the program's interface. The **Tasks** panel (the multi-purpose panel that houses most of the program's functions) is locked to the interface.

But, other than that, particularly if you've got lots of computer desktop space, you'll likely very much appreciate how much more accessible all of the program's tools are if you spread things out as much as possible.

And, if you ever do find the program misbehaving or if you just feel like you've lost control of your workspace, you can easily get back to the default look by simply going to the **Window** drop-down menu and selecting **Restore Workspace**.

### Minimum screen resolution

Because of the size of the panels and the number of tools that Adobe fits into some rather tight spaces, we recommend that this program not be used on a computer with a monitor with less than 1280x1024 resolution.

There's simply no room for it all to fit otherwise! And you'll waste far too much time scrolling panels around, trying to get to all the tools. (The **Monitor** panel alone, for instance, demands at least 665 pixels across in order to display its entire playback and tool set – and even on a 1024x768 monitor, that doesn't leave much horizontal space for the all-important **Tasks** panel!)

## What's a CTI?

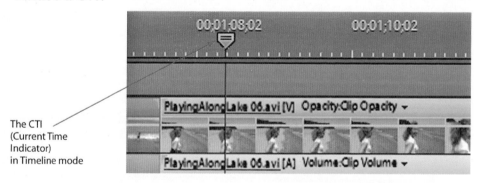

The CTI
(Current Time
Indicator)
in Timeline mode

Vital vocabulary alert! That thin, vertical, red line that moves along the Timeline as you play your video? It's called a **CTI**, which stands for "Current Time Indicator."

That's an all-important vocabulary term that you'll definitely want to know as we continue to work

Trust us on this. Especially since there's no other word that comes close to describing this thing – and we're going to use the term often throughout this book.

## Basic editing moves

No matter what you plan to do with your video and no matter how creatively you plan to do it, the video editing process itself will still fit the same basic structure.

Here's a brief review of the steps you'll take for creating any video project in Premiere Elements.

### Starting a new project in Premiere Elements 10

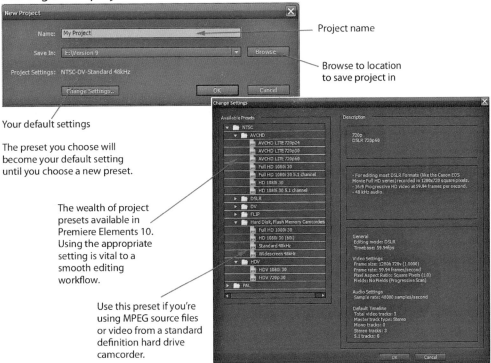

Project name

Browse to location to save project in

Your default settings

The preset you choose will become your default setting until you choose a new preset.

The wealth of project presets available in Premiere Elements 10. Using the appropriate setting is vital to a smooth editing workflow.

Use this preset if you're using MPEG source files or video from a standard definition hard drive camcorder.

## 1 Start a project

When you select the option to begin a new project, the current project settings will be listed on the lower left of the **New Project** panel. If you'd like to change them, click on **Change Settings** and select the appropriate settings from the list of presets.

Unlike a Word document, a Premiere Elements project must be *defined* as well as created. And the option to select the settings for your project is only available when you *first begin your project*. You can't change your project's settings midway through.

Which settings you choose should be based on what format of video you're going to be building your project from – and you may well use the same settings for all of your video projects.

But selecting the correct project settings now can very likely save you a lot of frustration later in your project.

In **Chapter 2**, **Start a New Project**, we'll show you how to ensure your project is using the right project preset.

Get Media options, under the Project tab

The DV, HDV and Webcam or WDM (Webcam) Device options launch the Capture workspace.

The DVD/DVD Camcorder and the Flip, AVHCD Cameras and Phones options launch the Video Importer, while the Digital Still Camera & Phones option launches the Photo Downloader.

The PC Files and Folders and Elements Organizer options allow you to browse to files on your computer.

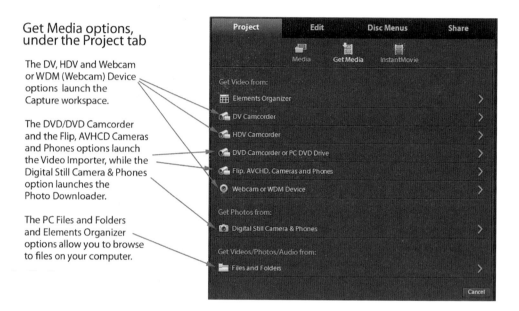

## 2 Gather your media

The assets, or media, you gather to create your movie can come from a variety of sources. It can be video, audio, music, photos or graphics. And, as you gather, or import, your assets into your project, they will appear in the media panel. This panel is accessed by clicking the **Media** button under the **Project** tab.

To import your media into your project, click on the **Get Media** button under the **Project** tab and then click the button representing your video's source device or location.

There are three ways to get your media into your project, all accessed by one of the seven buttons on the **Get Media** panel (illustrated above). We show you how and when to use each in **Chapter 3, Get Media Into Your Project**.

- **Stream, or capture, your video into your project.**

  The capture function works with tape-based camcorders, like miniDV (the **DV Camcorder** button) or HDV (the **HDV Camcorder** button), which are connected to your computer by a FireWire cable (aka IEEE-1394 or iLink). Video can also be streamed into the program using a DV bridge, like the ADS Pyro AV Link or Canopus ADVC units – although you will not be able to control the playback of these units from the capture screen.

Video captured from tape-based camcorders is streamed into your Premiere Elements project over a FireWire connection. The camcorder's playback is controlled by the software and you can select which segments to capture.

Video from non-tape-based sources – including hard drive camcorders, Flip and AVCHD camcorders and DVDs – is imported into your Premiere Elements project by the Video Importer, while still photos are downloaded from your digital camera or phone with the Photo Downloader.

Tape-based video, captured over FireWire, by the way, is by far the format that Premiere Elements works with most efficiently. Premiere Elements includes an option for streaming in and capturing video from a **Webcam or WDM Device**.

- **Download your video from a hard drive camcorder or other device.**

Hard drive camcorders, including high-definition AVCHD and Flip cam units (the **Flip, AVCHD, Cameras and Phones** button), download their video as files rather than stream it into the program. Media can also be downloaded from other sources, including DVDs (the **DVD Camcorder or PC DVD Drive** button) and **Digital Still Cameras & Phones**, although these files may need additional preparation or even conversion before they can be used effectively in Premiere Elements.

- **Browse to gather media files which are located on your computer's hard drive(s).**

When you select the **PC Files and Folders** button under **Get Media**, Windows Explorer or the Mac OSX Finder opens, allowing you to browse to video, stills, graphics or music files already on your computer's hard drive.

To add a clip to your timeline or sceneline, simply drag it from the Media panel.

In Timeline mode, the other clips will "ripple", moving aside if you add the clip in the middle of a project.

To override the ripple effect (as when you're adding music or a video clip to a parallel track) hold down the Ctrl key as you add the clip.

Zoom in or out on the timeline by pressing + or - or using the Zoom slider.

## 3 Assemble the clips on your timeline or sceneline

Once you've imported your media clips into a project, they will appear listed in the **Media** panel and you can begin the process of assembling your movie. This process is as simple, and as intuitive, as dragging the clips from the media panel to your timeline or sceneline and then arranging them in the order you'd like them to appear!

Once you add your files to your timeline or sceneline, you'll have a number of options:

- **Trim your clips.** Trimming means removing footage from either the beginning or the end of a clip. To trim a clip, click to select the clip on your timeline and then drag in either the beginning or end to shorten it, as in the illustration on the following page.

## Timeline mode is the more powerful editing workspace

Although there are some advantages to editing in **Sceneline** mode, the **Timeline** mode is by far the more powerful editing workspace, allowing you much more control over how your clips behave and, more so, how they interact with each other at specific points in your movie. We encourage you to make it your default editing workspace.

To slice a clip in two, click the Split (scissors) tool on the Monitor panel.

If a clip is selected on the timeline, only that clip will be split at the position of the CTI; If no clips are selected, all clips on every track on the timeline will be split at the position of the CTI.

◄**E** Trim from Beginning of clip          Trim from End of clip **E**►

To trim a clip on the timeline, hover your mouse over the beginning or end of a clip until the Trim from Beginning or Trim from End icon appears, then click and drag in or out.

- **Split your clips.** Splitting means slicing through your clips so that you can remove footage from the middle or delete one sliced-off segment completely. To split a clip, position the **CTI** (playhead) over your clip at the point at which you'd like the slice to occur and then click on the scissors icon at the lower right of the **Monitor** panel.

- **Place your clip on upper video or audio track**. An important feature of editing in **Timeline** mode is the ability to place your video or audio on tracks other than **Video 1** and **Audio 1**.

  The use of multiple tracks of video is, in fact, key to the creation of many of the more advanced video effects, including **Chroma Key** and **Videomerge.**

  We'll discuss how to assemble your movie on both the **Sceneline** and **Timeline** in **Chapter 5** and **Chapter 6**, respectively. We'll also show you how to use multi-track editing in order to create a a variety of effects and take advantage of a number of key storytelling techniques.

  In **Chapter 7,** we'll show you how to use both automatic and manual tools to work with your audio clips.

## 4 Add and adjust effects

Premiere Elements comes loaded with over a hundred video and audio effects as well as hundreds of preset effects for working magic on your movie. Most video and preset effects show you a thumbnail preview of the effect in action on the **Effects** panel.

Adding an effect in Premiere Elements is very easy, as we show you in **Chapter 11, Add Video and Audio Effects**.

## CHAPTER 1

There are several sets and categories of effects in Premiere Elements.

1  Click on the **Edit** tab and then click the **Effects** button.

   This will open the **Effects** screen in the **My Tasks** panel.

2  Select an **Effects** set.

   The **Effects** panel displays **Video Effects** by default. But, by selecting the drop-down menu on the upper left of the panel, you can set it to display **Audio Effects, Presets, Favorites** or even your custom-created **Presets**. If you've got a Plus account with Photoshop.com, there will be additional effects displayed under that option.

3  Select an effect.

   You can browse through the list of effects on the panel, select a category of effects from the second drop-down menu or quickly call up an effect by typing its name in the Quick Search box on the upper right of the panel.

4  Apply the effect.

   To apply the effect, either drag it from the **Effects** panel onto a clip on your timeline – or select the clip on the timeline, select the effect in the panel and click the **Apply** button.

5  Open the **Properties** panel.

   Although you may see an immediate change in your clip once you apply an effect to it, virtually all effects can benefit from some custom tuning in the **Properties** panel.

A clip's effects are adjusted and fine tuned in the Properties panel. The quickest way to access this panel is to right-click on the clip whose effects you want to adjust and select Show Properties.

There are four ways to open the **Properties** panel in Premiere Elements. And, because you may want to refer to them often, we've placed them in the box at the top of the facing page.

Throughout the book, I usually refer to the most efficient method for opening this panel: **right-clicking** on a clip on your timeline (**Ctrl-clicking** on a Mac) and selecting **Show Properties**.

Once the **Properties** panel is open, scroll down the list to locate the effect you've just added. Open up the effect's properties by clicking on the little triangle to the left of the effect's listing.

12

## Four ways to open the Properties panel

1 Click on the **Edit Effect** button on the **Effects** panel;

2 **Right-click** on the clip (**Ctrl-click** on a Mac) and select **Show Properties**;

3 Click on the **Properties** button on the top left of the **Timeline** or **Sceneline**; or

4 Select **Properties** from the **Window** drop-down on the program's Menu Bar

6   Adjust the effect's settings.

Settings for various effects can be changed numerically, by (depending on the effect) moving sliders, sampling colors or selecting presets from down menus. You should be able to see the change your new settings are making to your clip in the **Monitor** panel.

The **Properties** panel is a tremendously powerful workspace. Not only can you use it to change the settings for individual effects, but it is the main workspace for creating and adjusting **keyframes**, Premiere Elements' tool for creating animations, motion paths and effects that change over the course of the clip's playback.

This panel is probably second only to the **Timeline** itself as the most important workspace in the program.

In **Chapter 13**, we'll show you how to do basic effects adjustments in the **Properties** panel.

Then, in **Chapter 14**, we'll show you how to use the **Properties** panel to create effects and motion paths with keyframing.

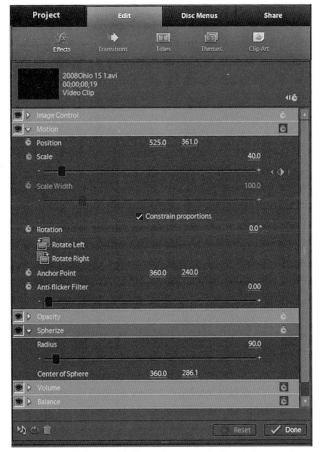

Effects that have been added to a clip appear in that clip's Properties panel, where they can be adusted and customized.

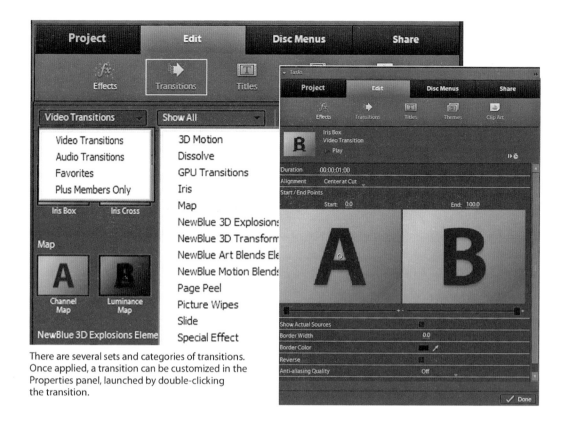

There are several sets and categories of transitions. Once applied, a transition can be customized in the Properties panel, launched by double-clicking the transition.

## 5 Add and adjust transitions

Transitions are the effects that take us from one clip to another. Some are gentle and nearly invisible – others are showy and draw attention to themselves. Most transitions are added to your timeline and adjusted similarly to effects:

**1** Click on the **Edit** tab and then click the **Transitions** button.

This will open the **Transitions** screen in the **My Tasks** panel.

**2** Select a **Transitions** set.

The **Transitions** panel displays **Video Transitions** by default. But, by selecting the drop-down menu on the upper left of the panel, you can set it to display **Audio Transitions**. If you've got a Plus account with Photoshop.com, there will be additional effects displayed under that option.

**3** Select a transition.

You can browse through the list of transitions on the panel, select a category of transitions from the second drop-down menu or quickly call an effect by typing its name in the **Quick Search** box on the upper right of the panel.

**4** Apply the transition.

Apply a transition by dragging it from the **Transitions** panel onto the intersection of two clips on your timeline or sceneline.

**5** Open the **Transition Properties** panel.

Transitions are customized in the **Transitions Properties** panel, illustrated on the facing page. To open this panel, double-click on a transition on your timeline or sceneline.

**6** Customize your transition.

Nearly all transitions include a number of properties that can be customized, depending on the nature of the transition. Virtually all include options for designating where the transition centers and the duration of the transition as well as an option for setting the transition to reverse its movement (i.e., wiping from right to left rather than left to right).

We'll show you just about everything there is to know about adding and customizing transitions – including why they sometimes seem to behave in very strange ways – in **Chapter 12**. And, as a bonus, we'll even show you how to use the **Gradient Wipe**, a tool for creating your own custom transition effects!

# 6 Add titles

Titles are text, and sometimes graphics, placed over your clips to provide additional visual information for your video story. In most cases, you'll create your titles in Premiere Elements' **Titles** workspace – a process that automatically places the title on an available video track on your timeline at the position of the **CTI** (playhead). To create a title:

**1** Open the **Titles** workspace.

The **Titles** workspace can be launched either by clicking the "**T**" icon on the lower right of the **Monitor** panel (which takes you directly to the main **Titles** workspace) or by clicking on the **Titles** button under the **Edit** tab (which takes you to the same **Titles** workspace, but by way of a panel offering optional title templates).

**2** Type your title over the placeholder "**Add text.**"

Additional text blocks can be created on the same title by clicking, with the text tool, on other locations on the **Titles Monitor** panel.

**3** Customize the text.

With your text selected, you can apply text attributes – including setting the font, size, style and alignment. You can also apply a style to your selected text by clicking on one of the **Text Styles** listed on the panel.

The Premiere Elements Titles workspace is launched by clicking on the "T" on the Monitor panel. It includes a number of tools for customizing your text and animating your titles.

**4** Apply a **Text Animation.**

By clicking on a **Text Animation** and then clicking the **Apply** button, you can apply an animation to your text. (Note that this feature only works on titles that are one line long. If your text runs more than one line, its **Text Animation** will not function.)

**5** Position the text and other elements.

By switching from the **Text Tool** to the **Move Tool** (by clicking on the arrow icon on the **Titles Toolbar**), your cursor will become an "arrow" tool for positioning text and other graphic elements you add to your title. Objects and text blocks on your title can be centered, both horizontally and vertically, by selecting these elements and then clicking on one of the two centering tools at the bottom of the **Titles Toolbar.**

**6** Exit the **Titles** workspace.

Once your title is finished, click on the **Done** button in the lower right corner of the **Titles** panel. The **Titles** workspace will close and you'll return to regular **Edit** mode. Your new title will appear as a clip on an upper video track at the position of your **CTI**, where it can be repositioned and customized like any other clip.

We'll show you how to create and customize your titles in **Chapter 10**.

## 7 Share your movie

When you're happy with the video project you've created, you'll find a number of options for outputting, or sharing it, as we discuss in **Chapter 18**.

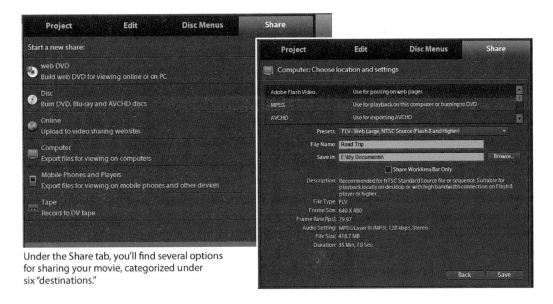

Under the Share tab, you'll find several options for sharing your movie, categorized under six "destinations."

- **Web DVD.** This option allows you to save your DVD files as Web site files that function just like an interactive DVD – complete with menus and scene link buttons – except that they can be posted online!

- **Disc.** Built into Premiere Elements are tools for creating menus and scene markers for creating DVD and BluRay disc projects.

- **Online.** The program comes complete with facilities for loading your finished video to your own personal Web site, YouTube, Facebook, Photoshop.com or podcast hosting site PodBean.

- **Computer.** The program will save your finished project as an AVI file, MPEG, Quicktime (MOV) file, AVCHD video, Windows Media (WMV) file and a Flash (FLV) file on your computer's hard drive. Once the output is complete, you can then share these files any number of ways, including posting them online or using them as segments in a larger video project.

- **Mobile Phone or Player.** You can output your movie to an iPod, iPhone, iPad, smartphone or virtually any other portable video player.

- **Tape.** Though this is rarely used anymore except as a means of archiving completed projects, the program will port your HDV or miniDV project back to your camcorder for storage on tape.

## And that's basically it!

You gather your assets; you assemble them on your timeline or sceneline; you add effects, transitions and titles; you share it with the world.

But between the lines of this simplicity are the countless variations that can elevate your movie project from the realm of a basic structure to something truly amazing!

## What's new in version 10?

Adobe continues to focus on improving performance as well as adding new features in Premiere Elements 10:

**Performance** with high-definition video – particularly AVCHD video – continues to improve. Timeline performance is also much snappier all around, and even timeline scrolling is much less likely to cause the program to lag.

The program also loads media clips into your project faster and opens and switches between projects more quickly and efficiently.

**Support for 64-bit operating systems.** In a very exciting move, Adobe has released not only separate Mac and PC versions of the program, but the PC version now comes in both 32-bit and 64-bit versions! Users of Windows 7 64-bit should see the most significant improvement in the program's performance as the program takes advantage of your computer's more advanced architecture.

### The Media panel now shows only the media in your project

The **Media** panel vs. **Project** panel confusion has finally been resolved!

In fact, the confusing and inefficient **Media/Organizer** panel has finally been *removed completely* from the multifunction **Tasks** panel. (Thank you, Adobe!) And, in the process, the old **Project** panel has been less ambiguously dubbed the **Media** panel.

Access to media in your **Organizer** catalog is now through the standalone **Elements Organizer** program (see **Chapter 15**) or by way of the **Elements Organizer** portal on the **Get Media** panel. (For more information on this feature, see **Chapter 3, Get Media into Your Project**.)

The **Media** panel now displays (rightfully) *only the video, stills and audio clips that have actually been added to your project.*

(The program also defaults to this panel whenever you add more media to your project.)

Additionally, the **Media** panel again has the option to display your media clips in either a list view or a large thumbnail/icon view.

The Media panel now displays only media clips that have been added to your project, and it can show these clips in either a list or icon view.

We'll talk more about this panel in **Chapter 4, Explore the Media Panel**.

## Pan and Zoom tool

A great new addition to version 10 is the **Pan and Zoom Tool**, a very intuitive workspace for creating Ken Burns-style pan and zoom motion paths across your photos and videos. We'll show you how to work this terrific new tool in **Chapter 6, Edit Your Video in Timeline Mode**.

## Advanced Color Correction Tools

Version 10 also includes two new, highly advanced tools for correcting and enhancing the color in your videos:

## AutoTone & Vibrance

The **AutoTone & Vibrance** tool automatically enriches the colors in your video, increasing contrasting, brightness, exposure and black and while levels. Each of these qualities can also be controlled manually, if you feel the need – although even the automatic settings do a very nice job of enriching your video's look. We'll show you how to use this very cool tool in **Chapter 11, Add Video and Audio Effects**.

The new new Pan and Zoom Tool makes creating motion paths much more intuitive.

The AutoTone & Vibrance effect automatically improves the brightness, contrast and white balance of your videos.

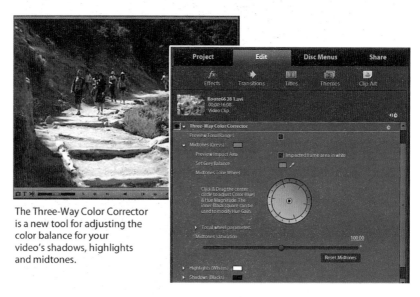

The Three-Way Color Corrector is a new tool for adjusting the color balance for your video's shadows, highlights and midtones.

## Three-Way Color Corrector

The new **Three-Way Color Corrector** is a professional-style tool for correcting the color in your shadows (blacks), highlights (whites) and midtones. Each tonal range includes a very intuitive color wheel tool for adjusting the hue, magnitude of color and color saturation. The tool makes it much easier to make precise color adjustments to your video. We'll show you how to use this tool in **Chapter 11, Add Video and Audio Effects**.

## AVCHD output

Finally, version 10 includes the option to output your video in true AVCHD format. This format can be used to output your video to disc (DVD or BluRay) or as a standalone AVC (Main Concept H.264) file.

This AVCHD output includes presets for outputting your video in standard television formats like 1440x1080, 1920x1080, 1280x720 and 720x480, both hi-def and standard Tivo® and also includes an online preset for outputting your video as an MP4 and for Vimeo and YouTube.

For more information on outputting your video, see **Chapter 18, Share Your Movie**.

Some of the new AVCHD output options in version 10.

**Starting a New Project**

**Opening an Existing Project**

**Using Project Presets**

Chapter 2

# Start a New Project
## Creating and opening your projects

When you first launch Premiere
Elements, you'll be greeted by the
"splash screen" – a Welcome Screen to
the program that serves as your starting
point for creating a new, or opening
your existing, video projects.

### Bypass the Welcome Screen

By default, when you launch Premiere Elements, the program will greet you with a **Welcome Screen**. (For more information on this screen, see page 22.)

In version 10 of Premiere Elements, however, you have the option of bypassing this **Welcome Screen** altogether and launching directly into either the Elements Organizer or a blank Premiere Elements project.

To select either of these alternate launch options, click on the purple launch configuration button in the upper right of the **Welcome Screen**.

In the panel that opens, select either the option to **Always Launch Elements Organizer Only** or **Always Launch Premiere Elements Only.**

21

Launch the Organizer    Start a new project    Open a previous project

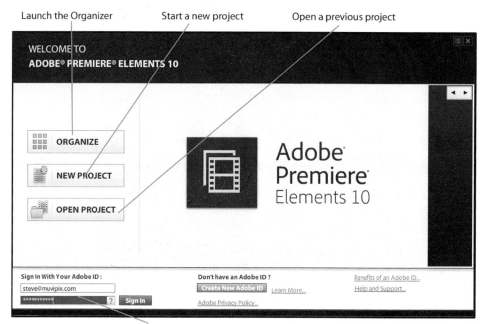

Registration and autologon to Photoshop.com, a site for displaying
photos and from which Premiere Elements accesses additional content.

## The Welcome Screen

When you first start up Premiere Elements, you'll be greeted by the
**Welcome Screen**. Very similar to the **Welcome Screen** in Photoshop
Elements, it is a launching point for the various workspaces for the
program.

From this **Welcome Screen** you can start a new Premiere Elements
project, open an old one or launch the Elements Organizer.

Additionally, this screen offers you the option of logging into (or creating
an account with) **Photoshop.com**, Adobe's online portal for a variety of
services and content.

Once you select the option to launch Premiere Elements or the Elements
Organizer, the **Welcome Screen** will close. You can re-open
the **Welcome Screen** at any time by clicking on the little house
icon that appears along the top of the Premiere Elements,
Photoshop Elements or Organizer workspace.

## Launch the Elements Organizer

The Elements Organizer is a powerful media file management program
that interfaces with both Premiere Elements and Photoshop Elements.

The Organizer allows you to catalog and search your media files based on
a wide variety of criteria. Additionally, the Organizer includes a number of
tools for creating and sharing your video and photo projects.

The Organizer reads the EXIF data off your digital photos, adds **Keyword Tags** (both manually and automatically) to your media clips, gives you the ability to sort your files into **Albums** and serves as a launching point for a number of Photoshop Elements and Premiere Elements functions.

We discuss its features and functions in more detail in **Chapter 15, The Elements Organizer.**

## Open a new project

Clicking the **New Project** button takes you to an option screen for setting up your Premiere Elements project.

The Elements Organizer is a separate file management and project tool that interfaces with both Premiere Elements and Photoshop Elements.

Part of creating a new project is selecting the project's settings. In most cases, these settings will be determined by the video format you are using as your movie's source.

It is very important that you choose the correct settings for your project. Doing so can save you a lot of frustration and heartache later!

It's also very important to note that these settings can only be selected when you *first create your project*. You will not be able to change them later! So determining and selecting the correct project settings at this point is a very critical step.

### Log on to Photoshop.com

Along the lower left of the Welcome Screen is a tool for logging on to **Photoshop.com**.

**Photoshop.com** is Adobe's free online photo-sharing and file back-up service. You can create an account right here, at this **Welcome Screen** or at the Web site.

Once you've signed on and created an account, you'll automatically be logged onto the site whenever you start one of the Elements programs.

**Photoshop.com** is a site on which you can share your photos and videos. Connecting to **Photoshop.com also** gives you access to the **Inspiration Browser**, a collection of tutorials and tips for Premiere Elements, Photoshop Elements and the Elements Organizer. You also get 2 megabytes of free space for backing up for your files. A **Plus membership** gets you additional storage space as well as access to additional movie themes and templates that are loaded automatically into your Premiere Elements program.

For more information on **Photoshop.com** and its services, see **Chapter 16, Photoshop.com.**

## Starting a new project in Premiere Elements 10

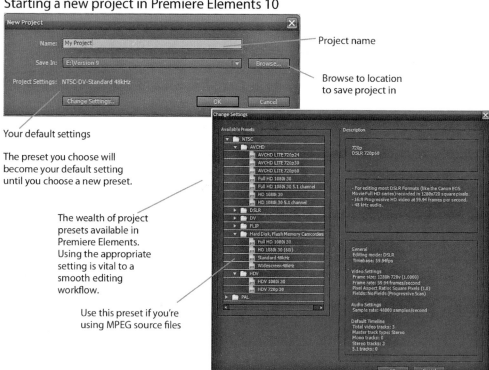

Project name

Browse to location
to save project in

Your default settings

The preset you choose will
become your default setting
until you choose a new preset.

The wealth of project
presets available in
Premiere Elements.
Using the appropriate
setting is vital to a
smooth editing
workflow.

Use this preset if you're
using MPEG source files

**1** Click the **New Project** button.

The **New Project** option screen will appear, as illustrated above.

Type the title for your new project in the box displayed at **Name**.

**2** Click the **Browse** button to choose a location to save your new
project file.

We at Muvipix recommend always selecting the **Browse** option
and, wherever you choose to save your file, *creating a new folder* for
every new project file.

This little bit of housekeeping keeps all of your new project's files in
one neat, little folder. And, when your project is done and you want
to clear it from your computer, you can then remove not only the
project file but all of the temp, render and scratch disk files Premiere
Elements has created for that project, simply by deleting that single
folder!

This makes post-project clean-up a much easier and neater process.

**3** Select your **Project Settings**.

**Project Settings**, at the bottom left of the **New Project** panel, will
display the last settings you used for a Premiere Elements project.

AVCHD Lite
camcorders

1920x1080 AVCHD

1440x1080 AVCHD

Digital SLR
camcorders
shooting 1080p

Digital SLR
camcorders
shooting 640x480

Digital SLR
camcorders
shooting 720p

MiniDV 4:3

MiniDV 16:9

Flip standard def
camcorders

Flip HD camcorders

Flash Memory
hi-def camcorders

DVD or Hard drive
standard DV 4:3

DVD or Hard drive
standard DV 16:9

HDV tape-based
video 1440x1080

HDV tape-based
video 1280x720

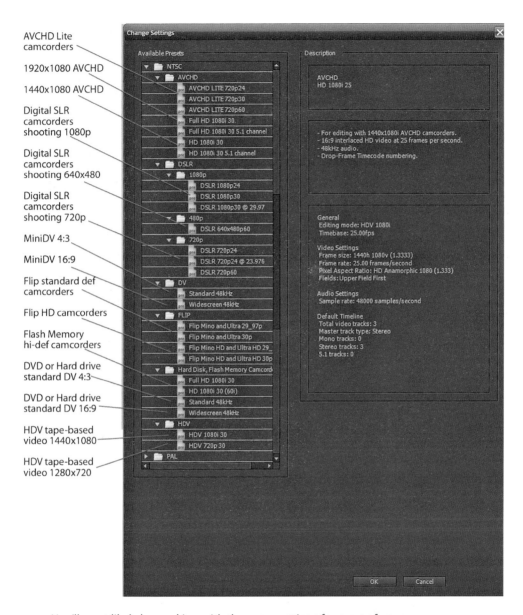

You'll most likely be working with the same settings for most of your
projects. But, if not, clicking the **Change Settings** button will display
a wealth of available project presets.

In addition to the option for switching from PAL to NTSC or vice
versa, this screen offers presets for a number of resolutions and
video formats. Each of these folders, in turn, can be opened to
reveal even more options, including the options for a widescreen
16:9 or standard 4:3 video frame and, in the case of high-definition
video settings, the HDV or AVCHD video format, vertical screen
resolution and audio channel format.

## Premiere Elements 10 project preset options

Below is an explanation of each of the presets available in Premiere Elements 10. The PAL and NTSC options are identical except that the frame rates for PAL presets are 25 fps rather than 30.

In addition to traditional video project settings, Premiere Elements includes support for both AVCHD Lite and video from DSLRs (digital still cameras). Many of these project settings are pretty precisely defined by their frame rates. For best results, fully check out your camera's specs and match your project's settings as closely as possible to the video that your camera records. (And note that some camcorders shoot in more than one format and resolution!)

For information on loading each of these formats into your Premiere Elements projects, see **Chapter 3, Get Media Into Your Project**.

| AVCHD | AVCHD Lite 720p24 | AVCHD video (1280x720) shooting at 23.976 progressive fps. |
|---|---|---|
| | AVCHD Lite 720p30 | AVCHD video (1280x720) shooting at 29.97 progressive fps. |
| | AVCHD Lite 720p60 | AVCHD video (1280x720) shooting at progressive 59.94 fps. |
| | Full HD 1080i 30 | AVCHD video (1920x1080 60i/30 fps square pixel, hard drive, high definition) from camcorders that shoot in stereo audio. |
| | Full HD 1080i 30 5.1 Channel | AVCHD video (1920x1080 60i/30 fps square pixel, hard drive, high-definition) from camcorders that shoot in 5.1 channel audio. *This is the most common format for most newer hard drive, high-definition camcorders.* |
| | HD 1080 30 | AVCHD video (1440x1080 60i/30 fps non-square pixel, hard drive, high definition) from camcorders that shoot in stereo audio. |
| | HD 1080 30 5.1 Channel | AVCHD video (1440x1080 60i/30 fps non-square pixel, hard drive, high-definition) from camcorders that shoot in 5.1 channel audio. This is the most common format for older hard drive, high-definition camcorders. *Note that, although this format uses less horizontal pixels, it produces the same high-quality, 16:9 image as 1920x1080 video. The pixels are just non-square, or wider than they are tall – as in the traditional television standard.* |
| **DSLR Presets** – Use these presets for working with high-quality video from digital still cameras (such as the Canon EOS Movie Full HD series). | | |
| 1080p | DSLR 1080p24 | 1920x1080 16:9 video shooting at 23.976 progressive fps. |
| | DSLR 1080p30 | 1920x1080 16:9 video shooting at 30 progressive fps. |
| | DSLR 1080p 30@29.97 | 1920x1080 16:9 video shooting at 29.97 progressive fps. |
| 480p | DSLR 640x480p 60 | 640x480 16:9 video shooting at 59.94 progressive fps. |
| 720p | DSLR 720p24 | 1280x720 16:9 video shooting at 24 progressive fps. |
| | DSLR 720p24 @23.976 | 1280x720 16:9 video shooting at 23.976 progressive fps. |
| | DSLR 720p60 | 1280x720 16:9 video shooting at 59.94 progressive fps. |
| DV | Standard 48 kHz | 720x480 4:3 video from a miniDV tape-based camcorders. |
| | Widescreen 48 kHz | 720x480 16:9 video from miniDV tape-based camcorders. |

*continued on facing page*

## More Premiere Elements project presets

| | | |
|---|---|---|
| **Flip** | Flip Mino or Ultra Flip 29.97 | Flip standard definition (640x480) video camcorders shooting at 29.97 fps. |
| | Flip Mino or Ultra Flip 30 | Flip standard definition (640x480) video camcorders shooting at 30 fps. |
| | Flip Mino HD or Ultra HD 29.97 | Flip high definition (1280x720) video camcorders shooting at 29.97 fps. |
| | Flip Mino HD or Ultra HD 30 | Flip high definition (1280x720) video camcorders shooting at 30 fps. |
| **Hard Disk, Flash Memory Camcorder** | HD 1080i 30 | High-definition video (1920x1080) from non-AVCHD hard drive or flash memory camcorders (such as the JVC GZ-HD7). |
| | HD 1080i 30 (60i) | High-definition video from (1440x1080) from non-AVCHD hard drive or flash memory camcorders that record in 60i format. (The PAL equivalent is, of course, 50i.) |
| | Standard 48kHz | Standard-definition (720x480) 4:3 video from hard drive camcorders as well as video from DVDs. *It is very important to use this or the following preset with standard-definition MPEG or VOB sources because it will automatically reverse the field dominance in your video, correcting an interlacing issue that can otherwise cause stuttering in your output videos.* |
| | Widescreen 48 kHz | Video from standard-definition (720x480) 16:9 hard drive camcorders and video from DVDs. |
| **HDV Presets** | HDV 1080i 30 | Video from tape-based, high-definition HDV camcorders that shoot full HDV at 1440x1080 pixels. |
| | HDV 720p 30 | Video from tape-based, high-definition HDV camcorders that shoot full HDV at 1280x720 pixels (progressive scan at 30 fps). |

Setting your project up using the proper preset is essential to a smooth workflow and the highest quality output results, so consider carefully the nature of your source files as you choose your settings.

The illustration on page 25 and the charts on these pages detail each setting and which video source it is designed to work with.

**Matching your project settings to your video source is vital to a successful video editing experience.**

4    Once you've chosen the settings, name and location for your project, click **Okay** and the program will open to the project workspace.

## Open an old project

Clicking the **Open Project** button on the **Welcome Screen** will get you access to any work-in-progress or old Premiere Elements project.

Your most recent projects will appear in the drop-down menu. Additional Premiere Elements projects on your computer can be accessed by selecting the **Browse** option.

## Open a project from within the program

Naturally, you don't have to go all the way out to the **Welcome Screen** to create a new project or to re-open an old one.

Both options are available from the **File** drop-down on the Menu Bar in the Premiere Elements workspace.

Selecting Ne**w Project** from this menu gives you access to the very same **New Project** settings as are available from the **Welcome Screen**.

## Open a project created by a previous version of the program?

Our advice: Don't do it.

It should work. And sometimes it does work. But, for the most part, Premiere Elements goes through such an overhaul from generation to generation, that it usually just leads to trouble. Only open version 10 projects with version 10, version 9 projects with version 9, etc.

Doing otherwise nearly always leads to buggy behavior – audio tracks that mysteriously disappear, clips that behave really strangely. A **Project** media panel that seems to have lost its mind.

Your best bet is to finish your Premiere Elements project in the same version of the program you began it in. Trust us on this.

Once it's far enough along that you consider it (or the segment you're working on) to be finished, you can export it – using **Share/Computer/AVI** (as we discuss in **Chapter 18, Share Your Movie**). You should then be able to import that AVI segment into your version 10 project with no problems, no bugginess and virtually no loss of quality.

But we very much recommend against opening even a version 9 project in version 10.

**Capture Video into Your Project**

**Download Media into Your Project**

**Add Media to Your Project**

**Work with Photos**

**Work with Music**

Chapter 3

# Get Media into Your Project

Capturing video and importing
video, audio and photos into your project

Before you can edit your video, you
need to get it (along with your other
source media) into your Premiere
Elements project.

This is a relatively simple process,
but unfortunately one that can
occasionally present some challenges.

Before you can begin editing your video, photo or audio sources, you need to import – or **Get Media** – into your Premiere Elements project.

As the chart on the facing page indicates, there are three ways to bring your media files into your project: **Capturing** your video over a FireWire connection; **downloading** your media from a device over a USB connection or from your computer's DVD/CD drive; or **importing** media already on your computer into your project.

Note that many of the formats you will be bringing into your Premiere Elements project must be uniquely processed by the program, and so it is very important to ensure that your project's settings match the format of the video you will be bringing into your project. (More information on selecting your correct project settings can be found in **Chapter 2, Start a New Project**.)

It is not possible to change your project's settings once you've begun your project, so it's very important that you set up your project correctly at the outset.

It can also be a challenging to combine formats that require different project settings in the same project. For this reason, it's not recommended, then, that you combine video from a miniDV camcorder and video from an AVCHD hard drive camcorder in the same project.

Once you've captured, downloaded or imported your media into your Premiere Elements project, it will appear listed in your **Media** panel (as we discuss in **Chapter 4**). Once the media is in your **Media** panel, you'll be able to begin assembling and editing it on your timeline or sceneline.

In this chapter, we'll look at each of the major media devices and sources and show you how to best gather your media from each.

We'll also show you how to work with photos, music and other media. And, as a bonus, we'll show you how to successfully capture video from analog camcorders and video players, as well as how and when to convert potentially troublesome formats.

We'll even include some troubleshooting steps for when things don't seem to go as they should.

## Three ways to the Get Media options

1. Click **Get Media** under the **Project** tab.
2. **Right-click** on a blank area in the **Media** panel (**Ctrl- click** on a Mac) and select the **Get Media** option.
3. Select **Get Media From** from the **File** drop-down menu.

## Getting Media

There are three basic ways to get media into your Premiere Elements project:

- **Capture your** tape-based video over a FireWire connection;
- **Download** your video or other media from a hard drive camcorder, camera or other device over a USB connection; or
- **Browse** to import media into your project from your computer's hard drive.

The chart below lists the methods of getting media from a number of devices.

| | |
|---|---|
| **MiniDV tape-based camcorder** | **Capture** video over a FireWire connection using the Premiere Elements capture interface. |
| **HDV tape-based hi-def camcorder** | **Capture** video over a FireWire connection using the Premiere Elements capture interface. |
| **Webcam** | **Capture** video using the Premiere Elements capture interface. |
| **AVCHD hard drive hi-def camcorder** | **Download** video to computer using the **Video Importer** with a USB connection. |
| **Flip Mino or Ultra camcorders** | **Download** video to computer using the **Video Importer** with a USB connection. |
| **Flash-based camcorders, such as the JVC-GZ series** | **Download** video to computer using the **Video Importer** with a USB connection. |
| **DVD camcorders or DVDs** | With the finalized disc in your computer's DVD drive, rip the video files to your computer using the **Video Importer**. |
| **Analog video** | **Capture** through a DV bridge or pass-through set-up using the Premiere Elements capture interface, as discussed on page 43. |
| **Digital still cameras** | **Download** stills using the **Photo Downloader** or video using the **Video Importer** over a USB connection. |
| **Music or audio from CDs** | Rip music to your hard drive from CD and then browse to the file(s) using the **Get Media** option **PC Files or Folders**. |
| **Video, music or still photos already on your computer's hard drive** | **Import** media into your project by browsing to it using the **Get Media** option **PC Files or Folders**. |

Whatever video or audio source you use, it is very important to ensure that your project's settings match your media's format or source. Information on setting your project up for a variety of media sources can be found in **Chapter 2, Start a New Project**. (Note that your project's settings can only be selected when a project is initiated. They can not be changed once a project has been started.)

Also note that some commercial DVD and music formats (including iTunes) include digital rights management, copy protection software that will prohibit their use in a Premiere Elements. Information on working around some forms of digital rights management can be found in **Add music files to a Premiere Elements project** on page 47.

**FireWire is the common term for an IEEE-1394 connection, also known as iLink.**

Get Media options,
under the Project tab

The DV, HDV and Webcam
or WDM (Webcam) Device
options launch the
Capture workspace.

The DVD/DVD Camcorder
and the Flip, AVHCD Cameras
and Phones options launch
the Video Importer, while the
Digital Still Camera & Phones
option launches the
Photo Downloader.

The PC Files and Folders
and Elements Organizer
options allow you to browse
to files on your computer.

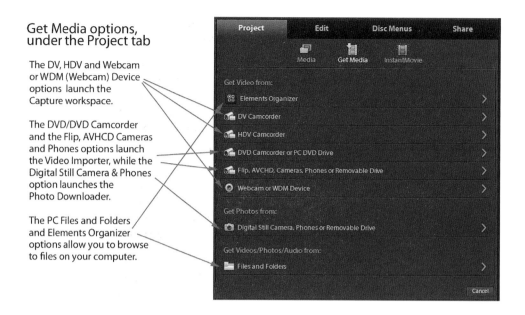

## Get media with the "Get Media" tool

To bring media into your Premiere Elements project – whether from a location on your hard drive or from a camcorder or other device – use the **Get Media** tool.

The simplest way to launch this tool is to click the **Project** tab in the **Tasks** panel and select **Get Media**.

At the **Get Media** screen, Premiere Elements offers eight options for bringing your media into your project (as illustrated above).

- The **DV Camcorder, HDV Camcorder** and **Webcam or WDM Device** options will launch the program's capture workspace.

  In the **Capture** workspace, the program interfaces with the video device. This usually gives you remote control of the device, allowing you to preview the video in real time and select only the segments you want imported into your project.

- The **DVD/DVD Camcorder or PC DVD Drive** and the **Flip, AVCHD, Cameras, Phones or Removable Drive** options launch the **Video Importer**, Adobe's interface for downloading videos from DVDs, camcorders and other devices, while the **Digital Still Camera, Phones or Removable Drive** option launches the **Photo Downloader**.

  Video or photo files are downloaded from the device to your computer using these interfaces. You will not have the option of capturing your video in real time with this software.

- The **PC Files and Folders** option will open Windows Explorer so that you can browse to your media files.

- The **Elements Organizer** option will launch the Organizer file management program (See **Chapter 15**).

A MiniDV camcorder connected via FireWire.

## Capture MiniDV, HDV Video or video from Webcams or WDM Devices

The process of capturing video to Premiere Elements is virtually the same, whether you're capturing from a miniDV camcorder, an HDV (hi-definition) camcorder or even from a DV bridge (see **Capture through DV bridges and pass-throughs**, below), as long as these devices are connected to your computer via FireWire (also known as IEEE-1394 and iLink).

You can also capture video from most Webcams.

1    With your camcorder in VTR mode, connect your camcorder to your computer's FireWire port (as illustrated above).

When your camcorder is properly connected, powered on and set to play, Windows should register the connection (usually with a "bing-bong" sound effect) and a camcorder icon should appear on the right end of your Windows Task Bar.

### Capture over a FireWire connection

All miniDV camcorders have FireWire connectors, even if they also offer a USB connection.

Our advice is to not bother with the USB connection, even if it means you have to buy your own FireWire cable. A few camcorders and some capture software will work with a USB connection, but with FireWire you'll know for sure you're properly connected.

Firewire is the common term for IEEE-1394 or iLink connections.

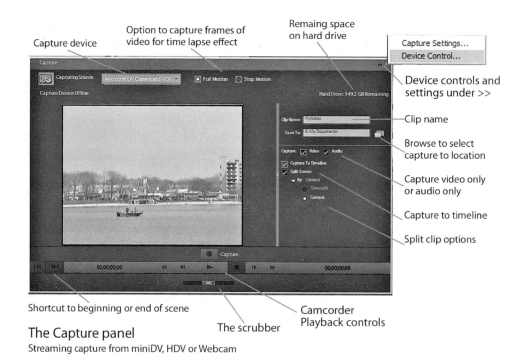

Capture device

Option to capture frames of video for time lapse effect

Remaing space on hard drive

Capture Settings...
Device Control...

Device controls and settings under >>

Clip name

Browse to select capture to location

Capture video only or audio only

Capture to timeline

Split clip options

Shortcut to beginning or end of scene

The scrubber

Camcorder Playback controls

### The Capture panel
Streaming capture from miniDV, HDV or Webcam

Windows should also launch an option screen offering you a handful of methods for capturing your video, among which Premiere Elements should be listed.

If this is not the case, something is wrong, possibly at a mechanical level, and you'll need to troubleshoot your FireWire connection and camcorder set-up before you proceed. (Troubleshooting steps are listed at the end of this chapter.)

If you have a good connection to your camcorder, cancel out of this Windows option screen and, if you're not already running Premiere Elements, launch the program.

2    In Premiere Elements, select the **Project** tab and click **Get Media**, then select the **DV Camcorder, HDV Camcorder** or **Webcam or WDM Device** option.

The **Capture** workspace will open, as illustrated above.

If your camcorder (or DV bridge) is properly connected to your computer via FireWire, the panel will show **Capture Device Online** in the upper left corner of the panel and the **Capturing Source** drop-down should list the camcorder or DV bridge you are interfacing with. If not, you may want to try some of the capture troubleshooting steps at the end of this chapter.

With a proper camcorder connection, the playback buttons along the bottom of this panel will remotely control your camcorder. (If you're using a DV bridge or a pass-through, the source device or camcorder isn't connected directly to the computer, so these buttons will have no function.) **Play, Fast Forward, Stop** and **Rewind** you'll recognize immediately. Once you press **Play**, your camcorder's video should display in the panel and the **Play** button should become a **Pause** button.

The buttons to the right of **Rewind** and to the left of **Fast Forward** are incremental advance and rewind buttons. They allow you to advance or back up your camcorder's playback one frame at a time.

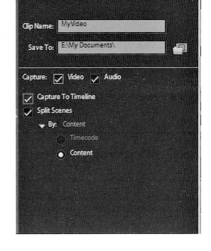

The slider under the playback buttons (called a **Scrubber**) allows you to advance or rewind your video at a variety of speeds, depending on how far you push it to the left or right.

At the lower left of the panel are two "shortcut" buttons. Clicking on these buttons will automatically advance or rewind your video to the previous or next scene (the last point at which your camcorder was stopped or paused).

Premiere Elements only reads these scenes when capturing from a miniDV camcorder, by the way, so these buttons will not function during HDV capture.

To the right of the screen are the capture options. Type the name you would like applied to your captured video in the **Clip Name** space.

(Premiere Elements will add numbers to the end of this name as it creates new clips during capture.)

You also have the option of designating a location for your captured video for this session. By default, the clips will be saved to the same folder as your project file.

- With the various checkboxes in the space below these options, you can designate that the program capture **Audio Only** or **Video Only**. If the **Capture to Timeline** option is selected, your video will be automatically added directly to your project's timeline or sceneline as it is captured.

- The **Split Scenes** option allows you to set whether the captured video is broken into clips based on **Timecode** (each time your camcorder was paused or stopped while shooting) or **Content** (when the video content changes significantly). Since, when you're capturing through a DV bridge or pass-through, timecode is not being streamed into your computer from the video device, you can not split scenes based on timecode while using a DV bridge or pass-through.

  If you elect the option to **Split Scenes** in your captured video based on **Content**, the Organizer's **Media Analyzer** will launch automatically once you've finished your capture. Your clips will automatically be **Smart Tagged** and will appear in your **Media** panel as shorter, trimmed clips, based on the changing content of the video.

  For more information on the **Media Analyzer** and its **Smart Tags** function, see page 172 of **Chapter 15, The Elements Organizer**.

To capture your tape-based or webcam video:

3    Use the playback controls to locate the segment you want to capture, pause your tape, then click the red **Capture** button.

4    When you want to stop your capture, click the **Stop Capture** button.

## Why tape-based miniDV and HDV are still the standards

MiniDV camcorders hit the market over a decade ago. HDV, a high-definition tape-based video format, was introduced a few years later. Based on the professional DV compression system still used in broadcast video, miniDV and HDV camcorders record to a tape cassette not much bigger than a Zippo lighter, each cassette holding about an hour's worth of video at standard speed.

There have been many formats introduced since – hard disk camcorders, DVD camcorders, flash memory camcorders – but none matches miniDV or HDV for their ability to interface with computers and PC-based video editing systems. This is as true for Macs as it is for Windows-based computers. Most home computer-based video editing software was designed to interface ideally with miniDV and HDV camcorders.

The chief advantage of miniDV and HDV camcorders is that, when connected to a computer by a FireWire cable (also known as an IEEE-1394 or iLink), video data is not so much *captured* from these camcorders as it is *streamed* into your computer.

The digital video data remains exactly the same as it flows from the camcorder to your computer (or back to the camcorder). The only change is that the capture software encapsulates the data from miniDV camcorders into AVI files (known more accurately as DV-AVIs) or DV-MOV files on a Mac. HDV video data is encapsulated into M2T files.

Since the video data is not *converted* during capture – as it would be if digitized by a capture device – there is no change to the video data itself, and hence no loss whatsoever of the data's quality in the move from camcorder to computer!

This is an ideal data flow system: A computer in the camcorder sending video data to your editing computer and vice versa – both speaking the same digital language!

Virtually all Windows and Mac professional style, computer-based editing systems are built around this DV workflow. When DV video files are used in programs like Premiere Elements, they are *not even re-rendered* by the program (unless an effect has been added to them).

This is not true of other video formats, many of which need to be continually rendered as you work with them on your timeline.

This means that video from miniDV and HDV camcorders flows smoothly and efficiently through the editing process.

Capture from miniDV and HDV camcorders is also done in "real time". That means that the capture software controls the camcorder remotely as you capture only the segments of your video that you actually want. You play the tape; you watch it on the **Capture Monitor.** You need capture only what you want to use in your video project.

Could you ask for a better marriage between software and camcorder?

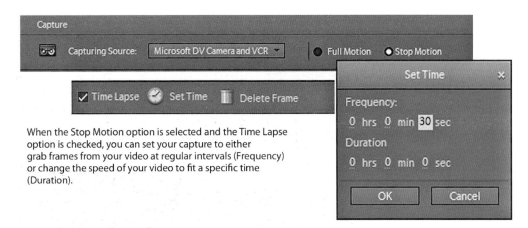

When the Stop Motion option is selected and the Time Lapse option is checked, you can set your capture to either grab frames from your video at regular intervals (Frequency) or change the speed of your video to fit a specific time (Duration).

Finally, at the top center of the **Capture** panel, you'll note that you have the option of capturing your video in **Full Motion** or **Stop Motion**.

The **Stop Motion** option will allow you to set up your capture so that it grabs frames from your video at regular intervals, rather than a continuous stream of video – the result being that the video will play very fast, as a "time lapse" sequence when placed on your timeline or sceneline.

Set your **Stop Motion**, for instance, to capture only one frame every 30 frames, and your captured video will seem to play at *30 times* normal speed.

This is great for showing clouds rolling through the sky or the sun quickly rising and setting, or a flower opening in mere seconds. Great visual effects, even if it does mean you go through a lot of tape to get a very short sequence!

## Get standard DV from an HDV Camcorder

Just because you're shooting your video in high-definition, it does not necessarily mean you'll need to edit it in high-definition.

And, unless you're planning to output your video as a BluRay disc or other high-definition media file, you can achieve excellent results on a standard DVD by *downsampling* your HDV video to standard DV within your camcorder before you capture it into Premiere Elements.

To capture downsampled video from your camcorder, connect your HDV camcorder to your computer via FireWire and set your camcorder to **DV** (called **iLink Conversion** or **DV Lock** on some brands), then capture it into your Premiere Elements project (using standard DV project settings) as if from a miniDV camcorder. The video quality, although no longer in high-definition, will remain excellent, usually much better than you would get from a regular miniDV video.

The overall quality of the results – compared to video captured in HDV and downsampled by Premiere Elements on output – will not be significantly better. However, working with standard DV puts a lot less demand on your system's resources, so you're likely to find it a much faster and more efficient workflow.

**The Video Importer**

Select the camcorder or device you're connecting to from the drop-down list (such as your computer's DVD drive, if "ripping" files from a disk to your computer).

**The Photo Downloader**

Select your camcorder or other photo device from the drop-down list at Get Photos From.

## Get video from DVDs and DVD Camcorders

Video from sources other than miniDV and HDV camcorders – including video from DVD camcorders and hard drive camcorders – is not captured into Premiere Elements the way miniDV is. That is, it's not *streamed* in and captured in real time, as miniDV and HDV video are.

Rather, video from non-tape sources, is *downloaded* into your computer and your Premiere Elements project using Adobe's **Video Importer** or **Photo Downloader** software.

To get video from a DVD or DVD camcorder:

1 Place the DVD into your computer's DVD drive

Note that discs from DVD camcorders must be *finalized* before Premiere Elements can rip the video from them.

2 Select the **DVD Camcorder or PC DVD Drive** option from the **Get Media** panel.

This will launch the **Video Importer**, as illustrated above.

3 Select your computer's DVD drive from the **Source** drop-down menu at the top of the **Video Importer**.

4 Click the **Browse** button to indicate where on your computer you'd like to save the DVD's files, then click the **Get Media** button at the bottom of the panel to rip the video files to your hard drive.

If you're going to use video from a DVD in Premiere Elements, we recommend you ensure you are using it in a project set to the **Hard Drive, Flash Memory Camcorder** project preset, as discussed on pages 26 and 27 of **New Media** in **Chapter 2, Start a New Project**.

## Get video from Hard Drive and Flash Drive Camcorders

As with video from DVDs and DVD camcorders, the video from hard drive and flash drive camcorders is *downloaded*, rather than captured, into Premiere Elements.

To get video from these types of camcorders

1   Connect your camcorder to your computer with a USB cable.

2   Select the **Flip, AVCHD, Cameras, Phones or Removable Drive** option from the **Get Media** panel.

    This will launch the **Video Importer**, as illustrated on page 38.

3   Select your camcorder from the **Source** drop-down menu at the top of the **Video Importer**.

4   Click the **Browse** button to indicate where on your computer you'd like to save the captured files, then click the **Get Media** button at the bottom of the panel to download your video.

If you're going to use video from a hard drive or flash drive camcorder in Premiere Elements, we recommend you use it in a project using the proper **Hard Drive, Flash Memory Camcorder** project preset, as discussed on pages 26 and 27 of **New Media** in **Chapter 2, Start a New Project**.

## Get video from Flip camcorders

Flip camcorders plug directly into your computer's USB port. As with hard drive camcorders, the video from Flip camcorders is *downloaded* rather than streamed or captured into Premiere Elements.

1   Connect your Flip camcorder to your computer's USB port.

2   Select the **Flip, AVCHD, Cameras, Phones or Removable Drive** option from the **Get Media** panel.

    This will launch the **Video Importer**, as illustrated on page 38.

3   Select your Flip camcorder from the **Source** drop-down menu at the top of the **Video Importer**.

4   Click the **Browse** button to indicate where on your computer you'd like to save the captured files, then click the **Get Media** button at the bottom of the panel to download your video.

If you're going to use video from a Flip camcorder in Premiere Elements, we recommend you use it in a project using the appropriate **Flip Mino or Ultra** or **Flip Mino HD or Ultra HD** project preset, as discussed on pages 26 and 27 of **New Media** in **Chapter 2, Start a New Project**.

## Get video from AVCHD camcorders

As with other hard drive camcorders, the video from AVCHD camcorders is *downloaded* rather than streamed or captured into Premiere Elements.

1   Connect your AVCHD camcorder to your computer's USB port.

2   Select the **Flip, AVCHD, Cameras, Phones or Removable Drive** option from the **Get Media** panel.

  This will launch the **Video Importer**, as illustrated on page 38.

3   Select your camcorder from the **Source** drop-down menu at the top of the **Video Importer.**

4   Click the **Browse** button to indicate where on your computer you'd like to save the captured files, then click the **Get Media** button at the bottom of the panel to download your video.

If you're going to use video from an AVCHD camcorder in Premiere Elements, we recommend you use it in a project using the appropriate **AVCHD** project preset, as discussed on pages 26 and 27 of **Chapter 2, Start a New Project**. There are four possible presets for AVCHD camcorders, and it is very important that you choose a preset that matches your audio (stereo or 5.1) as well as your video format.

## HDV (High Definition Video) versus AVCHD

One of the most exciting video formats to become available to consumers in recent years is high-definition video.

When configured to work with **HDV**, Premiere Elements handles the MPEGs from an HDV camcorder as smoothly and as efficiently as it does video from a miniDV source.

Though do note that HDV is much more compressed and contains much more video data than miniDV (approximately twice the horizontal and twice the vertical data). And that can put a lot more strain on your computer's resources.

The process of capturing HDV in Premiere Elements is essentially the same as capturing standard DV.

The newest type of high-definition video is an even more highly compressed format called **AVCHD**, which stores the video data to the camcorder's internal hard drive or to a memory card as MPEG4s.

Although this format can be more convenient to use, the fact that it is so highly compressed means that it puts *even more* strain on your system's resources. So it's very important to make sure you've got a powerful enough computer to handle these files!

Our **Appendix** offers our system recommendations for working with these more intensive formats and recommends tweaks for ensuring you're getting every bit of power your computer can muster.

## Get video from DSLR still cameras and other devices

Premiere Elements Media Downloader can also download media from other devices, including mobile phones.

**1**   Connect your device to your computer's USB port.

**2**   Select the **Flip, AVCHD, Cameras, Phones or Removable Drive** option from the **Get Media** panel.

    This will launch the **Video Importer,** as illustrated on page 38.

**3**   Select your USB-connected device from the **Source** drop-down menu at the top of the **Video Importer.**

**4**   Click the **Browse** button to indicate where on your computer you'd like to save the captured files, then click the **Get Media** button at the bottom of the panel to download your video or photos.

As we discuss in the sidebar below, when working with video from still cameras, you'll get the best results if you use the right project settings, as discussed on pages 26 and 27 of **Chapter 2, Start a New Project.**

## Get stills from digital cameras and cell phones

**1**   Connect your still camera to your computer's USB port.

**2**   Select the **Digital Still Camera, Phones or Removable Drive** option from the **Get Media** panel.

    This will launch the **Photo Downloader** as illustrated on page 38.

**3**   From the **Get Media From** drop-down menu at the top of the **Photo Downloader,** select your camera or other device.

**4**   Click the **Browse** button to indicate where on your computer you'd like to save the captured files, then click the **Get Media** button at the bottom of the panel to download your video or photos.

As we indicate in **Use photos in your Premiere Elements project** on page 45, for best results your still photos should be resized to an optimal, video resolution size.

### Video from still cameras

Adobe has added support for a wide variety of DSLR (digital still camera) video to Premiere Elements.  But, as with any video source format, you'll get the best results – and the program will function must effectively – when you match your project settings as accurately as possible to your source video footage.

The charts on pages 26 and 27 detail the project settings available in Premiere Elements. We strongly recommend you study your camera's specs carefully and select the project setting that best represents the format your camera is recording to.

## Work with standard definition MPEGs and VOBs

MPEGs and VOBs are essentially the same thing. VOBs are MPEG2s on a DVD.

They are both highly compressed video formats that provide excellent quality playback. Like DV-AVIs, they form video frames through interlacing – creating every frame of video in two passes, drawing every other horizontal line of pixels in each pass. This they do about 30 times every second (25 times every second on PAL video), too fast for your eyes to see.

The challenge is that MPEGs and VOBs usually create their interlaced frames with the *upper field* of lines first, while DV-AVIs create their interlaced frames with the *lower field* first.

That's not a significant issue *until* you bring an MPEG into a DV-AVI workflow, such as Premiere Elements. You may not see the difference when playing back your video in your project but, when you output your video or create a DVD from these types of files in Premiere Elements, the MPEG-based segments will often look very jumpy and jittery.

The old solution was to right-click on every MPEG clip on your timeline or sceneline and select **Field Options**, then **Reverse Field Order**. Very inconvenient and time consuming if you've got a lot of MPEGs in your project.

But, in Premiere Elements, Adobe has provided project settings especially for working with MPEGs as source files – the **Hard Disk, Flash Memory Camcorder** project preset. (For more information on project settings, see the **Open a new project** discussion in **Chapter 2, Start a New Project**.)

Video imported into a project using these settings will automatically have its field order reversed, and your MPEGs will render and output perfectly from Premiere Elements.

**If you use MPEGs or VOBs almost exclusively as your video source files, this is the project preset you want to use.**

Remember, however, if you mix DV-AVIs and MPEGs in the same project, you will have to change the field order for one of these video formats manually, as described above. Otherwise you may end up with a DV-AVI getting its field order reversed and playing all jumpy and jittery on your DVD!

That said, although Premiere Elements can work with MPEGs, VOBs and other video formats, the best – *the absolute best* – way to use these types of video files efficiently in Premiere Elements is to convert them to DV-AVIs, as described on the facing page.

## Import media from your PC files and folders

To load video, audio or stills already on your computer into your Premiere Elements project:

1   Click on the **Project** tab and select **Get Media**.

2   Select the **PC Files and Folders** option on the **Get Media** panel, or select the **Elements Organizer** option to launch the Elements Organizer program (see **Chapter 15**).

3   Browse to the file(s) you'd like to import on your hard drive.

You can also quickly open a browse screen from which to import your media files by double-clicking on a blank space (beyond the media listings) in your **Media** panel.

## Capture video through DV bridges and pass-throughs

There's a difference between a DV bridge and a plain old capture device or capture card. Capture devices merely digitize your video input to any of a number of video formats. DV bridges, on the other hand, are specifically designed to **convert any video and audio input into DV-AVI files**, the preferred video format for PC-based video editors. (Macs also prefer DV video, although they are saved as DV Quicktime files [MOVs] rather than AVIs. The video data content, however, is identical.)

DV bridges range from relatively inexpensive to high-end professional devices with time base correction and other video optimizers. The best value on the market in DV bridges and a Muvipix recommended "best buy" is the **Canopus ADVC Converter**, a favorite of many videographers.

### Convert non-DV-AVI files

For the cleanest results and smoothest operation in Premiere Elements, we recommend that, whenever possible, you use exclusively DV-AVIs as source files for your standard video projects.

If you're not shooting your video on a miniDV or an HDV camcorder, this may present a bit of a challenge. However, there are a number of very easy to use, very *free* programs available for converting almost any file to a DV-AVI, and we've listed a couple in our **Appendix**.

A favorite program for converting MPEGs and VOB files to DV-AVIs is the free utility **Super Video Converter**, from eRight Software. Instructions for downloading and using this program appear in this books **Appendix**.

This process of converting may seem a bit inconvenient at first. But the trade-offs in terms of improved performance, trouble-free operation and higher quality outputs from Premiere Elements will very soon convince you that it's well worth the little extra effort.

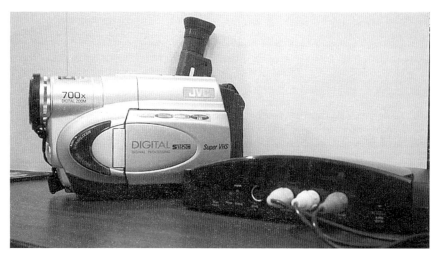

A DV bridge downloads DV video from a VHS camcorder over via FireWire connection.

The **Canopus ADVC** will take any AV input (a camcorder, a DVD player, a VCR or virtually any other video source, including live video) and port it into your computer as a high-quality DV-AVI or, on a Mac, DV-MOV file. This great device can be had for a street price of about $200, a great value if you plan to edit a lot of video from non-DV sources.

Capturing video from a DV bridge is easy. Just plug your camcorder's, DVD player's or VCR's AV cables (RCA jacks) into the DV bridge's inputs and plug the bridge (connected by FireWire) into your computer.

Your computer will recognize the device just as it would a miniDV camcorder connection.

The capture process itself is essentially the same as capture from a miniDV camcorder. The only difference is, since there's no direct connection between your video source device and the computer, you won't be able to control the device with the **Capture Monitor's** playback controls or break scenes by timecode.

But, once you've got the device cued up to the segment you want to capture, you just click the **Capture** button and you're good to go!

By the way, the **Canopus ADVC** can also be used with DVD camcorders and hard drive camcorders, so it's a great way to make any non-miniDV video 100% Premiere Elements compatible.

An alternative to a DV bridge is a set-up called a **pass-through**, which essentially uses a miniDV camcorder as a makeshift DV bridge.

To set up a pass-through connection, attach your non-DV camcorder to your miniDV camcorder via its AV input cables, then link the miniDV to your computer via FireWire.

With the miniDV camcorder in play mode (but without a tape inside) the non-DV camcorder's video flows through the miniDV and into the computer, where it's captured as DV-AVIs.

The biggest challenge to using this method is that fewer and fewer new miniDV camcorders support a pass-through connection. And it's very difficult to learn, from most spec sheets, which camcorders do.

But, if your miniDV camcorder is pass-through capable, this is a simple and effective method of digitizing almost any analog video input.

## Use photos in Premiere Elements

Premiere Elements can work with virtually any of the major photo or graphics formats, including JPEGs, GIFs, TIFs, vector art (EPSs and AI files) and PSDs (native Photoshop and Photoshop Elements files).

The exceptions are images using the CMYK color mode or RGB photo files using other than standard 8-bit color. But, if you are creating your graphics or using photos from a consumer graphics program (such as Photoshop Elements) or from a digital camera, scanner or other device, then you don't need to worry about these exceptions. Virtually all photo and graphics files from these sources are compatible with the program.

Premiere Elements will also support transparency (alpha channels) so that file formats like GIF, PNG, EPS, AI and PSD files with transparent areas will display, when used in a video project, with these areas transparent.

This is particularly useful if you're using one of these graphics file types on an upper video track with a video layer behind it (see **Use L-cuts, J-cuts and multiple tracks** no page 78 of **Chapter 6, Edit Your Movie in Timeline Mode**) or as a graphic added to a title (see **Add a graphic to your title** on page 116 of **Chapter 10, Add Titles**).

Photos make great source files for a Premiere Elements project, but you'll find the highest quality results and the best performance from the program if the sizes of your photos are properly optimized before you bring them into your project.

### Graphics and photo formats

For photos, the most size-efficient file format is the JPEG. As an alternative, PSD files and TIFs use less compression and, though larger, also produce excellent results.

Because JPEGs are highly compressed, they do not make the best format for graphics that include clean, distinct edges, such as logos or graphics that include text. In these cases, PSDs, TIFs, AIs, EPSs and even PNGs produce the crispest lines.

# CHAPTER 3

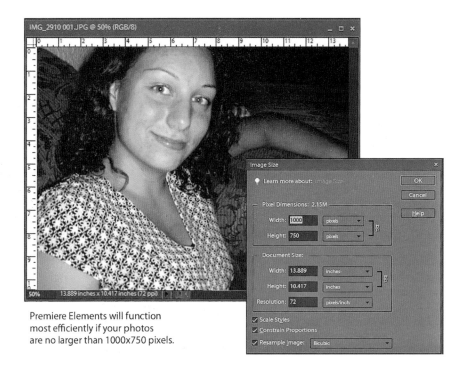

Premiere Elements will function
most efficiently if your photos
are no larger than 1000x750 pixels.

**We urge you to make sure that any photo you use (especially if you use several in a slideshow) has been resized to no larger than 1000x750 pixels before you bring it into your Premiere Elements project** to ensure the best quality and optimal program performance. (Photos taken directly from digital cameras can be 20 to 25 times that size!)

At first this may seem to go contrary to common wisdom.

Traditionally, the higher the resolution of your photo, the better the quality of the output. But remember that Premiere Elements is a *video* editing program, and video is a relatively low resolution medium (essentially the equivalent of 640x480 pixels). And, to a point, reducing the resolution of a photo or graphic to be used in a video actually *improves* the quality of the video output. (1000x750 pixels seems to be that point).

The reason for this has to do with a process called downsampling, the system a video program uses to bring high-resolution photos down

## Optimize photos for high-resolution video projects

For high-definition video slideshows, the optimal size for a photo is 2000x1500 pixels (approximately, since photos are usually 4:3 rather than 16:9) – although note that photos at this size will put a bit more strain your system's resources.

to video size. Premiere Elements does a fair job of this – but, as any pro knows, nothing that happens automatically will be as clean or as efficient as what you do manually. "Down-rezzing" is definitely one of those things.

There's also a more pressing reason for downsampling your photos yourself. The process of "down-rezzing," like the process of assimilating non-DV-AVI files into a video project, is a very intensive process. So intensive, in fact, that it is *the single biggest reason Premiere Elements crashes*, particularly during the disc burning process.

It also takes a lot longer for the program to down-rez, for instance, a 4000x3000 pixel photo than it does a 1000x750 pixel photo.

Much, much longer. And would you rather wait an hour or two for the program to create your DVD or 10 hours for a process that might end up with the program choking and dying anyway?

Trust us on this. Optimize your photo sizes to 1000x750 pixels before you import them into Premiere Elements. It will save you hours of anguish and misery in the end. (For high-definition video projects, you can go as large as 2000x1500 pixels.)

Photoshop Elements, by the way, has a very nice batch resizing feature that can resize a whole folder full of photos in just a few clicks. This feature is called **Process Multiple Files**, and it is located under the Photoshop Elements **File** menu.

## Add music files to a Premiere Elements project

Although Premiere Elements works with a variety of audio file formats, it's probably best to exclusively use **MP3s** and **WAVs** as your source files.

They seem to provide the most trouble-free operation.

One word of warning, though, in connection with using music files in your video projects: Many music download sites (iTunes, for instance) employ electronic **Digital Rights Management** (DRM) in their downloaded files.

This DRM system will throw up an error code if you try to load a copy-protected music file into your Premiere Elements project, blocking you from using the file. (Because many music sites, like Amazon.com, don't use such stringent DRM, even iTunes has relaxed theirs more in recent years – so these error codes are becoming less of a problem.)

There is software available on the Web for breaking this DRM. But probably the easiest way to get around this copy protection is to burn the music file to a CD and then use a program like Windows Media Player to rip the CD music file back to your computer as an MP3. The resultant MP3 should load right into Premiere Elements.

This process, of course, doesn't exempt you from respecting the rights of the artist who created the music. So please don't abuse the privilege.

Also, *before* you do bring those photos into your video project, go to **Edit/Preferences/General** in Premiere Elements and uncheck **Default Scale to Frame Size**.

Left checked, **Scale to Frame Size** automatically sizes your photo to fill your video frame, giving a false representation of your photo in the video frame in addition to really getting in the way when you're trying to add motion paths to your photos.

In the event this option was checked when you imported your photos into your project, you can also turn it off for your photos individually by **right-clicking** on each photo on the timeline (**Ctrl-clicking** on the Mac) and unchecking the **Scale to Frame Size** option on the pop-up menu.

For information on applying flicker removal to the photos and still graphics in your Premiere Elements project, see **Add still photos to your project** on page 76 of **Chapter 6, Edit Video in the Timeline Mode**.

## Troubleshoot Windows video capture in Premiere Elements

Video capture from a miniDV or HDV tape-based camcorder seems like it should be easy. And, since you can't do anything in Premiere Elements until you have your video captured into your computer, when capture fails it can be very frustrating!

I wish I could tell you that there was a magic bullet for making all the problems go away, but sometimes there just is no simple fix.

The following, though, can help you troubleshoot your problems. And, if they don't work, the third-party solutions we recommend below will get you through the day (and may ultimately become your preferred workflow!)

1   Before you blame the software, make sure your operating system and its components are optimized and up to date. Following the maintenance regimen on page 226 of our **Appendix** – which includes ensuring that your operating system, its firmware and drivers are up to date – is essential to the smooth operation of a process as intensive as video editing!

Remember, you're using a very intensive program on an operating system that's constantly changing, updating and evolving. Like a race car driver who knows that even a few pounds of pressure in one tire can mean the difference between a stable ride and one fraught with problems, you should always make sure your computer's operating system is in perfect working order.

And always make sure you have the latest version of **Quicktime** and the newest **RealTek drivers** on your system! This may not seem like an obvious solutions to your problems, but more times than not, a simple update makes all the difference.

**2**  As mentioned earlier in the chapter, if your operating system isn't even registering your camcorder as connected, you're dealing with a more fundamental problem than a Premiere Elements issue.

Check your connections. Make sure your camcorder is set up right for capture (i.e., is in VTR/play mode). Possibly even check the camcorder on another computer to see whether it's the computer, the FireWire cable or even your particular camcorder that's failing.

**3**  Make sure you're using a FireWire/IEEE-1394/iLink connection for capture. Some miniDV camcorders also offer a USB connection – but, most of the time, they won't work with Premiere Elements. Trust us on this. You want a FireWire connection if it is at all possible.

**4**  If all connections are working and Windows recognizes your camcorder but Premiere Elements doesn't, note the auto-launch window that Windows opens when you plug your camcorder into your computer.

What software does it offer to launch to capture your video? Some software (such as Nero) is less willing to share capture devices with any other software. And sometimes that means, unfortunately, that capturing directly into Premiere Elements may simply not be possible – at least not without way more work than it's worth. In that case, you may want to consider our third-party solutions below.

**5**  If all seems to be in order and Premiere Elements still isn't recognizing your camcorder, click on the **>>** button on the upper right corner of your **Capture** panel. (If this button doesn't show, go to Premiere Elements **Window** drop-down menu and select **Show Docking Headers**.)

Select the **Device Control** option and, from the panel that opens, click on the **Options** button.

This button will open another panel in which you can set the program to the exact brand and model of camcorder or DV bridge you're connected to. (There are **Standard** settings also, in the event your camcorder model isn't listed.)

In all honesty, changing these settings rarely revives a dead camcorder connection. However, it can "refine" a connection in which the camcorder is recognized but capture doesn't seem to be going quite right.

Finally, if none of these solutions works, you can use a third-party capture solution. Page 231 of our **Appendix** lists some great resources for free or low-cost **Capture Utilities** that can help.

Our personal favorite capture software utility for miniDV capture is **WinDV**. This free and fully-loaded capture utility will often work even when nothing else seems to (assuming Windows sees the camcorder connection).

Like Premiere Elements itself, WinDV captures miniDV video in small DV-AVI clips that are perfectly compatible with Premiere Elements and other editors.

Other options include the low-cost **Scenalyzer** and the absolutely free **Windows MovieMaker** (included with your Windows operating system). Both will capture your miniDV files in the DV-AVI format, which you can then import into your Premiere Elements project.

For high-definition video, **HDVSplit** is, like WinDV, free and yet very stable and nicely featured.

Because of the stability, reliability and sometimes extra features included with these free or low-cost utilities, many of our Premiere Elements users actually *prefer* to capture with these third-party applications and save Premiere Elements for what it does best.

Editing video!

## Automatically fix mismatched project settings

If you attempt to add to the timeline or sceneline of a new project a video clip that requires settings other than those that you have set for your project, a **Mismatched Media Settings Prese**t

notification window will pop up notifying you of the mismatch and offering to fix it for you.

If you click **Yes**, the program will automatically update the project's settings to match those of this footage.

This feature only works when this mismatched footage is the *first clip* you add to your timeline or sceneline in a project. And it doesn't correct issues that may arise from mixing more than one video format in the same project (something we strongly discourage you from doing). However – considering the liabilities of using the wrong settings for a project – it can prove a real lifesaver.

More information on project settings can be found in **Chapter 2, Start a New Project**.

**The Media Panel**
**The Preview Monitor**
**The Create Slideshow Tool**
**Color Bars and Countdown Leaders**

Chapter 4
# Explore the Media Panel
## The parts that will form your movie

The Media panel is the catalog from which you'll draw all of the video, audio and still clips that you'll use to create your movie.

If you select the Project tab and click on the Media button, the panel will display a list of all of the sound, video and graphics files that have been captured or imported into your Premiere Elements project.

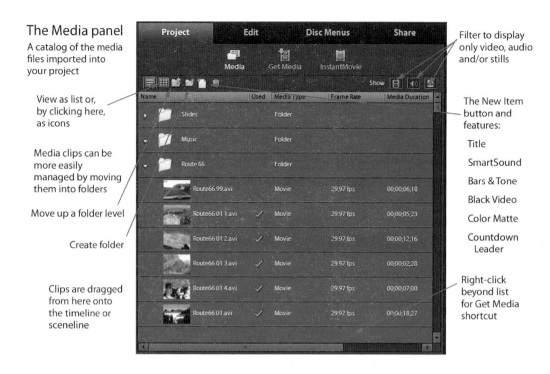

**The Media panel**
A catalog of the media files imported into your project

View as list or, by clicking here, as icons

Media clips can be more easily managed by moving them into folders

Move up a folder level

Create folder

Clips are dragged from here onto the timeline or sceneline

Filter to display only video, audio and/or stills

The New Item button and features:

Title

SmartSound

Bars & Tone

Black Video

Color Matte

Countdown Leader

Right-click beyond list for Get Media shortcut

The **Media** panel (opened by clicking the **Media** button under the **Project** tab) is the catalog from which you'll draw all of the video, audio and still clips that you'll use to create your movie.

Whenever you **Get Media** for your Premiere Elements project (as discussed in **Chapter 3**), it will appear listed in this panel.

To bring a clip from this panel into your movie, simply drag it from the panel to your movie's sceneline or timeline (as we discuss in **Chapter 5, Assemble Your Video in Sceneline Mode,** and **Chapter 6, Edit Your Video in Timeline Mode**.)

Media clips can be displayed in either a List View or an Icon View, set by the buttons in the upper left of the panel.

In fact, that's about 90% of what editing your video will consist of – simply dragging clips from here and placing them there.

But in addition to serving as a holding area for your video project's media, this panel includes a number of great tools for managing, ordering and preparing your clips for your movie's timeline or sceneline.

Different viewing modes (your media can be displayed in **List View** or **Icon View**) and folders make managing and keeping track of a large number of media files relatively simple.

Also, the **Preview Monitor** (page 56) is an invaluable tool for trimming your clips prior to adding them to your movie.

## Organize your media files with folders

The two folder icons in the list of controls along the top of the **Media** panel are for creating and navigating folders for your media files.

This is one of my favorite Premiere Elements features, extremely valuable when you're trying to sort through a large number of media files.

Click on the **Create Folder** icon to create and name a new folder.

Once you have a folder created, you can drag your media files into it – sorting your clips so that all of your files for a particular sequence of your project are in the same folder, for instance.

You can even create sub-folders within your folders – and even sub-sub-folders! – so that it becomes very easy to manage and locate the files you need without having to scroll through a long list of clips

Even as you're editing, you can drag your media clips around, and in and out, of folders to get them out of your way without affecting their positions or function on your timeline or sceneline.

Folders can be used to organize a large number of clips in your Media panel.

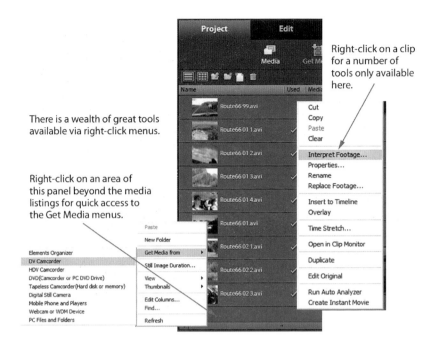

Right-click on a clip for a number of tools only available here.

There is a wealth of great tools available via right-click menus.

Right-click on an area of this panel beyond the media listings for quick access to the Get Media menus.

## Valuable Media panel right-click tools

There are a number of great tools available throughout Premiere Elements that can be (and sometimes can *only* be) accessed by **right-clicking** on clips or panels (or **Ctrl-clicking** on a Mac).

I do a thorough discussion of these tools in my *Steve's Tips* article "Powerful Tools in Premiere Elements' Right-Click Menus," available on the Muvipix.com product pages.

Here are a couple of my favorite right-click tools available exclusively in the **Media** panel.

Interpret Footage – Believe it or not, standard 4:3 video and widescreen 16:9 video use exactly the same number of pixels to create a video frame. The difference is that the pixels (the tiny squares of color that combine to create every frame of video) are shaped differently. Widescreen 16:9 pixels are much wider than standard 4:3 video pixels.

**Right-clicking** on a clip (**Ctrl-clicking** on a Mac) and selecting **Interpret Footage** gives you access to options for conforming a widescreen clip to fit in a standard video or vice versa.

This tool is invaluable if, for some reason, you find yourself with a clip that looks strangely squished, stretched or distorted.

Duplicate – This selection makes a duplicate of the clip you've right-clicked on. This is very helpful, for instance, if you've created a title slide with a style you'd like to re-use. You merely **duplicate** it and then revise the duplicate as needed. (Also see **Duplicate a title** on page 117.)

Rename – You can rename a clip by selecting this right-click option or by simply double-clicking slowly on the name of the file in the **Media** panel listing so that the name becomes highlighted. Renaming a clip doesn't change the name of the file on your hard drive, by the way. Nor does it affect the clip's position or function on the timeline. But it can make it easier for you to identify the file later.

## Create color mattes, bars and tone and countdown leaders

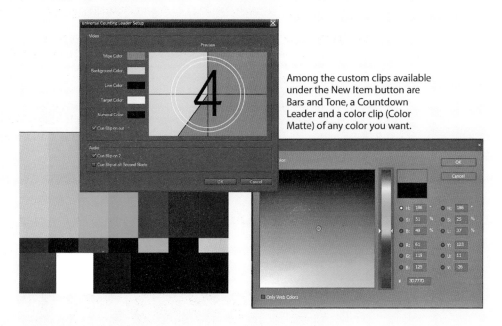

Among the custom clips available under the New Item button are Bars and Tone, a Countdown Leader and a color clip (Color Matte) of any color you want.

 The **New Item** button (the blank page icon) on the tool panel along the top of the **Media** panel launches options for creating a number of very valuable, short clips for your project.

Title launches the Premiere Elements **Title** workspace. We explore this tool in much greater detail in **Chapter 10, Titles.**

Bars and Tone creates a clip of bars and audio tone, which broadcasters often require at the beginning of every video in order to calibrate their equipment to your movie's sound levels and color profile.

Black Video and Color Matte create blank clips of whatever color you designate and which can be used behind titles or as blank spaces in your video.

Universal Countdown Leader creates a customizable countdown sequence (including an audio "blip" at two seconds) which can be placed at the beginning of your video – another feature broadcasters often require so that they can cue up the beginning of your movie.

You'll also find a link here for launching SonicFire Pro Express Track, the amazing third-party tool for creating custom, professional-sounding music clips for your project.

For more information about **SonicFire Pro Express Track**, see page 92 of **Chapter 7, Edit Audio on the Timeline**.

## Pre-trim your clips in the Preview Monitor

The **Preview Monitor** is a pop-up screen for previewing playback of a clip. It's also a work area in which you can trim a clip prior to adding it to your project by setting **In** and/or **Out** markers.

The **Preview Monitor** can be used to trim clips in the **Media** panel or clips that have already been added to your timeline or sceneline.

A clip's **Preview Monitor** is launched either by **right-clicking** on the clip (**Ctrl-clicking** on a Mac) and selecting the **Open in Preview Monitor** option – or by simply **double-clicking** on the clip.

As illustrated on the facing page, when you set **In** or **Out** markers in your **Preview Monitor**, only the segment of the clip between those markers will be displayed during the clip's playback in your movie.

In other words, if you have a 5-minute clip, you can set the **In** and **Out** markers so that only a 30-second segment of the clip is actually displayed in your movie – rendering the clip essentially a 30-second clip.

In the **Preview Monitor,** the "live" segment of the clip is indicated with a lighter, blue segment area on the **Preview Monitor's** mini-timeline. You can adjust this live area's length by either dragging the end points in or out, or by playing the clip using the playback controls at the bottom of the **Preview Monitor** and clicking on the **Set In** or **Set Out** buttons to isolate the segment you want to use.

The **In** and **Out** markers in the **Preview Monitor** can be used to isolate segments in audio clips as well as video.

You can not set **In** and **Out** markers on titles and still images, however, because they are stationary elements.

## Take a shortcut to "Get Media"

If you want to import additional media from your computer into your Premiere Elements project, or if you want to launch a video capture without leaving the **Media** panel, there is a shortcut to the **Get Media** option menu built right into the **Media** panel.

As illustrated at the top of page 54, if you **right-click** on a *blank* area of the **Media** panel (**Ctrl-click** on a Mac), beyond your media listings, you will have access to the same **Get Media** options available on the **Get Media** panel.

Additionally, you can quickly open a browse screen so that you can import media already on your computer by simply **double-clicking** on a blank area after your **Media** panel's listings.

The Preview Monitor launches when you double-click on any clip on the timeline or sceneline or in the Media panel.

Clips can be trimmed in the Preview Monitor either by dragging the in and out points on the mini-timeline or by playing the clip and clicking the Set In and Set Out buttons.

Although the original clip remains its original length, only the "trimmed" segment (the blue highlighted segment in Premiere Elements) will display when the clip is placed on the timeline.

Once the **Preview Monitor** has been launched, it will stay open as long as you keep your project open or until you manually close it.

Because this panel tends to pop up in the middle of the workspace whenever it launches, I usually launch it as soon as I open a project, position it off to the side and out of the way and leave it open. That way, if I later need to open a clip in this panel for previewing or trimming, the **Preview Monitor** will play this clip where I've positioned it instead of in the middle of my work.

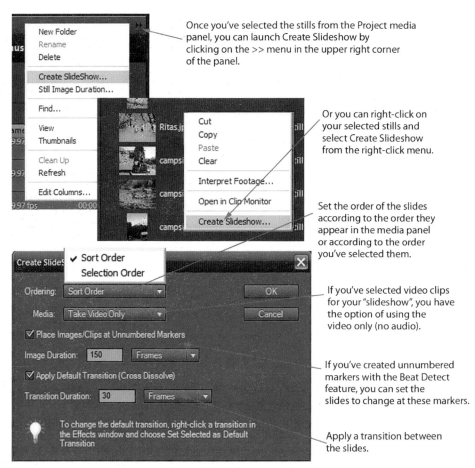

Once you've selected the stills from the Project media panel, you can launch Create Slideshow by clicking on the >> menu in the upper right corner of the panel.

Or you can right-click on your selected stills and select Create Slideshow from the right-click menu.

Set the order of the slides according to the order they appear in the media panel or according to the order you've selected them.

If you've selected video clips for your "slideshow", you have the option of using the video only (no audio).

If you've created unnumbered markers with the Beat Detect feature, you can set the slides to change at these markers.

Apply a transition between the slides.

The Image and Transition Durations can be set by frames or by seconds.

## Create a slideshow in the Media panel

One of my favorite automatic features in Premiere Elements is the **Create Slideshow** tool.

To create a slideshow automatically in Premiere Elements, you merely select a number of clips or stills from the **Media** panel (by holding down the **Ctrl** or **Shift** key as you select) and then either **right-click** on the selected clips (**Ctrl-click** on a Mac) or click on the **>>** button in the upper right of the panel and select **Create Slideshow**.

As you can see in the illustration of the **Create Slideshow** option screen, above, you can set the **Ordering** of your slides in a couple of ways.

**Sort Order.** In **Sort Order**, the **Slideshow Creator** places your slides in the same order as they appear listed in the **Media** panel.

**Selection Order.** In **Selection Order**, the **Slideshow Creator** places your slides according to the order you click-selected them in the **Media** panel.

On the **Create Slideshow** option screen, you also have a number of ways to set the duration of your slides:

**Image Duration**. You can set your slides to change after a designated interval of time.

**Unnumbered Markers**. You can set them to change at **Unnumbered Markers** on the **Timeline** (For more information on **Unnumbered Markers**, see **Detect Beats** on page 96 in **Chapter 7, Edit Audio on the Timeline**).

You can use either video or still clips in your slideshow – although only stills can be set to change at a given duration or at the unnumbered markers created by the **Detect Beats** tool.

If you use video clips in your slideshow, the **Create Slideshow** panel includes the option to remove the audio from the clips.

You can also select the option to apply a **Default Transition** between your slides. (For information on designating the **Default Transition**, see page 145 of **Chapter 12, Add and Customize Transitions**.)

For information on how to optimize your stills for a slideshow, see **Use photos in Premiere Elements** on page 45 of **Chapter 3, Get Media into Your Project**.

There are actually a number of different ways to create a slideshow in Premiere Elements, including a **Create Slideshow** tool built into the Elements Organizer and **InstantMovie** slideshow themes.

For more information on the tools and other methods of creating slideshows using features in both Premiere Elements, Photoshop Elements and the Elements Organizer – and the advantages of each – see my *Steve's Tips* article "Creating Slideshows with Photoshop Elements and Premiere Elements," available on the products page at Muvipix.com.

By the way, you can also create a slideshow using one of the **Slideshow InstantMovie** themes. For more information on creating **InstantMovies**, see page 104 of **Chapter 9**.

**Add Clips to Your Sceneline**

**Add Transitions**

**Add and Adjust Audio**

Chapter 5

# Assemble Your Video in Sceneline Mode
## The drag-and-drop editing space

Premiere Elements offers two workspaces
for assembling your video projects – the
professional-style Timeline panel and the
simple, drag-and-drop Sceneline.

There are advantages to each. But for
quickly assembling your movie, it's hard to
beat the Sceneline's simple drag-and-drop
interface.

In Sceneline mode, assembling your movie is as simple as dragging your video clips and stills to the area labeled Drag Next Clip Here. Transitions are added in the smaller blocks between the clips. Audio, music and narration are added to the tracks below the sceneline.

Narration track    Music Track    Transition placeholder    Video clip placeholder

The **Sceneline** is the simpler of the two workspaces for editing your Premiere Elements project. It's also, by nature of its simplicity, rather limited in its function and not always the easiest workspace for fine-tuning the elements of your movie. But, for the basic assembly of a single track of clips and three tracks of audio, it couldn't be easier to use.

While the **Timeline**, as the name implies, is about *time* – when things happen and how your clips interact with each other – the **Sceneline** is about *content*. It's about simply gathering your clips or slides together and creating a movie.

## Add video to your sceneline

Adding video clips to the **Sceneline** is as simple as dragging them from your **Media** panel (under the **Project** tab), and into the "**Drag Next Clip Here**" placeholders. Clips are not overlapped. They simply line up, one after another, as you add them, each clip represented by a single thumbnail.

Once your clips have been placed on your sceneline, you can trim them, removing undesired footage or audio from the beginning or end of each clip.

The "timeline" for your audio or video clips is displayed, in **Sceneline** mode, along the bottom of the **Monitor** panel, as illustrated to the right. The "live area" of the clip (the only part that will actually be played in your movie project) is represented by the light blue strip, with the end points for the "live" segment represented by markers at either end of this strip. By adjusting the positions of these **In** and **Out Point** markers, you can trim or extend each clip, from either the beginning or end.

In Sceneline mode, each clip's timeline appears as a blue line along the bottom of the Monitor. A clip can be trimmed by adjusting the In and Out Points at either end of this blue timeline.

## Add transitions

Between each clip on your sceneline is a placeholder for transitions. As with adding your video and audio clips, adding transitions is as simple as dragging them from the **Transitions** panel (under the **Edit** tab) to the placeholders between your sceneline clips.

A list of optional transitions can also be accessed by **right-clicking** on a transition placeholder on your sceneline (**Ctrl-clicking** on a Mac) and browsing through the transitions menus.

Each transition offers a variety of customizable options. To access these options, open the **Transitions** panel (by clicking the **Transitions** button under the **Edit** tab) and, with the transition you want to customize selected on your sceneline, click the **Edit Transition** button.

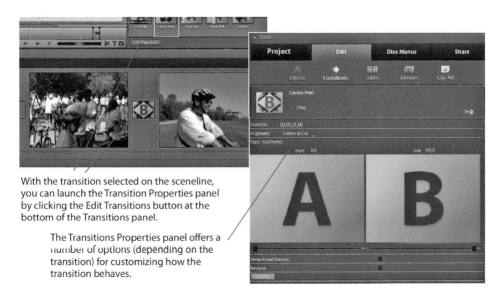

With the transition selected on the sceneline, you can launch the Transition Properties panel by clicking the Edit Transitions button at the bottom of the Transitions panel.

The Transitions Properties panel offers a number of options (depending on the transition) for customizing how the transition behaves.

Sceneline mode
includes two audio
tracks (in addition
to the "invisible"
track included with
your video clips).

Although labeled
Narration and
Soundtrack, any
audio can be
loaded onto
either track.

## Add audio to your sceneline

As you add your video clips to your sceneline, the accompanying audio
will be added automatically, as part of an unseen audio track.

In addition to the clip's audio, **Sceneline** mode offers two additional audio
tracks. (Although the icons to the left of each track imply that they are
for **Narration** and **Soundtrack**, any audio can be used on any track.) As
with your video clips, adding audio clips is as simple as dragging them
from your Media panel to one of these audio tracks. **Narration** can also be
added to your movie using the Premiere Elements narration recorder (as
we discuss on page 94 of **Chapter 7, Edit Audio on the Timeline**) or by
recording the narration separately and manually importing the audio clip
into your project.

If you drag a clip that includes both audio and video onto one of the audio
tracks, by the way, only the audio from that clip will be added to your
sceneline.

## Adjust your audio levels

There are a couple of ways to adjust the audio levels in **Sceneline** mode.
The simplest method is to adjust the level for the entire track. This is useful
if, for instance, you'd like to turn down your soundtrack music or the audio
on your video clips so that your narration can be better heard.

To turn down the audio for an entire track, click on the speaker or musical
note icon to the left of the track (as illustrated on the facing page). This will
reveal a levels slider, which you can adjust to the audio level you prefer.

But more often you'll need more precise audio level control, as when you'd
like your music to start at one level, then fade back when your narration
comes in. This can be accomplished by using the **Audio Mixer** (launched
by clicking the green speaker icon along the top of the **Sceneline** panel).

As you adjust the sliders in the **Audio Mixer** as your movie is playing, the
mixer will create audio keyframes, raising or lowering the audio levels at
precise points, based on your adjustments.

The audio level for a track can be adjusted by clicking on the icon to the left of the audio track and raising or lower the slider which then appears.

The speaker icon to the left of the video clips represents the video clips' audio

Audio can be adjusted more precisely by launching the Audio Mixer (by clicking the green speaker icon) and adjusting the sliders as your movie plays.

This can be a bit tricky though. And, if you don't like the way your audio has been adjusted, it can be challenging to reuse the **Audio Mixer** to undo your mistakes because the mixer merely adds more keyframes rather than replacing the old.

To adjust your audio levels with more precise control as well as the ability to re-adjust your settings, you'll be much better off if you use audio keyframes, as we discuss in **Adjust audio at specific points in your video** on page 88 of **Chapter 7, Edit Audio on the Timeline**.

## Add titles

As we discuss in greater detail in **Chapter 10, Add Titles**, the **Titles** workspace in Premiere Elements can be accessed in one of two ways.

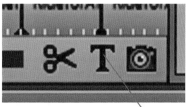

- Clicking the "**T**" icon at the bottom right of the **Monitor** panel takes you directly to the Titles workspace.

When the Titles workspace is launched by clicking the "T" in the lower right of the Monitor panel, a title is automatically created in your movie at the position of the CTI playhead.

- Clicking the **Titles** button (under the **Edit** tab) also takes you to this workspace, but it does so by taking you through the titles templates workspace first.

The presence of a title (or any video clip on an upper track) is represented in the upper right of a clip on your sceneline by a blue square.

The presence of narration or other audio on your audio track is represented in the upper right of a clip on your sceneline by a microphone icon.

Once you've created a title, it is automatically added to your sceneline at the position of the **CTI** (Current Time Indicator). The presence of a title over your clip is indicated by an icon which will appear in the upper right corner of the clip or clips on your **Sceneline**, as illustrated above.

Controlling the length of time the title displays and when in your movie it appears can be a bit challenging in **Sceneline** mode, however.

As we've said, **Sceneline** mode is mostly about assembling your clips into a movie. Switching to **Timeline** mode, you'll have much more control over when and how things happen. In **Timeline** mode, it is relatively simple to locate the title on an upper video track, position it precisely where you'd like it to appear and extend or reduce the time it is displayed.

## The limitations of Sceneline mode

Although many of the features discussed in **Chapter 6, Edit Your Video in Timeline Mode**, and **Chapter 7, Edit Audio on the Timeline**, are also available in **Sceneline** mode, many of the program's more advanced functions are limited or can only be used in **Timeline** mode.

Features that function to a limited degree or not at all in **Sceneline** mode include:

**Multi-track editing.** The **Sceneline** is limited to one video track. J-Cuts, L-Cuts, split screen and picture-in-picture effects can not be created in **Sceneline** mode.

**Chroma Key and Videomerge.** Because **keying** effects, including **Videomerge**, require at least two tracks of video in order to create their composite effects, these effects can not be effectively created in **Sceneline** mode.

**Time Stretch.** Because the **Time Stretch** effects are a function of time, fast motion, slow motion and reverse play effects can not be easily created in **Sceneline** mode.

**Titles.** Although titles can be created in **Sceneline** mode, they can not be precisely positioned, extended or trimmed to a specific length, or have effects or transitions – including fade ins and fade outs – applied to them.

**Audio Keyframing.** Audio can not be set to specific levels at specific points in a clip on the sceneline. Audio keyframes must be created and adjusted in the **Properties** panel.

**Add Clips to Your Timeline**

**Auto Enhance Your Clips**

**Split and Trim Your Clips**

**Work with Multiple Tracks of Video**

**Smart Trim Your Movie**

**Motion Tracking**

**The Time Stretch Tool**

Chapter 6

# Edit Your Video in Timeline Mode

## Where your movie comes together

Although every panel in Premiere Elements has its role in your editing workflow, the Timeline/Sceneline panel (or, as Adobe calls it, the My Project panel) is the arena where the real video editing action takes place.

It's where your clips are gathered, ordered, trimmed, sliced, rearranged, and where effects are applied. It's where your clips interact with one another.

In short, it's where your movie finally comes together.

In Timeline mode, your clips are dragged from the Media panel to any of up to 99 audio and/or video tracks. Transitions are added to points at which clips meet.

There are two workspaces in which you can build your movie in Premiere Elements. The **Sceneline**, as we discuss in **Chapter 5**, is the simpler of the two – a drag-and-drop workspace for quickly assembling your video project's parts.

The real power of the program, however, is in the **Timeline** workspace. In **Timeline** mode, you can not only arrange your clips into any order, but you can also control how and when they interact with each other. Further, you can control precisely how and when effects are applied or titles appear. And, with virtually an unlimited number of video and audio tracks at your disposal (officially 99 of each), you can create a variety of special effects – including transparent "keying" effects and **Picture-in-Picture** compositions – using techniques that otherwise are not be available in **Sceneline** mode.

In short, the **Timeline** is the more powerful, more professional-style video editing workspace.

(You can, of course, switch back and forth between the **Timeline** and **Sceneline** mode, taking advantage of the best features of each as you work.)

In **Timeline** mode, as in **Sceneline** mode, the Video 1 track appears by default with three audio tracks. Additional video tracks and audio tracks can be added, as needed, stacked above this basic set.

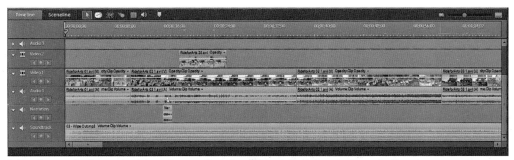

In Timeline mode, the emphasis is on time and how the different clips interact with each other.

## Override the timeline ripple function

The timeline in Premiere Elements is set, by default, to "**ripple**" as you add and remove clips from your project.

In other words, as you add and remove clips, the other clips on the timeline will move left or right to allow for inserted footage or to fill gaps.

- When you **Delete** a clip from your project, the clips to the right will slide to the left to fill in the gap (unless there is a clip filling this gap on a parallel track).

- When you **Insert** a clip into an assemblage of clips – even if on a parallel video or audio track – the clips to the right of that clip on the timeline will **split** and move to the right to accommodate the new clip.

In most cases, rippling will work to your advantage. If you've got an assemblage of audio and video clips in your movie and you decide to reorder it or add a clip to the middle of your project, you'll want the rest of the clips in your movie to stay in relative position, moving as a group to allow for the inserted clip.

But there may also be times when you'll want to override this ripple function – as when you've assembled a movie and you're trying to add background music to it or you want to add a video clip to the middle of your movie without changing the positions of any of its other clips.

**Holding down the Ctrl k**ey on a PC or the ⌘ key on a Mac as you add your new clip(s) to your timeline will override this ripple function.

When you override the ripple function, the rest of your clips will remain locked in their positions on your timeline as you add your new clip, and you'll be able to place your music on an audio track – or any clip on any other audio or video track – without disturbing the rest of your movie.

Particularly, if you're doing multi-track editing, holding down this **Ctrl** key on PC or **the** ⌘ key on a Mac is just about the only way to keep your movie clips in place as you continually add and remove clips on other tracks.

## Smart Fix your clips

When your clips have been Auto-Analyzed and Smart Tagged, the program will offer to apply a Smart Fix Auto Ehance when you place the clip on your timeline – correcting the contrast and brightness and, if necessary, stabilizing the camera movement.

Premiere Elements includes the option to have the program automatically apply a **Smart Fix** to your clips as you add them to your timeline or sceneline.

When this tool is enabled in the program's **Preferences** (under the **Edit** menu, as discussed below), an option panel will appear each time you add a new clip to your timeline or your sceneline, asking if you would like the program to "**Fix quality problems in your clips?**" (This option panel will only appear if your clips have been **Smart Tagged** prior to your adding them to your project, as discussed on the facing page.)

If you select **Yes**, Premiere Elements will automatically apply the necessary contrast levels to the clip and, if it judges the clip as too shaky, will apply automatic image stabilization!

If the clip is very long and has inconsistent quality issues, the program will even keyframe variations of contrast! (There is no way to set this feature to correct only contrast *or* only stabilization, by the way. Your options are only to have both applied or neither.)

In our experience, the results are usually very good (even if the applied effects mean that the program must then render the clips before they play back smoothly).

This feature can be turned off any time by checking the **Do Not Show Again** box in the **Smart Fix** pop-up panel, as illustrated above.

To re-activate this feature later, go to the **Edit** drop-down on the Menu Bar and select **Preferences**. On the preferences **General** page, check the box that says **Show All Do Not Show Again Messages**.

**Smart Fix** can also be applied manually to clips that are already on your timeline or sceneline. To apply this feature, **right-click** on a clip (**Ctrl-click** on a Mac) and select **Smart Fix** from the context menu.

As discussed in the sidebar on the facing page, the **Smart Fix** tool will only be available for clips that have been previously **Smart Tagged**.

## Timeline views

Premiere Elements includes a number of features for viewing your timeline, depending on how closely you want to look at your movie.

Using the zoom tool, for instance, you can zoom out to view your entire movie at once – or you can zoom in close enough to see your video's individual frames.

To zoom in or out on your timeline, drag the slider (on the upper right of the **Timeline** panel) left or right – or use the following keyboard shortcuts:

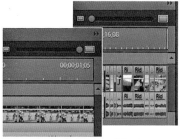

Using the Timeline zoom slider (or your +, – and \ keys) you can zoom out to see your whole project or or zoom in close enough to see individual frames.

 Pressing the **–** key on your keyboard zooms out.

 Pressing the **+** key zooms in.

 Pressing the **\** key (above the **Enter/Return** key) automatically zooms out to display your entire movie.

To make more efficient use of the panel's vertical space, individual tracks on the Timeline can be toggled between a compressed and an open view.

### Open or closed video and audio tracks

In Premiere Elements, you can also toggle the views of the individual tracks on your timeline to display as either open – which allows you to view your video clips as thumbnails and your audio clips as waveforms – or closed, reducing the amount of vertical space the **Timeline** panel requires when you are using multiple tracks of video and audio, as illustrated on the right.

### Clips must be Smart Tagged in order to be Smart Fixed

The **Smart Fix** option panel, discussed on the facing page, will only appear as you add your clips to your timeline or sceneline *if* these clips have been previously **Auto Analyzed** prior to your adding them to your project. This is because the **Smart Fix** tool takes its cue from information gathered by **Auto-Analyzer,** an Elements Organizer feature that automatically analyzes and records metadata to your clips based on content and quality issues.

The **Auto Analyzer** is set up in the Elements Organizer's **Preferences**, located under its **Edit** drop-down menu. (For more information, see **The Smart Tags Media Analyzer** on page 172 of **Chapter 15, The Elements Organizer.**) In this preference panel, you have the option of setting the **Auto-Analyzer** to automatically **Smart Tag** every clip in your Organizer catalog, or to only analyze clips meeting specific criteria. On most faster computers, the **Auto Analyzer** will work unobtrusively in the background, without interfering with your other editing work, running when you are not working on your computer.

You may, as an alternative to this automatic function, manually prep your clips for **Smart Fix** (or the other Premiere Elements tools that require **Smart Tagging)** by selecting these clips in the Elements Organizer **Photo Browser,** either one at a time or several at once, **right-clicking (Ctrl-clicking** on a Mac) and selecting the option to **Run Auto Analyzer** from the context menu.

To add a clip to your timeline or sceneline, simply drag it from the Media panel.

In Timeline mode, the other clips will "ripple", moving aside if you add the clip in the middle of a project.

To override the ripple effect (as when you're adding music or a video clip to a parallel track) hold down the Ctrl key as you add the clip.

Zoom in or out on the timeline by pressing + or - or using the Zoom slider.

## Add clips to your timeline

Adding clips to your project's timeline is about as intuitive as it can be. You simply drag in the clips from the **Project** or your **Media** panel (under the **Project** tab) onto a video or audio track.

You can reorder the clips on the timeline by dragging them around. Placing a clip to the left of another clip will cause it to slide it aside ("ripple" it) to accommodate the move. (See page 69 for information on overriding this feature.)

To delete a clip from your timeline, click to select it and press the **Delete** button on your keyboard or **right-click** on it (**Ctrl-click** on a Mac) and select **Delete**. Unless there are clips on parallel video or audio tracks, the timeline will ripple to fill in the gap.

To remove a clip *without* causing the other clips to ripple or fill in the gap, **right-click** on the clip (**Ctrl-click** on a Mac) and select **Clear** instead.

Once your clips are assembled, you can apply transitions between them by dragging a transition between them from the **Transitions** panel. More information on this feature can be found in **Chapter 12, Add and Customize Transitions**.

## Trim or split your clips

Once your clip is on your timeline, you can edit it to remove unwanted portions by **trimming** and/or **splitting** it.

**Trimming** removes footage from the beginning or end of a clip.

**Splitting** divides your clip into segments, which you can then remove or rearrange.

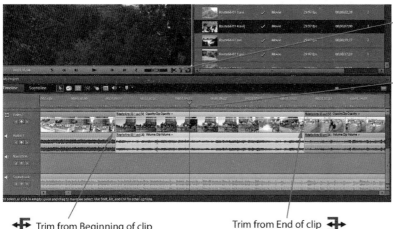

To slice a clip in two, click the Split Clip (scissors) tool on the Monitor panel.

If a clip is selected on the timeline, only that clip will be split at the position of the CTI; If no clips are selected, all clips on every track on the timeline will be split at the position of the CTI.

**⊢E** Trim from Beginning of clip          Trim from End of clip **Ǝ⊢**

To trim a clip on the timeline, hover your mouse over the beginning or end of a clip until the Trim from Beginning or Trim from End icon appears, then click and drag in or out.

### Trim a clip on your timeline

To **trim a clip**, click to select the clip on your timeline and hover your mouse over the clip's beginning or end.

As you hover your mouse over either end of a clip, it will switch to trim mode (becoming a **Ǝ⊢** or a **⊢E** cursor). Click and drag the end of the clip to trim it – removing footage from or adding footage to the clip's beginning or end.

The **Monitor** will preview the new in or out point as you drag. (For information on pre-trimming your clip before you drag it to the timeline or sceneline, see **Pre-trim your clips in the Preview Monitor** in **Chapter 4, Explore the Media Panel**.)

If you find, after removing a segment, that you've removed too much of a clip – or not enough – you can simply re-drag the end of the clip to replace or remove the extra frames. (In non-linear editing, nothing is ever permanently removed from a clip.)

### Split a clip on your timeline

To **split a clip** – either to remove a portion of it or to isolate a segment so that you can move, or add an effect to, it – position the **CTI** (Current Time Indicator) at the point on your timeline you'd like to slice and then click the **Split Clip** (scissors icon) on the lower right of the **Monitor** panel.

If you have a clip selected on your timeline, this tool will slice only that clip; if you have no clips selected, the tool will slice through *all* of the clips on all tracks at the **CTI's** current position.

If you then want to delete the segment you've sliced (or sliced on either side of), click to select the segment, **right-click** (**Ctrl-click** on a Mac) and choose **Delete** or **Clear**, depending on whether or not you'd like the timeline to ripple to fill the gap.

## Tools on the Timeline panel

Several editing tools can be found along the top left of the **Timeline/Sceneline** panel:

**Tools on the Timeline and Sceneline panels**

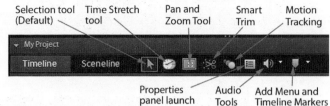

Selection tool (Default)  Time Stretch tool  Pan and Zoom Tool  Smart Trim  Motion Tracking

Properties panel launch  Audio Tools  Add Menu and Timeline Markers

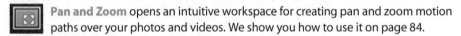

Smart Trim will trim a clip on your timeline, automatically indicating and offering to remove segments it sees as having quality issues. More information on the **Smart Trim** tool can be found below.

Time Stretch controls the playback speed of a clip. With **Time Stretch** you can set your clip to run in slow motion, fast motion or even reverse. We show you how to use this tool on page 81. (This **Time Stretch** tool is not available in **Sceneline** mode.)

Pan and Zoom opens an intuitive workspace for creating pan and zoom motion paths over your photos and videos. We show you how to use it on page 84.

Motion Tracking enables you to link a piece of clip art, title or even another clip to a person or object in your movie so that it follows it, him or her movement around your video frame. We show you how to use this tool on page 82.

Properties opens the **Properties** panel. We discuss this powerful workspace in detail in **Chapter 13**.

**Audio Tools** are discussed in detail in **Chapter 7, Edit Audio on the Timeline**.

## Smart Trim your video

The **Smart Trim** tool analyzes clips you add to your movie's timeline and then recommends trims to remove segments from your clips (or automatically trims the segments for you) which do not meet your indicated quality standards.

1    **Smart Trim** mode is enabled by clicking on the "magic scissors" icon on your timeline or sceneline.

Once this mode is enabled, a **Smart Trim Options** button will appear at the top of your **Monitor** panel, as illustrated on the facing page.

2    Click on the **Smart Trim Options** button to open the **Smart Trim Options** panel.

The **Smart Trim Options** panel allows you to set a **Quality Level** and an **Interest Level** for any new clips you add.

**Quality** automatically checks your clips for issues like blurriness, shakiness, brightness and contrast.

**Interest** searches through the segments that **Quality** recommends deleting and re-evaluates their content to see if they're actually worth saving, based on the level you've set.

In Smart Trim mode, clicking the Smart Trim Options button opens a panel for setting the levels of Interest and Quality for your potential auto-cuts.

In other words, the **Interest Level** and **Quality Level** balance each other out, according to the levels you set.

When you add a new clip to your timeline or sceneline with this mode enabled, **Smart Trim** automatically **Media-Analyzes** all of the clips in your **Media** panel – unless they have already been **Media-Analyzed** in the Elements Organizer – adding **Smart Tags** to the clips indicating whether they include areas that are out of focus, too dark, etc.

As these clips are added to your timeline or sceneline, a blue, diagonal line shading will be displayed over segments which are not up to the **Quality** and **Interest Levels** you've set, designating them as **Smart Trim regions** for potential deletion.

If you are in **Sceneline** mode, this shading will appear on the timeline that runs along the bottom of the **Monitor,** as illustrated on the right.

In **Timeline** mode, these **Smart Trim regions** will appear on the clip right on your timeline, as illustrated on the lower right.

- If you've selected the **Automatic** radio button in the **Smart Trim Options** panel, the program will then offer to automatically delete these segments.

- If you've elected not to have the program automatically trim these segments, or if you have the **Smart Trim Options** set to **Manual**, the program will not delete these segments. Rather they will remain shaded until you indicate what you'd like done with them.

As you hover your mouse over each **Smart Trim** region, the program will indicate the criteria for recommending the segment be removed, such as the segment is too blurry, too shaky, includes poor contrast, etc.

In Sceneline mode, the Smart Trim regions appear along the bottom of the Monitor.

If you hover your mouse over a Smart Trim region, Premiere Elements will suggest why the region should be removed.

Right-click on the Smart Trim region to select whether to cut the region or to override the recommendation.

3  Click on one of these overlayed **Smart Trim regions** to select it.

The diagonal shading will highlight in light blue.

By dragging on either end of this blue overlay, you can trim or extend the length of this **Smart Trim region**.

4  Once you've tweaked your **Smart Trim regions**, these segments can be manually removed or the feature disabled in a number of ways:

•   Right-click on a **Smart Trim region** and select **Trim** to remove that segment from your clip.

•   Right-click on a **Smart Trim region** and select **Select All** to select all of the clip's **Smart Trim** regions for deletion.

•   Right-click on a **Smart Trim region** and select **Keep** to turn off the **Smart Trim** option for this particular region.

In addition to **Smart Trimming** these regions from your clips, Premiere Elements can be set to automatically add a transition when you remove a **Smart Trim region**.

To exit **Smart Trim** mode, click again on the "magic scissors" icon on the **Timeline** or **Sceneline** panel.

## Add still photos to your project

Still photos are dragged to the timeline or sceneline just as video clips are. By default, the duration of a still photo in a Premiere Elements project is **five seconds**. (This default can be changed under **Edit/Preferences** – although changing it will only affect photos brought into the program *after* the preference has been changed.)

You can increase or decrease how long the photo displays on the timeline by dragging to trim or extend it, just as you would to trim or extend any video clip, as described in **Trimming and Splitting**.

As explained in **Use Photos in Premiere Elements** (page 45) in **Chapter 3, Get Media into Your Project**, you'll get the best performance from stills in a standard video project if they are sized to no larger than 1000x750 pixels.

Additionally, once you've placed a photo on your timeline, you can eliminate a somewhat common problem (related to interlacing) by **right-clicking** on the still on the timeline (**Ctrl-clicking** on a Mac) and selecting **Field Options** and then selecting the **Flicker Removal** option.

Applying this setting will preempt a fluttering problem that sometimes manifests itself in video outputs when highly detailed or high contrast photos are used in Premiere Elements projects.

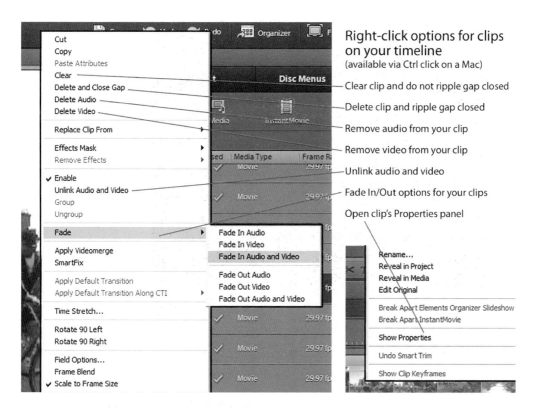

Right-click options for clips
on your timeline
(available via Ctrl click on a Mac)

Clear clip and do not ripple gap closed

Delete clip and ripple gap closed

Remove audio from your clip

Remove video from your clip

Unlink audio and video

Fade In/Out options for your clips

Open clip's Properties panel

## Remove audio or video from your clip

**Right-clicking** on a clip on your timeline (**Ctrl-clicking** on a Mac) gives you access to a number of helpful features, tools and options, as illustrated above.

Deleting a clip from your timeline is as simple as **right-clicking** on the clip and selecting **Clear** or **Delete and Close Gap**. Removing the audio track or video track from a clip is as simple selecting either **Delete Audio** or **Delete Video** from the right-click menu.

## Fade in and out of your clip

The simplest way to fade into or out of a clip is to **right-click** on it and select **Fade In** or **Fade Out** from the right-click menu. (Separate options are offered for fading in or out of your video and your audio, if your clip includes both.)

By default, your fades will last one second. You can, however, adjust the keyframe positions to lengthen or shorten that time.

To do this, look for the white dots that Premiere Elements has placed to create the fade on the thin, horizontal, yellow line that runs through your clip.

These dots are called **keyframes**, and we discuss them in much greater detail in **Chapter 14, Keyframing**.

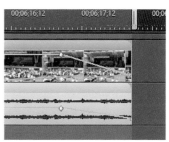

Fade ins and fade outs are really just keyframed Opacity and Volume properties. You can change the length of the fade by changing the positions of the keyframe points on the timeline.

By default, that yellow line represents **Opacity** on your video clips and it represents **Volume** on your audio clips.

See how the line slants down before or after that keyframe? That's your fade in or fade out of the clip's **Opacity** or **Volume** levels.

Adjusting that dot's position relative to the end of the clip, by clicking on it and dragging it, extends or shortens the duration of your fade in or fade out.

To find out more about adjusting your audio's volume and how to control it at specific points in your movie, see **Adjust audio levels at specific points on your timeline** in **Chapter 7, Edit Audio on the Timeline.**

## Use L-cuts, J-cuts and multiple tracks

The ability to compose your video using several audio and video tracks greatly expands your ability to use interesting and professional-style editing techniques in your video projects.

Multiple tracks of audio, of course, merely mix into a single soundtrack for your movie. (See **Mix Audio** in **Chapter 7, Edit Audio on the Timeline**.)

But, with multiple tracks of video you can combine elements from several video clips at once using a variety of properties and effects.

Think of multiple tracks of video as a stack, like layers in a photo. In most cases, only the uppermost track in the stack will be visible.

However, if you change the scale and position of the clips on the uppermost track – or on several tracks – you can display several tracks at once. (This **Picture-in-Picture** effect can be achieved using **Presets**, as discussed on page 134 of **Chapter 11, Add Video and Audio Effects**, or by adjusting their **Scale** and **Position**, as discussed on page 151 of **Chapter 13, Customize Effects in the Properties Panel**.)

You can also reveal portions of clips on lower tracks by using effects such as **Chroma Key** (as discussed on page 128 of **Chapter 11, Add Video and Audio Effects**), any of the **Matte** effects or even the **Crop** effect.

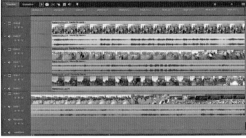

Using Scaling and Position settings with multiple tracks of video allows for Picture-in-Picture effects as well as the opportunity to do split screens, showing several video clips on screen at once

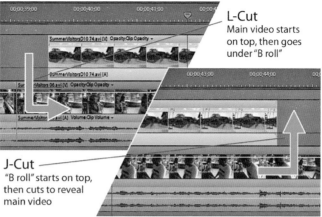

**L-Cut**
Main video starts on top, then goes under "B roll"

**J-Cut**
"B roll" starts on top, then cuts to reveal main video

As audio from main clip continues, video cuts to or from "B roll" footage.

By keyframing the effects in the **Properties** panel, you can also make these positions, sizings or other settings change over the duration of the clip. (For more information, see **Chapter 14, Keyframing**.)

Using multiple tracks of video and then scaling and positioning your clips on each, you can have any number of video images in your video frame at the same time. (Think of the grid of faces in the opening credits of *The Brady Bunch* – or see my multiple-panel illustration above.) The products page at Muvipix.com offers a wealth of tutorials describing techniques for achieving these effects using a number of video tracks and effects.

Additionally, two popular techniques that use multiple tracks of video are the **L-cut** and the **J-cut** – so named because, back in the days of single-track editing, when a segment of video had to be removed and the audio left in place to allow for the placement of alternate video, the primary video and audio clip resembled an "L" or a "J" (depending on which segment was removed).

Consider a TV news report that features video of a reporter shown standing in front of a burned-out building, describing the fire that destroyed it.

As he continues speaking, the video cuts away to footage shot earlier of the fire itself. That's an **L-cut**. (A **J-cut**, on the other hand, begins with the cut-away video and the reporter's voice heard on the soundtrack, then cuts to the reporter finishing his report.)

Creating an **L-cut** is easy with multi-track editing.

1   Put the main video, the clip of the reporter speaking to the camera (we'll call it **Clip A**), on Video track 1.

2   Holding the **Ctrl** key (to override the timeline's ripple function), place the second video – the footage of the fire (**Clip B**) – on Video track 2.

3    Overlap the latter part of **Clip A** with **Clip B**, as seen in the illustration on the previous page.

4    **Right-click** on **Clip B** (**Ctrl-click** on a Mac) and select **Delete Audio**, if you need to remove its audio track.

Voila! Tweak **Clip B**'s position for maximum effect and you're done! We begin with the reporter speaking to the camera and, as he continues to speak, we cut away to the footage of the fire.

**L-cuts** and **J-cuts** are very effective for news-style reports as well as for interviews, in which you cut away from the person speaking to separately shot footage of what he or she is describing. It's a great way to reinforce, with images, what's being presented verbally.

By the way, here's some professional vocabulary to impress your friends with. That secondary footage that plays as the main video's audio continues? It's commonly called "**B-roll footage**", a relic from the days when this kind of editing actually did involve pasting in footage from a separate roll of film or video.

## Output a segment of your video using the Work Area Bar

The Work Area Bar can be set to designate only a portion of your video project. Most Share options allow you to output the Work Area Bar segment only.

The **Work Area Bar** is the lighter gray area that runs along the ticker at the top of the timeline, defined by a silver marker on either end. Usually, this bar covers your entire video project and grows and shrinks with your project as you edit.

But, by dragging its beginning and end handles, you can manually set the **Work Area Bar** to cover only a portion of your video editing project, as illustrated above. In this way, you can designate only a portion of your project for output.

Nearly all of the output options under the **Share** tab include a checkbox option **Export Work Area Bar Only**, as in the illustration. Checking this option directs the program to output *only* the segment of your project you've defined with the **Work Area Bar**.

For more information on this function, see the discussions under each output option in **Chapter 18, Share Your Movie**.

## Use Time Stretch to speed up or slow down your video

There are actually two **Time Stretch** tools – one operates numerically, based on the speed percentage you designate, and the other operates more intuitively, based on how long you stretch your clip.

These are essentially two sides of the same tool, however, and you can use one tool to fine tune the results of the other.

**To Time Stretch numerically, right-click** on a clip on your timeline (**Ctrl-click** on a Mac) and select **Time Stretch** from the context menu.

- In the **Time Stretch** option panel, type the percentage of speed you would like your clip to play at. (50% means that your clip plays at half its normal speed, e.g.). As an alternative, you can type in the time duration (hours;minutes;seconds; frames) you would like your clip to play and the playback speed will set automatically.

- The **Reverse Speed** checkbox allows you to reverse your clip's playback.

Time Stretch for a clip can be set numerically by selecting the option from the right-click menu.

- **Maintain Audio Pitch** will apply a pitch shift tweak to your audio so that, for instance, if you speed the clip up, the voices won't sound quite so much like chipmunks.

**To Time Stretch using the Timeline tool**, click on the **Time Stretch** button (the clock) on the top left of the **Timeline** panel. (Because of how this tool functions, it is not available in **Sceneline** mode.)

- Drag the endpoints on the clip on your timeline inward or outward, as if you are trimming the clip. The shorter you make the clip, the faster it will play; the longer you stretch the clip, the slower it will play.

- To turn off the **Time Stretch** tool and return to normal editing mode, click on the **Selection Tool** button (the arrow) on the top left of the Timeline panel.

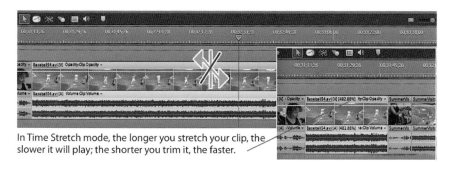

In Time Stretch mode, the longer you stretch your clip, the slower it will play; the shorter you trim it, the faster.

In Motion Tracking mode, click on Add Object to designate an object or person to be tracked.

The program will follow the object across the video frame.

## Follow an object with Motion Tracking

 Premiere Elements' **Motion Tracking** tool will lock onto an object or person you indicate in a clip and follow it, him or her around your video frame.

You can then link a piece of artwork, another clip or a title to that object or person and the program will automatically create a motion path so that it moves around the video frame along with the tracked object!

You can, for instance, link to someone running across your frame with clip art of a hat or a cartoon talk bubble, and that hat or bubble will stay with that person throughout the clip.

To use **Motion Tracking,** click to select a clip on your timeline or sceneline and then click the **Motion Tracking** mode button (the yellow ball icon) along the top of the **Timeline/Sceneline** panel.

1    The program will ask you if you want to **Media Analyze** the clip to track moving objects. **Media Analyzing** is related to the program's automatic metadata creation system and is not necessary for this tool to function.

2    Regardless of whether you elect to **Media Analyze** the clip, a box will appear over your clip in the center of the **Monitor** panel. This box will include four corner handles so that it can be reshaped and resized. Drag the corner handles and move the box to indicate the person or object in the frame you want to track.

3    Once you've framed the object or person to be tracked, click on the **Track Object** button at the top of the **Monitor** panel.

     The program will analyze the motion in the clip.

     When it has finished, if you play or scrub the clip (by dragging the **CTI** back and forth), The box should follow the indicated object or person around your video frame.

4    Once the **Motion Tracker** has completed its analysis, you can link an object to this motion track.

Under the **Edit** tab, Premiere Elements includes a collection of nearly 250 pieces of **Clip Art** that can be linked to a motion track. Titles and picture-in-picture clips can also be linked to a track.

To link artwork to motion track, drag your clip or **Clip Art** onto the **Motion Track** box on your **Monitor**.

The clip will be added to a video track above your current video. You can size or position this clip by dragging on the corner handles or dragging it around. As long as the object you are tracking in the main video has an active yellow box around it, the clip will follow the motion track once the program automatically creates the necessary keyframes.

In the same way, you can drag any clip from the **Media** panel onto your motion track. As long as the yellow rectangle is displayed when you drag the clip to the **Monitor**, the clip should lock to the motion track. (An indication that your clip is locked to a motion track is that the added clip will be noticeably smaller than its actual size.)

You can link several objects and clips, on a number of video tracks, to the same **Motion Track**. Just ensure that the main background clip is selected on your timeline and that the **Motion Track** mode is enabled. (The yellow rectangle will indicate that your motion track is active.)

You can also link text or a title to a motion track, although it takes an extra step or two.

1   Click the "**T**" on the **Monitor** panel to create your title (as we discuss in **Chapter 10, Add Titles**). Once your title is created and you have returned to **Edit** mode, locate the title on its video track and delete it. (It will remain in the **Media** panel.)

2   Select the clip that you've **Motion Tracked** and click on the **Motion Track** mode button so that the yellow rectangle is visible on the clip in the **Monitor**.

3   Drag the title you created earlier from the **Media** panel (under the **Project** tab) onto the yellow motion track rectangle. (As with any clip you add to a motion track, it will appear smaller than its actual size.)

    Size and position your title as needed.

When Clip Art, a title or a Picture-in-Picture clip is linked to the Motion Track object, the program creates keyframes so that the clip follows the object across the video frame.

Premiere Elements includes a set of animated clips that move or change shape as they follow your Motion Track across your video frame.

More than one clip can be linked to your Motion Track, combining, for instance, a cartoon thought bubble and a title.

The title should lock to the motion track and follow the tracked object around the frame.

You can have several **Motion Tracks** on the same video clip and link different clips to each **Motion Track**.

To create a new motion track, click the **Add Object** button that appears at the top of the **Monitor** panel while you are in **Motion Tracking** mode, then size and position the rectangle that appears over the object or person you want to track.

When more than one motion track appears on a clip, the active motion track will be highlighted with a blue rectangle. The other motion tracks on the clip – those that are present but not currently activated – will appear as yellow rectangles.

(Click on the various motion track rectangles displayed in your **Monitor** to select or to deselect them.)

When you link your clip or clip art, it will follow the **Motion Track** that was indicated with a blue rectangle when the clip or clip art was added.

## Create a Pan and Zoom motion path

A cool, new feature in version 10 is the **Pan and Zoom Tool**.

This tool allows you to create motion paths – pans and zooms across your photos – using a very intuitive interface. (It's, of course, not the only way to create motion paths. For more information on using keyframes to create custom motion paths, see **Chapter 14, Keyframing**.)

Although this tool can also be used on video, the effect will create the best results when used on photos that have a slightly higher resolution than the video project. As we explain in **Use photos in Premiere Elements** on page 47, you'll get the best balance of photo quality and system performance if your photos are no larger than 1000x750 pixels in size. (For high-definition video, you can go as large as 2000x1500 pixels.)

To demonstrate this tool, we'll create a simple motion path over a photo.

1   Click to select a photo still on your timeline.

2   Click on the **Pan and Zoom Tool** button along the top left of the **Timeline** or Sceneline panel.

   The **Pan and Zoom** workspace will open, as illustrated at the top of the facing page.

The concept behind this workspace is a simple one: You indicate the views you'd like for the beginning and end of your motion path and Premiere Elements will create the path of motion between them.

3   Create an initial motion path keyframe.

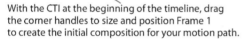

With the CTI at the beginning of the timeline, drag the corner handles to size and position Frame 1 to create the initial composition for your motion path.

Move the CTI to the end of the timeline and then drag the corner handles of Frame 2 to create the composition you'd like your motion path to end on.

Place the CTI at other positions on the timeline and click the New Frame button to create as many additional motion path keyframes as you need (including hold motion frames) to build your motion path.

Ensure that the **CTI** is at the beginning of the timeline that runs along the bottom of the workspace. (You should see a little, diamond-shaped keyframe on the timeline at the **CTI's** position.)

Drag on **Frame 1** (the green box) and on its corner handles to size and position the frame to create the initial composition you'd like for your motion path.

4    Move the **CTI** to the end of the timeline.

There will be another diamond-shaped keyframe at this position on the timeline. When you move the **CTI** over this keyframe, **Frame 2** (a second green box) will become highlighted.

Size and position **Frame 2** to create the composition you'd like to end your motion path with. (A little blue line will indicate the duration (in seconds) of your motion.)

Click the **Play Output** button along the bottom of the panel to preview your motion path.

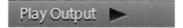

You may add additional keyframes to create additional movements if you'd like. To do this, move the **CTI** to other positions on the timeline and click the **New Frame** button in the upper left of the workspace, as illustrated above.

5    When you are finished, click **Done** to return to the regular editing workspace.

If you'd like to further customize this motion path, you can do so by opening the clip's **Motion Properties**, as described in **Chapter 14, Keyframing.**

## Render your timeline

When you initially set up your Premiere Elements project (see **Chapter 2, Start a new project**), you set the program to use a certain workflow, based on a given video format.

In standard definition video, for instance, your workflow is based on the DV-AVI video format. That means that, whatever video clips or photos you put into your standard definition video project, Premiere Elements assimilates them and renders them as DV-AVI video before it outputs them as another video format.

And that's true even if you put an MPEG in and then output an MPEG from the project you've created with it. *Everything* in a standard definition project goes through the process of becoming a DV-AVI before Premiere Elements encodes it as anything else.

Premiere Elements also includes components that allow it to work natively with a number of high-definition formats, including HDV and AVCHD.

When your project settings ideally match your source video, *you will not see any red lines* above the clips on your timeline until you add effects or transitions to them.

As you add effects and transitions to your project or you add other video sources to your project (including photos), you will see red lines appear above the clips, as illustrated below, indications that these segments of your timeline need to be rendered – converted to the workflow video format. As more of your project requires rendering, your computer will begin to operate more sluggishly and the program may even notify you that your system is running low on memory. Your preview video will also suffer a reduction in quality.

This is because, until you manually render these segments, the program is continually creating "soft renders" of them –"on the fly" previews of your unrendered files. And that puts a lot of strain on your system.

Manually rendering your project will create temporary videos based on these segments in the ideal format for your project. The program will then use these rendered videos to create your preview playback – providing you a much cleaner representation of what your final video will look like and greatly reducing the strain on your system's resources.

To **Render** your video projects' timeline, press the **Enter** key on your keyboard, or select **Render Work Area** from the **Timeline** drop-down on the Menu Bar.

A red line just below the ticker along the top of the timeline indicates a segment that requires rendering.

Once your clip has been rendered, the red lines above the clip will turn green and your playback will be much cleaner and smoother.

You can render your clips continually as you're working. Or you can wait until your playback performance starts to lag. It's up to you.

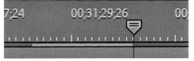

Once the sequence is rendered, the red line will turn green.

But do be aware that, if you're having playback problems and your **Timeline** has a lot of red lines running across the top, a few seconds of rendering can usually do a lot to improve the program's performance.

**Adjust Audio Levels with Keyframes**
**Monitor and Mix Your Audio Levels**
**Smart Mix Your Audio Levels**
**SonicFire Pro Express Track**
**Detect Beats**

Chapter 7
# Edit Audio on the Timeline
## Working with sounds and music

Great sound is as important as great
visuals in your video project. And
Premiere Elements includes a number
of tools for adding and enhancing
your audio and music files.

Premiere Elements 10 even includes
SonicFire Pro Express Track, an
amazing tool for creating musical
tracks – based on your custom
specifications– for your movies!

## Audio tools on the Timeline panel

A number of powerful audio tools can be accessed by clicking on the green speaker button on the top left of the **Timeline/Sceneline** panel:

Audio tools on the Timeline and Sceneline panels drop down from under the green speaker button.

**Smart Mix** will automatically mix the audio levels for your movie, based on criteria you set. We show you how to use this tool on page 91.

**Audio Mix** launches the **Audio Mixer**, which we discuss on page 90.

**Add Narration** launches a tool for creating narration for your video. We show you how to use it on page 94.

**Detect Beats** will drop markers on your timeline based on the beat of a music track you've selected. These markers can be used as a cue to change slides when you use the **Create Slideshow** feature (discussed in **Chapter 4, Explore the Project Media Panel**). We show you how to use **Detect Beats** on page 95.

**SonicFire Pro Express Track** is an amazing tool for creating custom music tracks for your videos of specific lengths, based on your style and tempo specifications. We show you how to use it on page 92.

## Adjust the audio levels at specific points in your video

The audio levels of the clips on your timeline is represented by thin, horizontal, yellow lines that run through your clips. You can easily raise or lower the volume level for a clip by dragging that line higher or lower. (See also **Monitor and mix your audio levels** on page 90.)

But what about if you want to raise and lower the audio levels for a clip at specific points?

Say you want to fade your music down for a few seconds so that your narration track can dominate? Or you have a conversation recorded in which one person speaks very quietly and you need to raise the audio level for his part of your clip, while leaving the audio level for the rest of the clip as is?

That's when you use audio keyframes. (For a more detailed discussion of keyframes, see **Chapter 14, Keyframing**.)

Audio **Volume** keyframes can be created and adjust in **Properties** panel (as discussed in **Chapter 13**) or, more conveniently, right on your timeline.

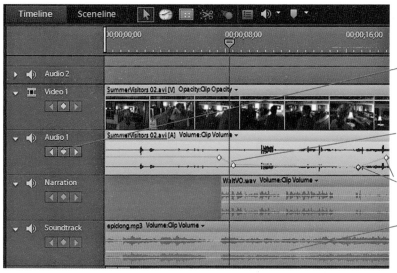

**Audio keyframes adjust audio levels at specific points**

When a clip is selected (clicked on), audio keyframes can be added with the timeline's Add/Remove Keyframe button.

Keyframes are added at the position of the CTI, but can be dragged to any position.

Dragging the keyframes higher raises the clip's audio level; dragging them lower reduces the audio level.

Dragging the yellow line with no keyframes applied raises or lowers audio level for the entire clip.

## Create audio volume keyframes on the Timeline

To create **keyframes** for your audio clips:

1    Click to select an audio or audio/video clip on your timeline and position the **CTI** (Current Time Indicator) over the approximate spot where you want to add a keyframe.

(A clip must be selected and the **CTI** positioned over it in order to create a keyframe on the timeline.)

2    Click on the little, diamond-shaped **Make Keyframe** button on the track header, left of the video or audio track, as illustrated above.

This will create a keyframe point, which will appear as a white dot on your audio clip at the position of the **CTI**. You can drag this dot to any position on the clip, or change or delete it at any time.

3    Adjust the keyframe point's position to adjust audio levels.

• Positioning the keyframe higher on the clip increases the audio volume level at that point.

• Lowering it decreases the audio volume level.

In the illustration above, the audio on the Audio 1 track has been temporarily lowered so that the narration can be heard.

You can create as many keyframes as you need, using several to set the audio level higher for some segments, and lower for other segments, on your clips.

To delete an audio keyframe, **right-click** on the white diamond keyframe point (**Ctrl-click** on a Mac) and select **Delete** from the context menu.

## Monitor and mix your audio levels

The **Audio Mixer** can be used to monitor your audio levels as well as adjust them.

To open the **Audio Mixer**, click on the green speaker icon on the top-left of the **Timeline** or **Sceneline** panel and select **Audio Mix** from the drop-down menu.

The **Audio Mixer** displays the audio levels for each of your active audio tracks and offers controls for raising and lowering these audio levels.

The Audio Mixer will display separate controls for each audio track. If adjustments are made while playback is stopped, adjustments will affect the entire clip. If made during playback, audio keyframes will be created.

The **Audio Mixer** is a great panel to keep open as much as  possible so that you can monitor your movie's audio levels, particularly as you begin the final phases of editing your project. For best results, never let your audio levels peak in the red. Overmodulated audio can sound distorted and fuzzy.

The **Audio Mixer** can also be used to adjust the levels for your individual audio clips:

- When you're not playing your video project, click to select a clip on the timeline at the position of the **CTI** (Current Time Indicator). Raising or lowering the **Audio Mixer** sliders will raise and lower the volume level for that entire clip.
- If you adjust the sliders as your video is playing, keyframe points will be added to the clip so that the audio is raised or lowered only at the point at which you adjusted the slider.

As you play your project, watch the meters for each track, adjusting the sound levels as necessary to keep these levels as much as possible in the green, with the bulk of the audio peaking at zero or a little beyond.

An occasional peak in the red will probably not cause problems, but too much will cause your video output to sound distorted.

In our opinion, this tool serves much more effectively as an audio meter than an audio level adjustment tool.

If used to adjust audio levels while the video is playing, it simply places too many hard-to-adjust audio keyframes on the timeline. You'll get much neater and much more effective results if you use the technique we describe in **Adjust audio levels at specific points in your video** on page 88.

## Smart Mix your audio

Premiere Elements' **Smart Mix** tool will automatically adjust the levels of several audio tracks, to allow one track to dominate over the others.

In other words, if you've got a sequence that includes music, narration and the original audio from a video clip, **Smart Mix** will automatically lower the music and clip levels wherever there is a narration clip (a feature sometimes called "auto ducking").

1   To set the criteria for your audio clip adjustments, click on the green speaker button on the upper left of the **Timeline** or **Sceneline** panel and, from the drop-down menu, select **Smart Mix**, then **Options**.

The **Smart Mixer Options** panel displays each audio track in your Premiere Elements project and allows you to indicate, with drop-down menus, which tracks will serve as your audio **Foreground**, which will serve as **Background** and which will be **Disabled** completely.

In Smart Mix Options, you designate which audio tracks will dominate and which will be lowered or eliminated completely.

2   Once you've set your preferences for the tool, activate the **Smart Mix** feature by clicking on the **Apply** button on the **Smart Mixer.**

(You can also start the **Smart Mix** tool without opening this mixer by selecting **Apply** from the **Audio Tools/Smart Mix** button on the **Timeline** or **Sceneline** panel.)

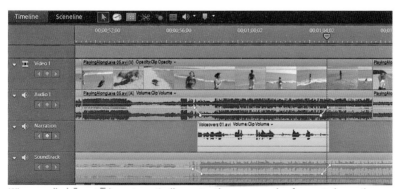

When applied, Smart Trim automatically creates the necessary keyframes to lower the audio on the tracks you've designated as Background.

The **Smart Mixer** will create the necessary audio keyframes – which appear as little white diamonds on your audio clip(s) – to lower the volume of the audio clip(s) that you've designated as **Background** audio.

Further, if you move or change a clip you've indicated as your **Foreground** and re-apply **Smart Mix**, the **Smart Mixer** will automatically remove or revise the audio keyframes!

To set preferences for the **Smart Mixer** – including how much the **Background** audio is reduced in volume and if the **Foreground** audio is automatically **Normalized** – go the Premiere Elements **Preferences** under the **Edit** drop-down on the Menu Bar and select **Audio.**

## Create custom music clips with SonicFire Pro Express Track

**SonicFire Pro Express Track** is a terrific third-party music creation feature for Premiere Elements. (It replaces the old SmartSound QuickTracks plug-in.)

A free, limited edition of the program is included with Premiere Elements – although you will need to activate the product by entering its serial number the first time you use it. To receive a free serial number, follow the instructions under **Step 1** below.

**SonicFire Pro** actually includes to elements:

**Express Track**, your free tool for creating custom-designed, royalty-free music tracks for your videos.

**SoniceFire Pro Scoring Edition**, a workspace for editing and enhancing music clips, including those created by **Express Track**. (This component is a 21-day trial.)

**Express Track** will create custom, professional-style music tracks, based on criteria you select, in whatever time duration you designate – from a short bumper of a few seconds to a full-length musical score.

1   To launch **Sonicfire Pro Express Track**, click the green speaker button on the upper-left of the **Timeline** or **Sceneline** panel and select **SonicFire Pro**.

    The first time you launch **SonicFire Pro**, you will need to activate it. To do so, click on the **Request Free Serial Number** button on the screen that appears when you launch the program and follow the prompts to the SmartSound Web site. Once you sign into the site, there will be some back-and-forth between the site and your e-mail and eventually you will be sent your serial number. (Most likely, once you activate the program, it will also need to apply some updates. Be patient. This can take a while .)

2   On the **SmartSound Express Track** option screen (illustrated on the facing page) ensure that **Owned Titles** is selected. (Ten sample **Titles** are included free with the program.)

3   Select a **Title** or filter your **Titles** by selecting a **Style** or **Keyword** in the panels along the top of the program interface. You can sample any selected **Title** by clicking the blue button **Play** on the lower right of the panel.

4   Once you've selected a **Title**, select a **Variation** and **Mood** from the drop-down menus (most **Titles** include several of each) – then set a custom **Length** for it.

## SonicFire Pro Express Track for Premiere Elements

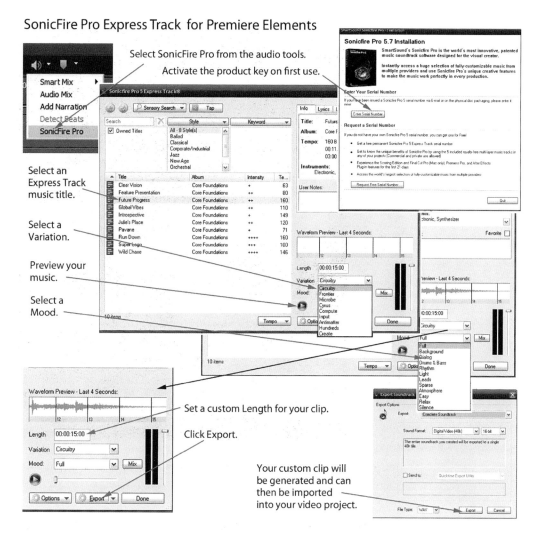

Select SonicFire Pro from the audio tools.

Activate the product key on first use.

Select an Express Track music title.

Select a Variation.

Preview your music.

Select a Mood.

Set a custom Length for your clip.

Click Export.

Your custom clip will be generated and can then be imported into your video project.

**5**   Click the **Export** button to output your musical clip. (You'll be prompted to designate a location for the file.) Once it's been created, you can further enhance the track in **SonicFire Pro's Scoring** workspace or import it into your Premiere Elements project.

The program will custom-create a rich, professional-style musical track, precisely to your specifications. And, best of all, the track is royalty-free, so you can use it in any of your productions without restriction!

### Purchase more music

In addition to the clips included free with the program, **SmartSound.com** offers hundreds of high-quality, professional-style musical clips and even sound effects for purchase.

These can be purchased individually (for typically around $14.95), or you can buy an entire package of similar music styles for $99. (Their Web site offers frequent discounts.)

Add Narration panel

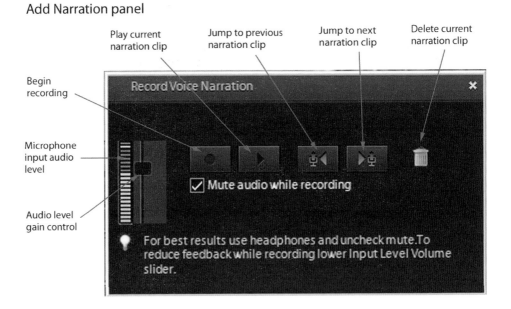

Play current
narration clip

Jump to previous
narration clip

Jump to next
narration clip

Delete current
narration clip

Begin
recording

Microphone
input audio
level

Audio level
gain control

Mute audio while recording

For best results use headphones and uncheck mute. To reduce feedback while recording lower Input Level Volume slider.

## Add Narration

With this tool, you can add narration to your project – and even record it as you watch your video playing.

1    To launch the **Record Voice Narration** tool, click on the green speaker button on the upper left of the **Timeline** or **Sceneline** panel and, from the drop-down menu, select **Add Narration**.

The **Record Voice Narration** panel will open.

The microphone recording level displays on the meter that runs along the left side of the panel.

You'll want to keep it green and full, adjusting the slider as necessary for optimal sound.

Turn down your computer's speakers or select the option to **Mute Audio While Recording** so that you don't get feedback from the speakers as you record.

2    To record your narration, click the red **Record** button.

The panel will display a three-second countdown and then will begin recording as your movie plays.

Click the same button again to stop the recording.

The program will place the narration clip that you've recorded on the **Narration** audio track, at the current position of your **CTI** (Current Time Indicator), on the timeline or sceneline.

## Normalize: A great audio tool

One other audio tool that merits mentioning is the **Normalize** tool. Although it will override any other adjustments you've made to your clip's audio volume, it's a powerful and easy-to-use way to bring up or down the audio level for an entire clip with just a couple of clicks of the mouse.

To use it, **right-click** on your audio clip (**Ctrl-click** on a Mac), select **Audio Gain** from the right-click menu and then click the **Normalize** button on the option screen. The tool will automatically analyze your clip and optimize the audio level for that clip, raising it as much as necessary to create a full sound. (You can also set the **Gain** numbers manually).

Because it sets levels based on the loudest sound on the clip, and affects the entire clip equally, it's not the perfect solution in every case. But it is a great quick fix for improving a clip with a low but even audio level.

The two shortcut buttons on the panel will jump you back to the beginning of the clip you've just recorded (or to the next or previous narration clip). You can then click the play button to hear the results.

3    If you're unhappy with the results, you can click the shortcut button to jump back to the beginning of the clip and record new narration. (Your new narration will replace the old automatically.) Or, by clicking the trashcan icon, you can delete the current narration clip completely.

A good microphone and good, quality sound card are essential to getting a good strong narration recording.

Premiere Elements seems to work best with microphones that are connected through your audio card.

Microphones attached via USB can prove problematic.

To ensure your microphone is properly configured in the program, go to Premiere Elements' **Edit** drop-down menu and select **Preferences/Audio Hardware**.

Click the **ASIO Settings** button, and adjust whatever settings are necessary there.

Finally, if you can't get the **Narration** feature to work at all in Premiere Elements, you can, as an alternative, record your narration into **Windows Audio Recorder** (usually under **Accessories/Entertainment** under your **Start** menu) or similar software and then import the audio clip into your project.

I've found I get the best quality for the narration for my videos by just recording myself with my camcorder and then capturing the video as **Audio Only** (as described in **Capture MiniDV, HDV Video or Video from Webcams or WDM Devices** on page 33 of **Chapter 3, Get Media into Your Project**.)

The Detect Beats Tool

Adjust settings as needed
for your music

Click to select your musical clip on the timeline
or sceneline, then select Detect Beats from the
Audio Tools drop-down menu

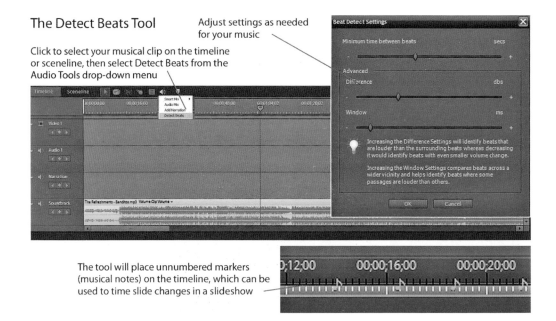

The tool will place unnumbered markers
(musical notes) on the timeline, which can be
used to time slide changes in a slideshow

## Detect Beats in your music

This cool tool can be used as part of the process of creating a slideshow
that changes in rhythm with a music clip.

To use the **Detect Beats** tool:

**1**    Click to select a music clip on your timeline or sceneline.

When a clip is detected on your timeline, it will be highlighted.

**2**    Click on the green speaker button on the upper left of the **Timeline**
or **Sceneline** panel and, from the drop-down menu, select **Detect
Beats**.

The **Beat Detect Settings** option screen will open, as illustrated
above.

**3**    Set the sensitivity and limitations of your beat detection.

**4**    Click **OK**.

The tool will then analyze your music clip and create unnumbered markers
along the timeline to the beat of the song. (They'll look like little musical
notes, as in the illustration.)

Once these markers have been created, you can use them as indicators for
the **Create Slideshow** tool in the **Project** media panel so that your slides
change in rhythm with the music.

For information on this **Create Slideshow** tool, see page 58 of **Chapter 4,
Explore the Project Media Panel**.

**Safe Margins**

**Playback Buttons**

**Add Clips Through the Monitor**

**Split a Clip**

**Add a Title**

**Grab a Freeze Frame**

Chapter 8
# Edit with Monitor Panel Tools
## Viewing, splitting, adding clips and adding titles

The Monitor panels displays the video you've assembled on your timeline or sceneline.

The majority of the controls available on this panel's toolbar, along the bottom of the panel, control playback. However, the Monitor panel also includes some valuable video editing tools.

The Monitor panel
Playback of Timeline and Sceneline, plus some editing tools

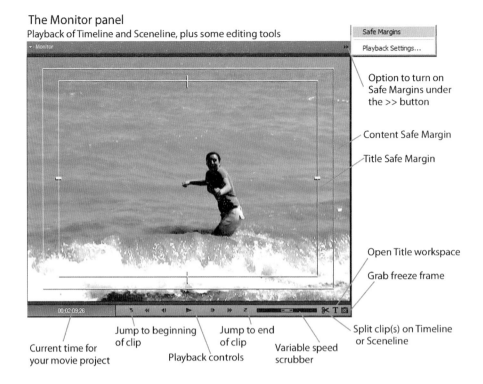

Safe Margins
Playback Settings...

Option to turn on
Safe Margins under
the >> button

Content Safe Margin
Title Safe Margin

Open Title workspace
Grab freeze frame

Jump to beginning
of clip
Current time for
your movie project

Jump to end
of clip
Playback controls

Variable speed
scrubber

Split clip(s) on Timeline
or Sceneline

## Play and navigate your video

The **Playback Control** buttons, along the bottom of the **Monitor** panel, control the playback, rewinding and fast forwarding of the video on your **Timeline** or **Sceneline**.

In addition to the common playback buttons you no doubt recognize, between **Play** and **Rewind** and between **Play** and **Fast Forward** are buttons which look like this: and this: .

These buttons will advance or rewind the playback incrementally – a single frame at a time – for precise navigation of your video.

On either end of the playback button set are the and buttons. These buttons will quickly jump you to the beginning or end of your current clip.

The numbers to the left of the playback buttons are **timecode**. This timecode represents the current time position of the playhead (**CTI**) in your project.

The numbers are displayed as 00;00;00;00, which represents hours; minutes; seconds; video frames. There are roughly 30 frames in each second of NTSC video and 25 frames in each second of PAL video. That's why the last set of numbers will only advance to 29 (or 24) before rolling over to zero again and advancing the seconds count.

This timecode indicator is also a dynamic tool which you can use to jump to specific points in your video, as discussed in the sidebar on page 101.

To the right of the playback controls is a slider called the **Scrubber**. The **Scrubber** will advance or rewind your video at various speeds, depending on how far to the right or left you slide it.

## Use Safe Margins

If you've selected **Show Docking Headers** from the **Window** drop-down menu, as we recommended in **Chapter 1**, you'll see the **>>** button in the upper right corner of the **Monitor** panel.

Click on it and you'll see the option to turn on your **Safe Margins**. (You can also find the option for turning on **Safe Margins** by **right-clicking** on the **Monitor** itself.)

**Safe Margins** will display as a pair of rectangular guides over your video display, as illustrated in the **Monitor** panel illustration on the previous page. (These guides will not be on your final output. They're just for your information as you edit your video.)

**Safe Margins** are great helps for ensuring that what you want to have on screen during your video's play will *definitely* be on screen in your final video output.

The challenge is that televisions can vary in how much of a video they actually show onscreen. All TVs cut off a little of the video image from around the edges of your screen (technically called "overscan") – and some cut off more than others.

The purpose of these margins isn't so that you will resize your entire video so that it fits inside the inner margin, of course. But you should use them as guides to make sure that your *essential* video information falls within your "safe area", ensuring that it will appear on all TV displays.

The outer rectangular guide represents the **Video Safe Margin**. As you edit, you'll want to make sure all of the "must-see" video falls inside this rectangle.

Otherwise – well, you know that big group picture of everyone at your family reunion waving to the camera? Well, if you've not ensured everyone in the picture is inside the **Video Safe Margin**, some TVs may not show Cousin Bill, standing off to the side of the picture, outside the **Safe Margin**!

The inner rectangular guide is your **Text Safe Margin**. This is for your titles, subtitles and captions.

**Never place any text or titles outside of the Text Safe Margin!**

Otherwise, some TVs may display your "Gone With the Wind" title as simply "one With the Win"!

We recommend that, as much as possible, you work with both of these **Safe Margins** turned on.

## Add media options on the Monitor panel

In addition to dragging video clips to your timeline or sceneline from your **Project** panel, you have the option of adding your clips to your movie through the **Monitor** panel.

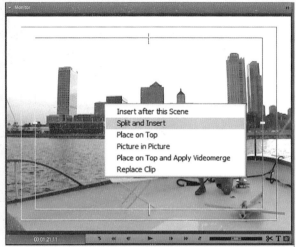

When a clip is dragged from the **Project** media **panel** onto the **Monitor**, it will automatically be added to the end of your timeline or sceneline.

This is true regardless of where the **CTI** (Current Time Indicator) is in your project timeline at the time.

If you hold down the Shift key as you drag a clip from the Media media panel onto the Monitor, you'll be offered several options for loading the clip to your project's timeline.

Even more options are available if you hold down the **Shift** key as you drag your clip from the **Project** media panel onto the **Monitor:**

**Insert After Scene** – The new clip will be added immediately after the scene currently displayed in the **Monitor**. If there is already another scene following the current scene, the new clip will be inserted in between the two.

**Split and Insert** – The current clip displayed in the Monitor will split at the position of the **CTI** (Current Time Indicator) and the new clip will be inserted within the split.

**Place on Top** – The new clip will be placed on the video track above the currently-displayed clip.

**Picture-In-Picture** – The new clip will be placed on the video track above the currently-displayed clip and will be scaled to 50% of its actual size. Once this new clip appears in the **Monitor**, you can click on it and drag it, and/or resize it (by dragging the corner handles), to any position you'd prefer.

**Place on Top and Apply Videomerge** – The new clip will be placed on the video track directly above the currently-displayed clip and **Videomerge** will automatically make the background transparent. (More information on **Videomerge** can be found in **Chapter 11, Add Video and Audio Effects**.)

**Replace Clip** – The new clip will replace the currently-displayed clip on the timeline. If the new clip is a different length than the previous clip, the program will automatically trim it or add black so that it fills exactly the same space on the timeline.

## Editing tools on the Monitor panel

### Split a clip

 The scissors icon in the lower right of the panel is the **Split Clip** tool.

Clicking this tool will slice through the clip(s) on your timeline or sceneline at the position of the **CTI** (Current Time Indicator), cutting the clip(s) in two.

How this tool functions with several layers of video or audio clips depends on whether or not you have a clip on your timeline selected.

If you have a clip selected on your **Timeline** (it will be highlighted if you have it selected), selecting the **Split Clip** tool on the **Monitor** panel will slice through *only that clip.*

If you have no clips selected, the **Split Clip** tool will slice through every clip on every Video/Audio track at the **CTI's** position. (This excludes clips on the **Narration** and **Soundtrack**, which will not be split unless specifically selected.)

### Add Text (Title)

 Clicking the "**T**" icon in the lower right of the **Monitor** panel launches **Add Text** (better known as the **Title** tool).

When you select this tool, you will be taken to the **Titles** workspace and default text ("**Add Text**") will appear on the **Monitor** screen. Typing over this text creates your new title.

We discuss this workspace in much greater detail in **Chapter 10, Add Titles**.

### Jump to a position using timecode

You can jump your **CTI** to very precise positions on your timeline – positioning it, for instance, to exactly one second from the end of the clip – by using the timecode in the lower left of the **Monitor** panel.

When you click to select this timecode, the numbers become dynamic, and you can overwrite them with whatever minutes, seconds or even frame numbers that you'd like. When you press **Enter** afterwards, the **CTI** playhead will jump to that precise position on your timeline!

## Grab a Freeze Frame

 The camera icon in the lower right of the **Monitor** panel is called the **Freeze Frame** tool. (Although it might more accurately be called a "frame grab" tool, since it doesn't so much *freeze* a frame of your movie as it *grabs* a frame from it.)

Clicking on this tool brings up an option screen which displays the grabbed frame from your video (based on the position of the **CTI** on your timeline) as well as a number of options for saving it, as illustrated below.

- You can choose to simply **insert** the still in your movie. The inserted still will display in your video project at whatever duration you've indicated in **Freeze Frame Duration**.

- Selecting the option to **Edit In Photoshop Elements After Inserting** loads the still into your movie and simultaneously launches it in the edit space of Photoshop Elements.

  Once you've made any adjustments to the photo in Photoshop Elements and saved the file, the updates will automatically appear in the photo in Premiere Elements.

- Whether or not your choose to insert the still into your movie, your **Freeze Frame** will be saved to your hard drive as a Bitmap (BMP) file and will appear in your current **Project** media panel.

If you'd like to save a **Freeze Frame** of your movie as a JPEG or TIF for use in either another video, Web or print project, use the **Share** output option that we discuss in **Output a still of your current video frame** on page 217 of **Chapter 18, Share Your Movie**.

### Freeze Frame options
Grabbing a still photo from your video

Clicking the camera icon on the Monitor panel launches the Freeze Frame option screen

Duration of still if added directly to timeline

Option to launch in Photoshop Elements editor

Option to export as a BMP picture file

Option to insert still directly to movie's timeline or sceneline

**Create an InstantMovie in the Media Panel**

**Use Themes to Create Movies on Your Timeline**

Chapter 9

# Use Movie Themes and InstantMovies

## The easy way to create movies

Themes are a tool in Premiere Elements that can be used for creating automatic or InstantMovies.

Themes include a combination of titles, music and special effects that can be customized in a variety of ways and then applied to a set of clips you've gathered or selected.

In addition to their use in creating InstantMovies, Themes can also be applied to a sequence of clips already on your timeline or sceneline.

Creating an InstantMovie is as easy as grabbing video clips or photos from the Premiere Elements Media panel, clicking the InstantMovie button and applying a Theme.

## Create an InstantMovie in the Media panel

**Themes** can be used to create an **InstantMovie** from scratch, or they can be applied to clips already on your timeline.

To create an **InstantMovie** from scratch, using files you've selected in the **Media** panel, click on the **Project** tab.

1  Click, on the **Project** tab and select **Media.**

The **Media** panel will display the video clips, audio clips and in stills in your project.

Hold down the **Shift** or **Ctrl** key and click to select the clips you would like to include in your **InstantMovie**, or click and drag your mouse over the panel to "lasso" the clips you'd like it to include.

2  Click the **InstantMovie** button.

The panel will display a library of movie **Themes**.

The drop-down menu at the top of the panel (set to **Show All** by default) will allow you to filter the **Themes** displayed in this panel by category or to access additional themes available from **Photoshop.com**.

You can see an animated preview of any **Theme** by clicking on the thumbnail representing it.

3  Once you've selected a **Theme** for your **InstantMovie**, click the **Next** button in the lower right of the panel.

**4**   The panel will display a list of the optional elements that make up your **Theme's** template, as illustrated on the right.

Type the titles you'd like included in the boxes provided, then select or deselect the elements you'd like applied to your movie.

You can even swap out music by selecting the **My Music** option and browsing to a music file on your computer.

(You may need to scroll down to see the entire list of optional elements, then click on the little white triangles to the left of the listed categories of options to see the entire options list.)

Once you've selected and customized the elements you'd like included, click the **Apply** button in the lower right corner of the panel.

Premiere Elements will process all of the options and apply the elements you selected to the clips you selected.

After your automatically-generated movie appears on your timeline or in your sceneline, the program will offer to render it for you.

It's a good idea to accept this offer, as your movie will likely need to be rendered before it will play at full quality.

The rendered video will provide you with a much cleaner representation of what your final video output will look like.

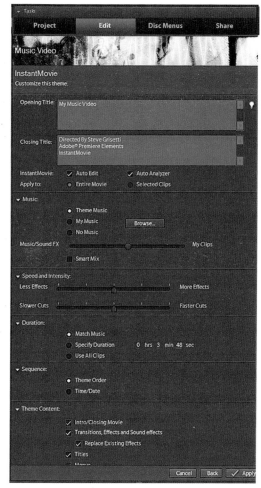

Once you've selected a Theme, you can customize it by including your own text and selecting which elements will be applied.

For more information on the rendering process, see **Render your timeline** on page 86 of **Chapter 6, Edit Your Video in Timeline Mode**.

Instant Movie Themes include sliders for setting the speed of the cuts and the intensity of the effects.

To "lasso" (select) a sequence of clips on your timeline, click and drag from beyond
the end of your movie across the clips.

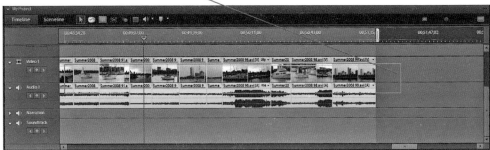

## Apply a Theme to clips on
## the Timeline or Sceneline

**Themes** can also be applied to clips that you've already gathered on the
**Timeline** or **Sceneline**. (In **Timeline** mode, these clips must all be on the
Video 1 track.)

1   To apply a **Theme** to clips on your project's timeline or sceneline,
    select the clips on your timeline by "lassoing" the clips you'd like to
    include in your **InstantMovie**.

    To lasso clips on the **Timeline**, click on an area of the **Timeline** in
    which there are no clips, then drag your mouse across the clips
    you'd like to select, as illustrated above. (Or, to select all of the clips
    on your timeline, press **Ctrl+a** on a PC or ⌘**+a** on a Mac.)

    Once you've selected a group of clips, click the **Edit** tab in the Tasks
    panel and select **Themes**.

2   The **Tasks** panel will display available **Themes** for your
    **InstantMovie**.

    Select your **Theme**, then proceed as described in **Create an
    InstantMovie in the Media panel** on page 104.

**The Titles Workspace**
**Title Templates**
**Text Attributes and Styles**
**The Titles Toolbar**
**Text Animations**
**Roll/Crawl Options**

Chapter 10

# Add Titles

## Using title templates and text

With Titles, you can create opening or closing credits for your movie.

Or you can use them to add subtitles or captions to your videos.

The Titles workspace can be launched by clicking the "T" on the Monitor panel (which takes you directly to the Titles workspace)

Or by clicking the Titles button under the Edit tab (which takes you to the Titles Templates area first)

There are actually two different routes to the **Titles** panel and workspace.

You can create your title from scratch – or you can use one of the colorful **Title Templates** bundled with the program.

## Create a title

To go directly to the **Titles** workspace and create your title from scratch, click on the "**T**" icon on the toolbar that runs along the bottom of the **Monitor** panel.

To go to the **Titles** workspace by way of the **Title Templates** panel, click on the **Edit** tab and then click the **Titles** button on the Tasks panel, as discussed in the sidebar on the facing page.

Whichever route you take, once you select a template or enter the **Titles** workspace by way of the button on the **Monitor** panel, a title clip will automatically be added to your project's timeline or sceneline, as illustrated below.

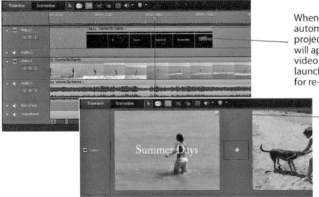

When you create a title, it is automatically added to your movie project. In Timeline mode, the title will appear on the lowest available video track. Double-click it to launch the Titles workspace for re-editing.

In Sceneline mode, if overlayed on a video clip, the title will be indicated by an icon in the upper right corner of the thumbnail.

**Titles and Title Templates**

Titles

## Use Title Templates

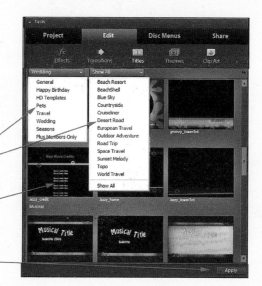

The Title Templates drop-down gives you access to the various categories of title templates.

Title Templates can be searched by category or specific template, using drop-down menus

Many templates are animated, and you can preview the animation by hovering your mouse over the template's thumbnail.

To apply a template and proceed to the Titles workspace, click Apply.

Clicking the **Titles** button under the **Edit** tab in the Tasks panel displays a library of title templates, each shown as a thumbnail. (Black areas in these thumbnails usually represent transparency, through which your main or background video will be displayed.)

Using the drop-down menus, as in the illustration above, you can isolate your templates by category or select a specific template. You also have the option of downloading additional materials from **Photoshop.com**, if you have a **Plus** premium membership.

The templates usually include a graphic design and placeholders for adding your own custom text – and many are animated! Once you've clicked on a template to select it, click the **Apply** button in the lower right corner of the panel. The title template will be applied, the title will appear on your timeline or sceneline and you'll move into the **Titles** workspace.

In **Timeline** mode, you will be able to see the new title clip on an upper track of your project's timeline at the position of the **CTI** (Current Time Indicator). Premiere Elements will place the title on the lowest video track in your project that contains no other clips.

As with any video clip, you can shorten or lengthen your title's duration by dragging on its ends, or you can slide it to any other position on the timeline. (See **Trim or split a clip** on page 73 of **Chapter 6, Edit Your Video in Timeline Mode.**)

In **Sceneline** mode, you will only be able to see the title as a separate clip if it has been added to a movie in a space with no other video. Otherwise, it will be displayed in the **Monitor** and will be indicated in the sceneline by a small icon in the upper right corner of your clip's thumbnail.

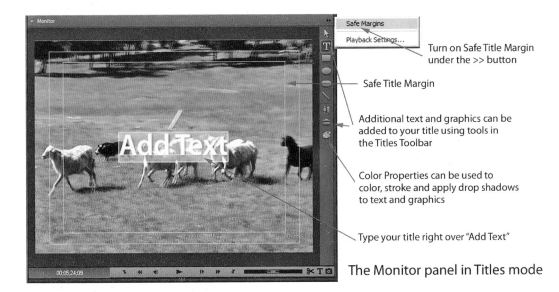

Turn on Safe Title Margin under the >> button

Safe Title Margin

Additional text and graphics can be added to your title using tools in the Titles Toolbar

Color Properties can be used to color, stroke and apply drop shadows to text and graphics

Type your title right over "Add Text"

The Monitor panel in Titles mode

## Open the Titles workspace

The **Titles** workspace is loaded with tools for creating and customizing your project's titles.

If you've come to the **Titles** workspace directly, by clicking on the "**T**" icon on the toolbar along the bottom of the **Monitor** panel, the words "**Add Text**" will be displayed in the **Monitor**.

This placeholder text will already be selected when you launch this workspace and, when you start typing, your new text will replace it.

If you've come to this workspace by way of the **Title Templates** workspace, your title is already well underway, and you can click on any of the placeholder text boxes on your template to replace the text with your own.

You can also move or remove any of the text or graphics on your template by switching to the **Selection Tool** (the arrow) on the **Titles Toolbar** (see page 112), to select the element or text box. Once you've selected it, you can drag the text block or graphic to a new position or remove it completely by pressing the **Delete** key.

## Show Title Safe Margins

If you haven't turned on the **Safe Margins** on the **Monitor**, make sure you do so before building your titles.

To turn on the **Safe Margins,** click on the **>>** button in the upper right corner of the **Monitor** panel and check the option for **Safe Title Margin**, as in the illustration above.

(If the **>>** button isn't visible, go to the **Window** drop-down and select **Show Docking Headers**.)

The **Safe Title Margin** (the inner rectangle of the two sets of rectangular guides that are displayed on your **Monitor**) won't show up on your final video output. It's purpose is to offer a guide to protect you from TV screens that cut off the edges of your video image (quite common).

Keeping all of your onscreen text within the bounds of the inner **Safe Title Margin** ensures that it will always be displayed completely, with no chance of any accidental cut-off. (See page 99 for more information.)

## Set Text Options

While in the **Titles** workspace, the Tasks panel displays a number of options for stylizing your title's text. Drag over your text to select it or use the **Selection Tool** (the "arrow" icon in the **Toolbar**) to select a text box in order to apply these options to it.

The basic options for your title's text are **Font**, **Size**, **Baseline Shift** (raising or lowering the selected text relative to the unselected text), **Left Align/ Center/Right Align** and **Font Style**.

Once you've applied these settings to your selected text and colored it (using the **Color Properties** on the **Toolbar**, discussed on page 112), you can then save it as a permanent style in your **Text Styles** menu.

To save a custom style, select the text, click the **Save Style** button on the panel and then name your style. It will then appear as an "**Aa**" thumbnail among the other **Text Styles**.

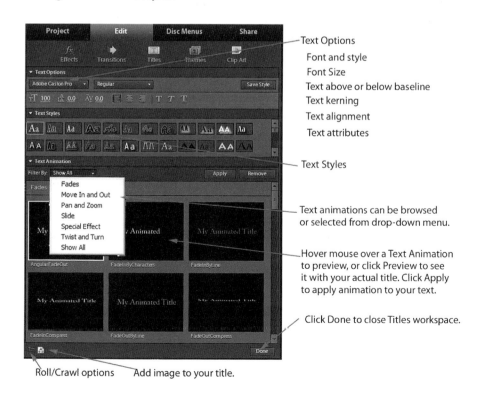

Text Options
  Font and style
  Font Size
  Text above or below baseline
  Text kerning
  Text alignment
  Text attributes

Text Styles

Text animations can be browsed or selected from drop-down menu.

Hover mouse over a Text Animation to preview, or click Preview to see it with your actual title. Click Apply to apply animation to your text.

Click Done to close Titles workspace.

Roll/Crawl options    Add image to your title.

**111**

## Customize your title with the Titles Toolbar

Selection Tool, for repositioning text and graphics

Text Tool, for revising or adding text

Shape Tools, for adding basic shapes

Center text or graphic vertically

Center text or graphic horizontally

Launch Color Properties for selected text or graphic

No fill
White
Black

Color Picker

Fill color selector

Stroke color selector (available only with certain Text Styles)

Gradient fill controls

Drop Shadow control (available only with certain Text Styles)

**The Titles Toolbar**                    **Color Properties**

The **Titles Toolbar** is displayed along the right side of the **Monitor** in the **Titles** workspace. The tools include:

The Selection Tool (the arrow) – Clicking the **Selection Tool** allows you to use your mouse to drag the text blocks and graphic elements to new positions on your title.

The Text Tool (the "T") – The **Text Tool** changes the mode of your cursor to a text editor. If you click on an existing text box on your title, you will be able to edit the text; if you click any place else on your title space, you will create a new text box (although it will be a part of the same title clip) into which you can add more text.

The Shape Tools (the **Rectangle**, the **Oval**, the **Rounded Rectangle**, the **Line**) – Selecting a **Shape Tool** allows you to draw a basic geometric shape on your title by clicking and dragging.

You can recolor these shapes by clicking to select them and then using the **Color Properties** tool, as described below.

The Center Vertical and Center Horizontal Tools – If you've selected a text box or graphic element on your title using the **Selection Tool** (above), clicking on either of these tools centers it in your video frame.

Color Properties (the artist's palette) – After you've dragged over text to select it, or used the **Selection Tool** (above) to select a text box or shape, you can recolor it by clicking on this icon.

*Continued on facing page*

## Use Text Styles

**Text Styles** are fonts, font styles and colors that can be applied to your selected text simply by clicking on the "**Aa**" thumbnail representing the style.

Some of the styles include outlined or "stroked" text. If you apply a **Text Style** that includes an outline, or "stroke," you will have the option to change the color and weight of the stroke in **Color Properties** (as discussed in the **Titles Toolbar** sidebar).

If you **right-click** on any of these **Text Styles** in the **Titles** panel (**Ctrl-click** on a Mac), you will find the option to set it as the **Default Style**. The **Default Style** is the font, color and font style that will appear whenever you create new text for a title, and will appear as your default font and color whenever you create a new Premiere Elements title.

## Select a Text Animation

**Text Animations**, as the name implies, are ways of animating how your title text is introduced onto or removed from your video frame.

Premiere Elements' **Text Animations** are in several categories, and you can filter the animations displayed in the panel by selecting a category from the drop-down menu that displays **Show All** by default.

To see a preview of how the animation looks, hover your mouse over the animation thumbnail until a **Play** button appears, then click on this **Play** button.

### *The Titles Toolbar (continued)*

On the **Color Properties** panel that opens, Fill is the color of the shape or text itself; Stroke is the outline around it. The Stroke Weight is the thickness of that **Stroke**.

A Gradient is a fill that is blended from one color to another.

Clicking the Drop Shadow option creates a shadow below your text or graphic. The characteristics of the gradient and the drop-shadow can be customized with the various settings.

- **Fill**, **Gradient** and **Drop Shadow** can be applied to any shapes drawn with the **Shape Tool**.

- **Fill**, **Gradient** and **Drop Shadow** can also be applied to any text. However, in order to apply a **Stroke** (outline) to the text, you *must* first apply to that text a **Text Style** that includes a **Stroke** outlining the text.

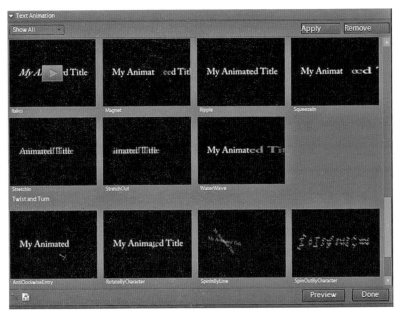

Premiere Elements Text Animation workspace includes nearly 40 ways to add life and excitement to your titles.

**Text Animation** is a pretty intensive function, and the performance of this feature, including previews, can be limited by your computer's RAM load and graphics card power.

In order to apply, or even *preview*, a **Text Animation** for your title:

- Your text or text block must be selected on the **Monitor** in the **Titles** workspace;
- Your text block must *not* be more than one line long; and
- A **Text Animation** must be selected.

To see a preview of **Text Animation** using your actual text or to apply a **Text Animation** to your text:

1   Select your text on the **Monitor** in the **Titles** workspace.

2   Click to select a **Text Animation.**

3   Click the **Apply** button.

4   Click the **Preview** button at the bottom right of the panel.

5   Before you apply a new **Text Animation** to your title, you must select the text again and click the **Remove** button.

6   Once you're satisfied with the **Text Animation** you have applied, click the **Done** button.

The program will return to the **Edit** workspace and your title, with any styles or animations you've applied, will appear on your timeline or sceneline at the position of the **CTI** (Current Time Indicator).

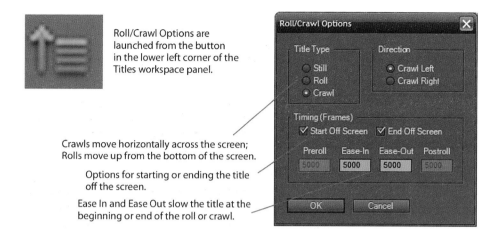

Roll/Crawl Options are launched from the button in the lower left corner of the Titles workspace panel.

Crawls move horizontally across the screen; Rolls move up from the bottom of the screen.

Options for starting or ending the title off the screen.

Ease In and Ease Out slow the title at the beginning or end of the roll or crawl.

## Create rolling or crawling titles

Any titles you create can automatically be made to **roll** (move up over a video frame) or **crawl** (move left to right, or right to left, across a video frame).

To access the **Roll/Crawl Options** screen, click on the **Roll/Crawl Options** icon in the lower left corner of the **Titles** panel – or select **Roll/Crawl Options** from the **>>** button on the upper right corner of the **Titles Monitor** panel. (If this button isn't visible, select **Show Docking Headers** from the **Window** drop-down menu.)

The options on this screen are fairly intuitive. If you select **Crawl**, for instance, you have the option of setting it to either **Crawl Left** or **Crawl Right** across the video frame.

The **Timing** options allow you to set the roll or crawl to start and/or end off screen.

- You have the options of setting your title to **Start Off Screen** or **End Off Screen.** Alternatively, you can manually set the **Preroll** or **Postroll** time for how long the title is off the screen before or after it rolls or crawls.

- The **Ease In** and **Ease Out** options allow you to change the rolling or crawling movement from a steady speed to one that begins slowly and then speeds up (**Ease In**), or vice versa (**Ease Out**).

The speed at which the title rolls or crawls is determined by how long the title is on your timeline. Extending (by dragging one end to lengthen) the title on your timeline will **increase its duration and thus slow the speed** of the roll or crawl; dragging in one end of the title to **decrease its duration will increase the speed** of the roll or crawl. (Note that changing the duration of a clip is a function of **Timeline** mode editing only.)

As an alternative to using these automatic roll and crawl options, you can manually keyframe the movement of your title so that it is revealed through any movement or effect you can imagine. To learn more about using keyframing, see **Chapter 14, Keyframing.**

## Add a graphic to your title

To add a graphic to your title, click the Add Image icon on the Titles panel and browse to your custom graphic file.

To add a graphic or any image or photo from your computer to your title, click the **Add Image** icon on the lower left of the **Titles** panel and browse to the picture file.

Once you've added the graphic, use the **Selection Tool** to size and position it in your video frame. (See **The Titles Toolbar** on page 112.)

### Re-edit a title

If, after you've created a title, you need to re-edit it, you can re-open that title's workspace by double-clicking the title on your project's timeline.

In Sceneline mode, you can usually re-open a title by double-clicking it on the **Monitor** panel.

## Duplicate a title

If you like how your title looks and you want to re-use the look and style for another title, you can duplicate it and then edit the duplicate.

To duplicate a title, **right-click** on it in the **Media** panel (**Ctrl-click** on a Mac) and select **Duplicate**. You can then drag the duplicate title to your timeline and double-click on it to re-open its **Titles** workspace for editing.

It's important that you *duplicate* your title in the **Media** panel rather than merely doing a copy-and-paste on the timeline.

If you create a *copy* of your title rather than a duplicate, you've merely created a "clone" – and any changes you make to *one* title will be made to *both*.

And that's likely not how you intend to use the title's copy.

**Duplicating** creates an *independent* and editable copy of your title.

Duplicating a title creates a copy of it, which you can use as a template for a new title. Copying a title, on the other hand, creates a "clone" of your title, such that any changes you make to the original are made to both titles.

## Render your title

Your title will likely look a bit rough when you first play it back from your timeline or sceneline. To get a better idea of what the segment will look like when you output your movie, press the **Enter** key or select the option to **Render Work Area** from the **Timeline** drop-down menu to render your video or select the **Render Work Area** option from the **Timeline** drop-down on the program's Menu Bar. (For more information, see **Render your timeline** on page 86 **Chapter 6, Edit Your Video in Timeline Mode**.)

**Video Effects Defined**

**Chroma Key**

**Videomerge**

**Audio Effects Defined**

**Customizing Audio and Video Effects**

Chapter 11
# Add Video and Audio Effects
## Bringing excitement to your movie

There is an amazing number of effects
available in Premiere Elements 10 –
too many, in fact, to display in a
single panel.

The program includes nearly 90 video
and 23 audio effects as well as nearly 275
automatic, or "Preset" effects, that include
applied effects as well as keyframed
effects and motion paths – all of which
are infinitely customizable.

The Effects panel in Video Effects mode

Eyeball button toggles view of effects preview as applied to your selected clip.

The Effects drop-down menu offers access to the other Effects sets

The categories filter drop-down gives you quick access to any category of effects

Quickly call up any effect by typing its name in the search box

>> Menu option to display only local or only downloadable content

Hover your mouse over any thumbnail to preview the effect

After effect is applied click Edit Effects to adjust it in the Properties panel

Click to apply effect to your selected clip or simply drag the effect onto a clip on your timeline or sceneline

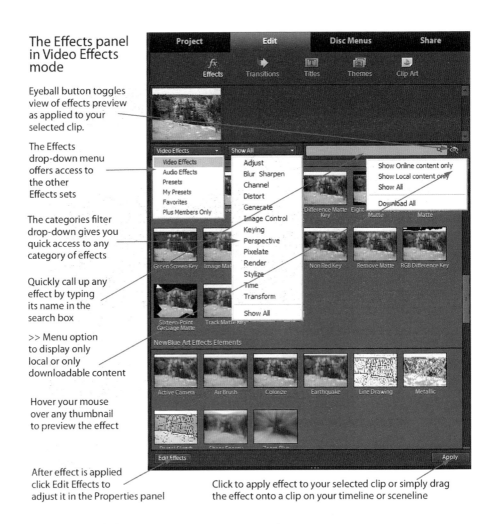

To open the **Effects** panel, click the **Effects** button under the **Edit** tab.

In addition to **Video Effects** and **Audio Effects**, the **Effects** panel includes categories in which you can store your own custom created effects and motion paths (**My Presets**), and your most-often used effects (**Favorites**), for easy access.

**Presets** and **Video Effects** will display in the panel as thumbnails, demonstrating their effect. Animated effects can be previewed by clicking on the thumbnail image. And, if you have a clip selected on your timeline or sceneline when you open the various **Effects** panels, your clip will appear as the effect preview!

At the drop-down menu for each effect, you'll also find the option to access additional effects from Photoshop.com listed under **For Plus Members Only**. (See page 192 of **Chapter 16, Photoshop.com.**)

If you have a **Plus** premium account at **Photoshop.com** and you are logged into the site at the Premiere Elements **Welcome Screen** (see **Chapter 2, Start a New Project**), you will regularly find additional effects automatically loaded into this panel category.

## Apply an effect to several clips at once

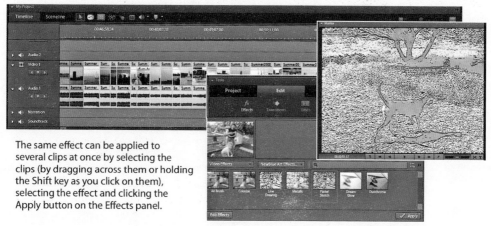

The same effect can be applied to several clips at once by selecting the clips (by dragging across them or holding the Shift key as you click on them), selecting the effect and clicking the Apply button on the Effects panel.

Premiere Elements includes the ability to apply an effect to several clips at once.

To apply an effect to several clips in one move:

**1** Select your clips, either by holding the **Shift** or **Ctrl** key as you click to select clips on your timeline or sceneline or by dragging across your timeline from beyond your clips to "lasso" the clips you'd like to apply the effect to. (You can also use **Ctrl+a** on a PC or ⌘**+a** on a Mac to select all of the clips on the timeline.)

**2** Once the clips are selected, go to the **Effects** panel (by clicking on the **Effects** button under the **Edit** tab) and locate the effect you want to apply.

Click the **Apply** button in the **Effects** panel.

The effect will be applied to all of your selected clips.

You can fine-tune the effects in the **Properties** panel by **right-clicking** each clip (one clip at a time) – **Ctrl-clicking** on a Mac –and selecting the option to **Show Properties**. (For more information on adjusting effects settings, see **Chapter 13, Customize Effects in the Properties Panel.**)

To create and customize an effect on one clip and then apply the same effect and settings to several other clips, use the **Paste Attributes** feature, as we also discuss on page 154 of **Chapter 13, Customize Effects in the Properties Panel**.

You can apply any number of effects to a clip. In fact, you can even double-up the same effect on the same clip (such as **Volume** on an audio clip) to increase its intensity. Sometimes the way effects interact with each other on a clip can create a new effect all its own.

(For information on how to turn effects on a clip off and on, see **Disable or remove an effect** on page 154 of **Chapter 13, Customize Effects in the Properties Panel**.)

## Premiere Elements' video effects

By default, when you select **Effects** under the **Edit** tab, the **Video Effects** catalog will be displayed, as seen in the illustration at the beginning of this chapter.

Video effects are arranged in categories, and you can use the second drop-down menu on the panel to display only effects from one particular category.

Here are the various categories as well as brief descriptions of how some of the key effects in that category work.

> **Adjust.** The **Adjust** effects work primarily with color. These are the effects you'll use if you want to change or correct color in your clip.
>
> Additionally, **Lighting Effects** imposes a spotlight-like effect on your clip.
>
> **Posterize** reduces the number of colors in your clip, making it appear more cartoon-like.
>
> And the **Shadow/Highlight** effect is a great way to decrease contrast in a clip (e.g., the sky is too bright and the shade is too dark). Also available in Photoshop Elements is **Shadow/Highlight,** one of my personal favorite picture-saving effects!
>
> **Blur & Sharpen.** These effects soften or sharpen your picture.
>
> The **Ghosting** effects leaves a very cool trail behind objects that are moving in your clip.
>
> **Channel. Invert**, the single **Channel** effect, turns your video's picture into its negative.
>
> **Color Correction.** Brand new to version 10, the two effects in this set – **AutoTone & Vibrance** and the **Three-Way Color Corrector** – are advanced tools for enhancing and correcting the color in your video. We discuss their workings in detail on page 125.
>
> **Distort.** The **Distort** effects warp, twist and/or bend your video image.
>
> **Generate.** The **Lens Flare** effect in this category adds a bright, white flare to a spot on your video picture, as if a light is being shone back at the camcorder.
>
> **Image Control.** These effects offer tools for color, contrast and light adjustments. Among this set are tools for tinting, replacing and even removing the color completely from your video.

## Mac video effects: A limited edition

The Mac version of Premiere Elements 10 does not include all of the effects available in the PC version. For a list of the omitted effects, see page 224 in the **Appendix**.

**Keying.** **Keying** effects remove or make transparent a portion of your video's picture.

A powerful tool in this category is the **Chroma Key** effect, which we discuss in detail on page 128.

Other effects in this category are essentially the **Chroma Key** preset applied to certain colors (**Green Screen Key, Blue Screen Key**). The **Non Red Key** can be used to remove some of the "fringe" around the edge of a keyed area on a clip to which **Chroma Key** has been applied. (Yes, you can add more than one **Key** effect to a clip to fine tune the effect!)

The very cool, new NewBlue Cartoonr effect.

Others, like the **Garbage Mattes**, create transparent areas in a clip that can be shaped with user-defined corner handles.

**NewBlue Art Effects, NewBlue Film Look, NewBlue Motion Effects**. These effects categories include high-level image effects created by NewBlue, one of the world's top video effects companies.

One of the most popular of these is the **Old Film** effect, a highly customizable effect which makes your video look like a damaged, worn, old movie.

**NewBlue Cartoonr Plus Elements**, An effect for making your videos look cartoon-like, as in the illustration above right!

**Perspective**. These effects can be used to make your video image look as if it is floating or rotating into space.

**Pixelate**. The **Facet** effect in this category reduces your video picture to a group of large color blocks.

**Render**. The **Lightning** effect is great fun, although it takes a lot of computer power to create and customize it!

The **Ramp** effect fades your video out across the screen in a gradiated pattern.

**Stylize.** The effects in this category, as the category name implies, can be used to create a highly stylized video.

**Time.** Effects in this category change how your video displays motion by reducing or affecting the look of the frame rate.

Note that this is *not* the place to go if you want to slow down or speed up a clip. That's the **Time Stretch** effect (see page 81), available by clicking on the clock icon on the **Timeline/Sceneline** panel.

**Transform.** A real hodgepodge of effects, this category includes some stylized effects, some 3D transformations and, for some reason, **Clip** and **Crop**, two effects for trimming off the sides of your video picture.

(For the record, **Clip** trims away the sides of your video and replaces them with color while **Crop** trims away the sides and replaces them with transparency – a significant difference, if you're using your cropped clip on an upper video track with another clip on a track below it).

To learn more about using the **Crop** tool (or **Clip** tool, since you use the same method to adjust both) see **Types of effects settings** in **Chapter 13, Customize Effects in the Properties Panel**.

**Video Stabilizer.** The **Stabilize** effect can be used to take some of the shake out of a handheld camera shot.

**Videomerge.** This effect is essentially a more automatic version of the **Chroma Key** effect. When applied to a clip, it removes what it interprets to be the background in a single step. We show you how to use it on page 130.

For information on changing settings for effects, see **Adjust settings for effects and properties** in **Chapter 13, Customize Effects in the Properties Panel.** For information on keyframing effects to change over time, see **Chapter 14, Keyframing**.

## Find and apply an effect

Effects are displayed as thumbnails representing the effect's effect. These effects are stored within categories, and you can filter the listing of any type of effect to display a specific category by selecting that category from a drop-down menu at the top of the panel (which, by default, is set to **Show All**).

You can also quickly call up an effect simply by typing its name in the **search box** to the right of the drop-down menus, as illustrated on page 120.

Applying an effect to a clip is as simple as selecting the clip on your timeline or sceneline, selecting the effect by clicking on it and then clicking the **Apply** button in the lower right corner of the panel. (You can also just drag the effect onto your clip.)

Some effects will cause an immediate change to your video. But nearly all effects can also be customized in the **Properties** panel and/or include settings that can, or will need to, be tweaked once the effect is applied to a clip in order to show any change.

## Close Up: Premiere Elements 10's new Color Correction tools

With Premiere Elements 10, Adobe introduces two exciting, new effects for correcting and enhancing the colors in your videos (located in the **Color Correction** category of **Effects**).

### AutoTone & Vibrance

The **AutoTone & Vibrance** effect will automatically enrich and intensify the colors in your videos. In fact, simply applying the effect (by dragging it from the **Effects** panel onto a clip on your timeline or sceneline) will often do a more than adequate job.

To further adjust the intensity of the effect, **right-click** on the clip on your timeline or sceneline and select **Show Properties,** or select the clip and click the **Edit Effects** button on the **Effects** panel.

In the **Properties** panel, locate and open the effect's properties and adjust the **Vibrance** slider as needed. (Alternatively, if you uncheck the **AutoTone** checkbox on the **Properties** panel, you can manually adjust the clip's brightness, contrast, exposure and black and white levels.)

### Three-Way Color Corrector

A much more advanced tool for adjusting and correcting your video's color is the **Three-Way Color Corrector.** Modeled after color correctors in professional video editing software, this effect allows you to adjust the hue, saturation and lightness for your video's individual **Shadows (Blacks), Midtones (Grays)** and **Highlights (Whites).**

To adjust the effect's levels, **right-click** on the clip on your timeline or sceneline and select **Show Properties,** or select the clip and click the **Edit Effects** button on the **Effects** panel.

Locate the **Color Corrector** listing on the **Properties** panel. Under each of the effect's three tonal levels, you will find a color wheel.

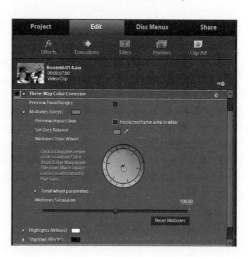

To adjust that tonal level's hue and lightness, drag the center circle point around within the color wheel. To adjust the hue's saturation, move the slider below the wheel.

To see which areas of your video image are being affected with each adjustment, check the **Preview Impact Area** checkbox.

For best results, we recommend you adjust **Shadows (Blacks)** first, then **Highlights (Whites),** then **Midtones (Grays)**.

**CHAPTER 11**

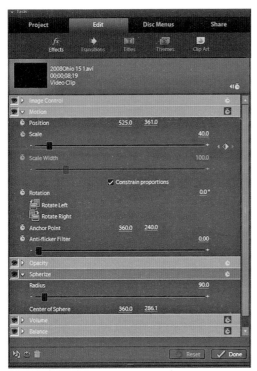

Effects that have been added to a clip appear in that clip's Properties panel, where they can be adusted and customized.

## Adjust an effect or property

To adjust the effect's settings, click to select the clip to which an effect has been applied on the timeline or sceneline and, on the lower left corner of the **Effects** panel, click **Edit Effects**. This will open the **Properties** panel for your clip.

You can also open the clip's **Properties** panel by **right-clicking** on the selected clip on your timeline or sceneline (**Ctrl-clicking** on a Mac) and selecting **Show Properties,** or by clicking on the **Properties** icon at the top left of the **Timeline**.

The **Properties** panel is a very useful and powerful workspace in Premiere Elements.

With it you can not only customize your effect's settings (see **Adjust an effect or property** on page 152 of **Chapter 13, Customize Effects in the Properties Panel**) but you can also create keyframed effects that change over the course of the clip or motion paths that move your entire clip around your video frame (as discussed in **Chapter 14, Keyframing**).

## Isolate an effect area with the Effects Mask

The **Effects Mask** enables you to isolate an area of your video and apply an effect to it without effecting the other areas of the clip.

You can see an example of how it works on the following page.

In other words, you can define a rectangular area any place in your video frame and apply the **Black & White** effect to it.

The area within the rectangle will be black & white while everything in the video frame outside this rectangle will remain in color.

The way this effect works is that, when applied, it creates a duplicate of your selected clip and adds it to your timeline, directly above your selected clip.

The area you define with the **Effects Mask** is actually the clip on the Video 2 track – with the area around your defined area "masked," or made transparent, revealing the clip on the Video 1 track below it, as illustrated on page 127.

(Because of the way it functions, the **Effects Mask** will only work in **Timeline** mode.)

When the Effects Mask is applied (by right-clicking on a clip on the timeline), any effects are applied only to the area you define.

The tool actually creates a duplicate of the clip on a track directly above it, with any effects applied to the duplicate and seen through a mask you shape with corner handles.

To create an **Effects Mask**:

**1**  **Right-click** on a clip on your timeline (**Ctrl-click** on a Mac) and select **Effects Mask** and then **Apply** from the context menu.

A duplicate of your clip will appear on the Video 2 track and a rectangle, with four active corner handles, will appear in your **Monitor.**

**2**  Click and drag the corner handles to define the mask area.

This area can be moved and re-shaped later, if you'd like.

**3**  Select a **Video Effect** (from **Effects**, under the **Edit** tab) and click the **Effects** panel's **Apply** button. The effect will be applied only to the area defined by the rectangular mask only.

To fine tune the effect, select the clip(s) (they'll be grouped, and when you select one, you'll select both) and open the **Properties** panel by **right-clicking** on the clips (**Ctrl-clicking** on a Mac) and selecting **Show Properties**

Adjust your added effect as described in **Adjust an effect or property** on page 152 of **Chapter 13, Customize Effects in the Properties Panel**.

- To re-edit the position and shape of the **Effects Mask**, **right-click** again on the clips and select **Effects Mask** then **Edit** from the context menu. The corner handles will again become active and you will be able to drag them, or the mask box, to any new position on the **Monitor** display.

- To remove the **Effects Mask**, **right-click** on the clip group on your timeline and select **Effects Mask** then **Remove**. The duplicate clip will be removed from the Video 2 track and any effects you've added will be applied to the entire original clip.

  The effect(s) can then be removed from the original clip by **right-clicking** on the clip and selecting the **Remove Effects** option.

## Close-Up: Chroma Key

Whether you're aware of it or not, you've encountered **Chroma Key** (and its variations in **Green Screen** and **Blue Screen**) countless times.

Every time you watch a televised weather report – the weather person apparently standing in front of satellite video and moving maps – you're actually seeing a **Chroma Key** effect. That weather person is, in reality, standing in front of a plain green screen, electronics removing this green background and replacing it with the weather graphics for the broadcast.

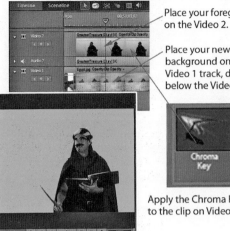

Place your foreground clip on the Video 2.

Place your new background on the Video 1 track, directly below the Video 2 clip.

Apply the Chroma Key effect to the clip on Video 2.

Virtually every movie that includes scenes of live actors interacting with special effects is using some form of **Chroma Key** – as the actors, like the weather person, perform in front of a green or blue background which is later swapped out with some new background or effect.

Creating the effect is fairly simple. And once you understand how it works (and maybe how to combine it with keyframed motion), you'll be able to create many of these same big-screen Hollywood effects at home. (Strangely, this effect is not available on the Mac version of the program.)

Here's how it works: You shoot your subject standing in front of an evenly-colored screen – usually bright green or blue (colors that are not present in human skin tones). This clip is placed on an upper video track. Your new background is placed on a lower video track, directly below it on your timeline.

The **Chroma Key** effect is then applied to the clip on the upper track and its "key" color is set to the color of the background. **Chroma Key** then renders that "key" color transparent, revealing the video on the track below it through it – making it appear that your subject is standing in front of whatever video you've placed on the video track below it!

The **Chroma Key** effect actually appears in a couple of forms in the **Key** category of Premiere Elements' **Effects**. Also known as the **Blue Screen Key** and the **Green Screen Key**, though the function of the effect is essentially the same – a designated color, or range of colors, on a clip is made transparent. The **Green Screen** and **Blue Screen Keys** are merely preset to the two most commonly used "key" colors. (Also see **Videomerge** on page 130.)

To create a **Chroma Key** effect, you'll need two things: A video clip that has been shot with a subject standing in front of an evenly-colored, evenly-lit green or blue background and a second clip with a background you'd like to swap in.

By the way, you can only effectively do a **Chroma Key** effect in **Timeline** mode, because it requires two video tracks, as shown in the illustration.

*Continued on facing page*

## Chroma Key (continued)

**1** Place the video you shot in front of a green or blue screen (we'll call it your **Key Clip**) on the Video 2 track, as illustrated on the facing page.

Right-click on the "key" clip (on Video 2) and select the option to Show Properties to open the Properties panel.

Place the video or still of the background you want to swap in on the Video 1 track, directly below the **Key Clip**.

**2** Apply the **Chroma Key** effect to your **Key Clip**.

**3** With the **Key Clip** selected on your timeline, click the **Edit Effects** button on the **Effects** panel or **right-click** on the clip and select **Show Properties**.

In the Properties panel, locate the Chroma Key effect listing. Click to select the Sampler (eye dropper) and use it to sample the green background on the clip in your Monitor. It will become transparent – revealing the new background on Video 1.

**4** In the **Properties** panel, click on the little white triangle to the left of the **Chroma Key** effect listing to open its properties, as illustrated above.

**5** Click to select the little **eye dropper** icon next to the color swatch on these properties (technically called the **Color Sampler**). Your cursor will become a little **eye dropper**.

Use this eyedropper to click on the colored background in your **Key Clip** in the **Monitor**.

**6** Once you've selected your **key color**, most of the **Key Clip**'s background will become transparent, revealing the new background you've placed on Video 1 through this area.

You'll likely need to do some fine tuning with the sliders in the **Chroma Key** properties to remove the **Key Clip**'s background completely and smooth the edges between the keyed area and the subject in the foreground.

One very effective way to fine tune your **Chroma Key** is to check the **Mask Only** option in the **Chroma Key** properties.

This will display your keyed foreground as a white silhouette so that you can focus on removing the keyed area while maintaining the integrity of your foreground subject.

It's usually best to adjust only the **Similarity** and **Blend** levels in **Mask Only** mode. Once you've got these properties adjusted as well as possible, uncheck the **Mask Only** box to return to regular view before adjusting the other properties.

You may also find that the **Green Screen Key**, **Blue Screen Key** or even **Videomerge** (page 130) will work more effectively for your particular needs or situation than the **Chroma Key** effect.

Don't be afraid to experiment and see which **Keying** effect works best for your situation!

## Close-up: Videomerge

As with **Chroma Key**, **Videomerge** works by making areas on a clip transparent – and it tends to do this fairly automatically.

Videomerge can be applied by right-clicking on the clip on your timeline.

You'll find access to the **Videomerge** effect in several places throughout the program:

- **When you drag a potential "key" clip to your timeline** – If you drag to your timeline a clip that includes a flat, evenly-colored background, the program will launch a pop-up panel asking if you'd like **Videomerge** to be applied to the clip.

- **On the Effects panel** – Like **Chroma Key**, **Videomerge** can be applied to a clip by dragging the effect from the **Effects** panel onto a clip (or by selecting the clip and the effect, then clicking the panel's **Apply** button).

- **Right-click on a clip** – **Right-click** (**Ctrl-click** on a Mac) on any clip on the timeline and you'll find the option to **Apply Videomerge** in the context menu.

- **On the Monitor** – If you drag a clip onto the Monitor while holding down the **Shift** key (as we discuss in **Add media options** page 100 of **Chapter 8, Edit with the Monitor Panel**), the

The Properties settings for Videomerge are much simpler than those for Chroma Key.

pop-up menu will offer you the option of adding the clip to the track, directly above the currently-displayed video clip, and applying **Videomerge** to it.

Once applied to a clip, the **Videomerge** effect has a greatly simplified "key" adjustment tool.

Open the **Properties** panel for the clip the effect has been applied to (by either **right-clicking** on it – or **Ctrl-clicking** on a Mac – and selecting **Show Properties**, clicking the **Properties** button on the **Timeline** or clicking the **Edit Effects** button on the **Effects** panel).

Click the white triangle to the left of the **Videomerge** listing to open its settings control panel.

The **Videomerge** effect's control panel includes only a few simple adjustments:

- An **eyedropper** for designating the color to be keyed. (Check the **Select Color** box to use the eyedropper to sample a color on the **Monitor's** display.)

- A **drop-down Preset list** for controlling how detailed the **Videomerge** key is.

- A **Tolerance** slider for setting the range of colors to be keyed.

- The option to **Invert Selection**, which makes the clip transparent *except for* the designated key area.

In our experience, **Videomerge** is easy to use and surprisingly effective. In many situations, it's a great alternative to the **Chroma Key, Blue Screen** and **Green Screen Key** effects.

**The Effects panel in Presets mode**

Eyeball button toggles view of effects preview as applied to your selected clip.

The Presets drop-down menu offers access to the other Effects sets.

The categories filter drop-down gives you quick access to any category of presets.

Quickly call up any preset by typing its name in the search box.

>> Menu option to display only local or only downloadable content.

Hover your mouse over any thumbnail to preview the preset.

After preset is applied, click Edit Effects to adjust it in the Properties panel.

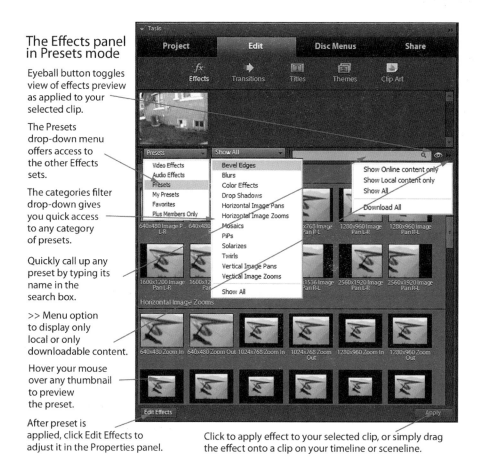

Click to apply effect to your selected clip, or simply drag the effect onto a clip on your timeline or sceneline.

## Preset Effects

To access Premiere Elements' **Preset Effects**, click the **Edit** tab, then click the **Effects** button and chose **Presets** from the **Effects** drop-down menu.

**Presets** are represented as thumbnails in the panel and, if you hover your mouse over those that are animated, a preview of the animation will play.

**Presets** are, essentially, effects to which settings have already been applied. Some of these presets change the size or texture of your video clip, or create a **Picture-in-Picture** effect. Others include keyframed effects so that your video image moves or changes scale, or the setting for the effect changes over the course of the clip. (For more information on motion paths and keyframed effects, see the **Chapter 14, Keyframing**.)

In fact, once you apply a **Preset** to a clip, you can open the clip's **Properties** panel and adjust the settings or keyframe positions to tweak it. (For information on making these adjustments, see **Adjust settings for effects and properties** on page 152 of **Chapter 13, Customize Effects in the Properties Panel**.)

Presets are pre-set Effects, often with keyframed motion.

Applying a Picture-In-Picture preset to a clip on Video 2 is a quick and easy way to create a PiP composite of the clips on Video 1 and Video 2

Presets, like all effects, can be further adjusted in the Properties panel by clicking the Edit Effects button.

To apply a preset effect to a clip, click to select the clip on your timeline or sceneline, then either drag the preset from the **Presets** panel or click the **Apply** button in the lower right corner of the panel.

The nearly 275 **Presets** fall into a number of categories.

**Bevel Edges.** These presets create the illusion of a raised edge along the sides of your video clip.

**Blurs.** Animated **Blur** presets go from blurry to clear or clear to blurry, and can be applied to the beginning or end of a clip.

When using multi-track editing (See **Use L-Cuts, J-Cuts and multiple tracks** in **Chapter 6, Edit Your Video in Timeline Mode**), you can use these keyframed blurs as transitions between video tracks.

**Color Effects.** These presets can be used to tint your clip or to increase the color saturation.

**Drop Shadows.** These presets reduce your clip's scale and create a shadow effect so that your clip appears to be floating – an effect that's most effective when applied to a clip on Video 2 track, casting a shadow over a clip on Video 1 track.

Some of these presets use motion paths so that the shadow moves around over the course of your clip.

**Horizontal Image Pans, Horizontal Image Zooms, Vertical Image Pans, Vertical Image Zooms.** These presets are pre-programmed motion paths for panning and zooming around your photos – their names describe which size photo they are preset to pan or zoom across.

## Create a custom preset

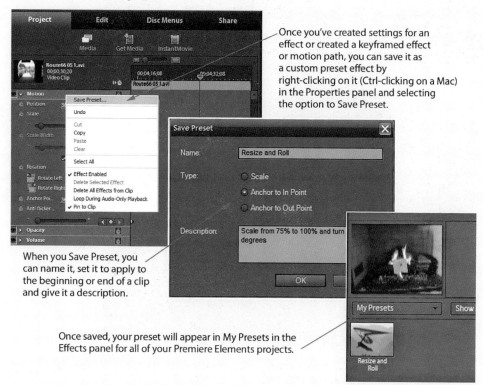

Once you've created settings for an effect or created a keyframed effect or motion path, you can save it as a custom preset effect by right-clicking on it (Ctrl-clicking on a Mac) in the Properties panel and selecting the option to Save Preset.

When you Save Preset, you can name it, set it to apply to the beginning or end of a clip and give it a description.

Once saved, your preset will appear in My Presets in the Effects panel for all of your Premiere Elements projects.

You can easily create your own presets, saving your custom effects settings, animations or motion paths for future use.

To create a custom preset, **right-click** on the effect it represents in your clip's **Properties** panel (**Ctrl-click** on a Mac) and select the **Save Preset** option, as illustrated above.

Once you have saved the preset, it will be available under **My Presets** on the **Effects** panel.

Applying a custom preset to a clip is just like applying a default preset.

Click to select the clip on your timeline or sceneline and then either drag the preset from the **My Presets** panel or click the **Apply** button in the lower right corner of the panel.

They'll do the job in a pinch, but you'll have much more control over the process if you use keyframing to create your own motion paths, as explained in **Chapter 14, Keyframing**.

The biggest challenge to using these preset pans and zooms is that they are designed for specific sizes of photos (as indicated in each preset's name). If the photo you are panning and zooming around is smaller than the effect, for instance, the effect may pan right off the edge of your photo!

With **keyframing** – and even the **Pan and Zoom Tool** (page 84) – you have the ability to control *precisely* how your motion path behaves.

**Mosaics.** These animated presets go to or from a mosaic pattern and can be applied to the beginning or end of your clip.

**Picture-in-Picture (PiP).** The **PiP** presets, when applied to a clip on the Video 2 track with another clip on the Video 1 track under it, automatically reduce the scale of the clip on the Video 2 track and reposition it in the video frame, such that both it and the clip under it are on screen at the same time (as illustrated above).

Some **Picture-in-picture** presets will even add motion, changing the scale or position of **PiP** over the course of the clip – sometimes even incorporating an elaborate animation effect, such as spinning.

**Solarizes.** These animated presets go to or from a bright **Solarize** effect, and can be applied to the beginning or end of a clip.

**Twirls.** These animated twirling effects can be applied to the beginning or end of a clip.

## Cool Tricks & Hot Tips for Adobe Premiere Elements

There is practically no limit to the special video and audio effects you can create with Premiere Elements.

If you'd like to learn some advanced tricks – like creating explosions in the sky or making a person appear to confront his identical twin, making your photos look three-dimensional or creating amazing titling effects – check out our *Cool Tricks & Hot Tips for Adobe Premiere Elements*.

Full of bright, colorful illustrations and step-by-step instructions for creating 50 very cool special effects, with dozens of helpful "Hot Tips" thrown in for good measure, it's a book that will show you the amazing potential of this simple, inexpensive program.

The book is available through major online book stores as well as at the Muvipix.com store.

For more information as well as examples of some of the effects you can learn to create, see Muvipix.com/CoolTricks.

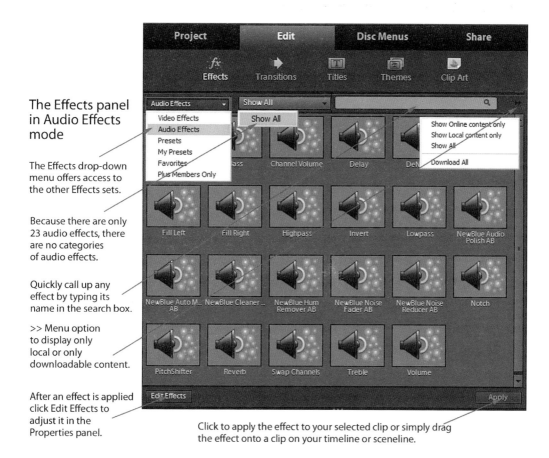

The Effects panel in Audio Effects mode

The Effects drop-down menu offers access to the other Effects sets.

Because there are only 23 audio effects, there are no categories of audio effects.

Quickly call up any effect by typing its name in the search box.

>> Menu option to display only local or only downloadable content.

After an effect is applied click Edit Effects to adjust it in the Properties panel.

Click to apply the effect to your selected clip or simply drag the effect onto a clip on your timeline or sceneline.

## Audio effects

To open the **Audio Effects** catalog, click the **Effects** button under the **Edit** tab and then select **Audio Effects** from the panel's drop-down menu.

Premiere Elements offers 23 audio effects which can be used to improve the sound quality in your project. (The Mac version of the program offers a reduced set of **Audio Effects**, as discussed on page 224.)

A number of these effects (**Bass, Treble, Volume** and **Channel Volume**) can easily be identified by their names. Others (**Denoiser, Highpass, Lowpass** and **Notch**) are filters for removing certain frequencies of sound. **Dynamics** and **Invert** are processors for "sweetening" your movie's sound.

Premiere Elements also includes six audio enhancement effects from NewBlue – high-end, professional-style tools for reducing noise and sweetening your audio: **NewBlue Audio Polish, NewBlue Auto Mute, NewBlue Cleaner, NewBlue Hum Remover, NewBlue Noise Fader** and **NewBlue Noise Reducer**.

**Balance** raises or lowers the volume of each stereo channel relative to the other. **Swap** switches the left and right channel's audio.

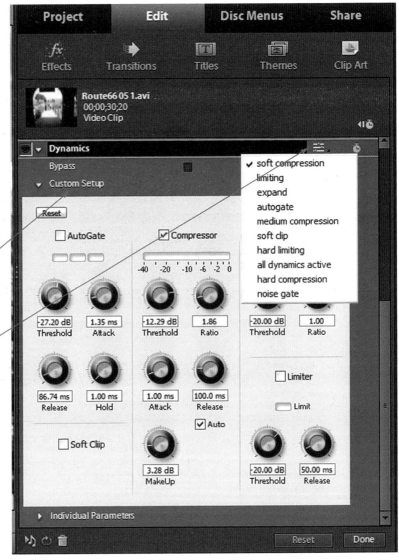

Many audio effects can be customized either by opening Custom Setup and adjusting their individual parameters...

Or by selecting a preset from the drop-down list.

Fill Left and Fill Right are very helpful effects for those times when you have audio on only one of your stereo channels. Applying **Fill Left** or **Fill Right** takes the mono audio from one channel and uses it for both stereo channels.

Delay and Reverb create echo effects.

The Dynamics effect can be used to compress the sound of your audio by reducing the difference between the highest and lowest levels in a clip. **Dynamics** also lets you "sweeten" the sound by removing some background noise, reducing distortion or otherwise balancing the dynamic range. Well tuned dynamics can give your video a richer, more professional, more big-screen movie-like sound.

The **DeNoiser** effect likewise reduces noise in your audio clip. The **DeNoiser** is primarily designed to clean up tape hiss that may have crept into your audio.

And just for fun, there's the **PitchShifter**, which changes the pitch of an audio track, usually in very unnatural and often comic ways, as indicated by some of the names of some of its presets: **Female Becomes Secret Agent, Cartoon Mouse, Boo!, Sore Throat, A Third Higher, Breathless, Slightly Detuned, A Quint Up** and **A Quint Down**.

As with video effects, audio effects can be applied constantly, for the entire duration of a clip or, by using keyframing, you can vary the intensity or settings for your effects or properties over the course of the clip – making the audio louder in some portions of the clip and quieter in others, for instance.

For more information on changing settings for effects, see **Adjust an Effect or Property** on page 152 of **Chapter 13, Customize Effects in the Properties Panel.**

For information on keyframing effects, see **Chapter 14, Keyframing**.

As with video, there are a few basic adjustments that can be made using the **default properties** for any audio clip. Adjustable settings for **Balance** and **Volume** can be found in the **Properties** panel for any clip that includes audio by **right-clicking** on the clip on your timeline or sceneline (**Ctrl-clicking** on a Mac) and selecting **Show Properties**.

Additionally, audio levels can be controlled, and even raised and lowered at specific spots, right on your project's timeline. We explain how in **Adjust the Audio Levels at Specific Points in Your Video** on page 88 of **Chapter 7, Edit Audio on the Timeline.**

**Transitions Defined**

**Fading In and Out**

**How Transitions Work**

**Customize Your Transitions**

**The Gradient Wipe**

Chapter 12
# Add and Customize Transitions
## Cool ways to get from one scene to the next

Transitions in Premiere Elements are very easy to use.

However, like most of Premiere Elements' tools, there is also a surprising amount you can do to customize them, if you know where to look.

The Transitions
panel in
Video Transitions
mode

The Transitions
drop-down menu
offers access to
the other
Transitions sets.

The categories filter
drop-down gives
you quick access to
any category of
transitions.

Quickly call up any
transition by typing
its name in the
search box.

>> Menu option
to display only
local or only
downloadable content.

Click on any thumbnail
and hover your mouse
to preview the
transition's animation.

After a transition is
applied, click Edit
Transition to
adjust it in the
Properties panel.

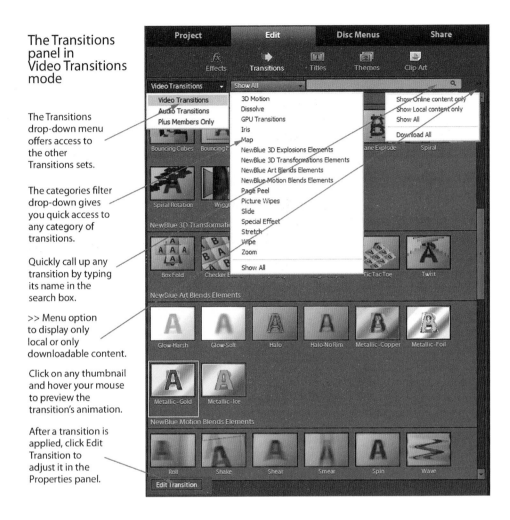

To open the **Transitions** panel, select the **Edit** tab and click on the
**Transitions** button.

From the left drop-down menu, you can access the **Video Transitions,
Audio Transitions** or transitions downloaded from **Photoshop.com.**

At this drop-down menu, you'll also find the option to access additional
transitions from **Photoshop.com,** if you have a **Plus** premium account at
**Photoshop.com** and you are logged into the site at the Premiere Elements
**Welcome Screen** (see **Photoshop.com** on page 23 of **Chapter 2, Start a
New Project** and **Chapter 16, Photoshop.com**).

As with many of Premiere Elements' tools, **Video Transitions** are  arranged
in categories.

By default, the filter drop-down menu is set to **Show All**, displaying all 100
or so of the program's **Video Transitions**. By selecting a category from
this drop-down menu, you can filter the list to display only the **Transitions**
from a particular category.

## Fade in or out of a clip

Fades, in and out of a clip, are most easily achieved by **right-clicking** on a clip on your timeline or sceneline (**Ctrl-clicking** on a Mac) and selecting a **Fade In** or **Fade Out** option.

This works for audio as well as video clips. By **right-clicking** on a clip which includes both audio and video, you'll find separate **Fade In** and **Fade Out** options for both the clip's audio and its video.

A fade in or fade out can be easily added to any video or audio clip by right-clicking (Ctrl clicking on a Mac) on on the clip and selecting the option from the pop-up menu.

For quick access to any transition, you can also type the name of a transition in the **search box** to the right of these drop-down menus (as seen in the illustration on the facing page), and the transition will be brought to the top as you type.

## Video transitions

**Video Transitions** are displayed in the **Transitions** panel as thumbnails representing their effect. If you click or hover your mouse over any thumbnail, you will see an animated representation of the **Transition** in action.

The categories of **Video Transitions** are:

**3-D Motion.** These transitions give the illusion that your video clips are transitioning by turning around or flipping over in three-dimensional space.

**Dissolve. Cross-Dissolve** is the most basic transition, a dissolve from one clip to the next.

The **Dip to Black** transition fades the first clip to black before fading the next clip in from black.

### Mac transitions: A limited edition

The Mac version of Premiere Elements 10 does not include all of the transitions available in the PC version. For a list of the omitted effects, see page 224 in the **Appendix**.

## Apply a transition to several clips at once

In Premiere Elements you can add a transition between several clips in one move.

To apply the **Default Transition** to several clips at once:

The Default Transition can be applied to several clips at once by selecting the sequence and choosing the option from the right-click (Ctrl click) menu.

1  Select your clips, either by holding the **Shift** or **Ctrl** key as you click to select clips on your timeline or sceneline, or by dragging across your timeline from beyond your clips to "lasso" the clips you would like to select. (You can also use **Ctrl+a** – ⌘**+a** on a Mac – to select all of the clips on the timeline.)

2  Once the clips are selected, **right-click** (**Ctrl-click** on a Mac) on the group and select **Apply Default Transition** from the context menu.

You may get a warning that your selected clips include "Insufficient media. This transition will contain repeated frames."

This means that one or more of your clips lacks enough "head" or "tail" material and that, if you proceed, some of your transitions will be composed of freeze frames. (For more information on why this happens and what you can do about it, see the discussion of **How transitions work** on page 146.) The only alternative to letting the program generate freeze frames is to trim back your clips so that at least one second of transitional material exists beyond the in and out points on each clip.

There is currently no way to add a transition other than the **Default Transition** (or to add random transitions) to multiple clips in one move.

However, *any* transition can be designated as the **Default Transition**. As illustrated on page 145, to designate a transition as the default, locate the transition on the **Transitions** panel, **right-click** on it (**Ctrl-click** on a Mac) and select the option to **Set Selected as Default Transition**.

Iris. **Iris** transitions change from one clip to another through a shape.

Map. These transitions map their transitional phase to your clip's luminance values.

**NewBlue 3D Explosions, NewBlue 3D Transformations, NewBlue Art Blends, NewBlue Motion Blends.** These categories contain very cool effects created by NewBlue, one of the world's top video effects companies.

Page Peel. These transitions give the illusion of a page peeling or rolling away between clips.

Slide. **Slide** transitions push one clip out of the way so that another is revealed or they transition between clips through sliding boxes or swirls.

Picture Wipes. These transitions use graphics (such as stars, travel signs or wedding dress lace) to transition from one clip to another.

Special Effects. A hodge podge of very showy transitions.

Stretch. These transitions seem to twist or stretch one clip away to reveal another.

Wipe. A variety of transitions that replace one clip with another with a clear line of movement. (See **Create custom transitions with the Gradient Wipe** on page 145 for information on the unique features of this transition.)

Zoom. High energy transitions that suddenly shrink or enlarge one clip to reveal another.

## Audio transitions

To display the **Audio Transitions**, select **Audio Transitions** from the **Transitions** panel's drop-down menu.

There are only two **Audio Transitions** – **Constant Gain** and **Constant Power** – both variations of an audio cross-fade.

The difference between the two is minor, having to do with whether the effect transitions from one audio clip to another in a linear fashion or by varying the audio levels as they crossfade.

Of the two, **Constant Power** is generally considered to provide the smoother transitional sound – though, in reality, most people can't really tell the difference.

The Transitions panel in Audio Transitions mode

The Transitions drop-down menu offers access to the other Transitions sets.

There are only two audio transitions, subtly different audio crossfades.

After a transition is applied, click Edit Transition to adjust it in the Properties panel.

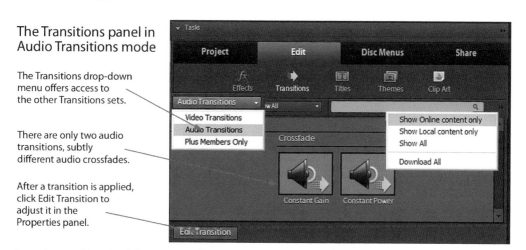

To apply a transition, drag it between two clips on your project's timeline or sceneline.

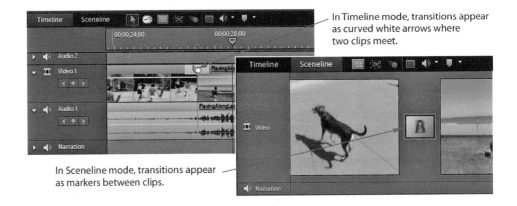

In Timeline mode, transitions appear as curved white arrows where two clips meet.

In Sceneline mode, transitions appear as markers between clips.

## Add a transition to your movie

Adding a transition to your Premiere Elements project is as simple as dragging it from the **Transitions** panel to the point where two clips meet on your timeline or sceneline.

In **Sceneline** mode, there is even a placeholder in which to drag the transition between the clips.

In **Timeline** mode, you drag the transition onto a spot where two clips meet. The transition you've added between two clips is represented by a graphic overlapping one or both of the clips. (See **How transitions work**, on page 146, for information on why transitions position themselves where they do on your clips.)

Transitions, by default, are one second long. However, you can make them as long or as short as you'd like.

If you'd like to increase or decrease the speed of a transition on your timeline, you can do so by clicking on it and dragging it wider or narrower.

You can also customize virtually all of your transitions by changing their properties.

## Customize your transition

Once you've placed a transition, you can also customize it in the **Transition Properties** panel. To open this panel, right-click on the transition on your timeline or sceneline and select **Show Properties** – or simply **double-click** on it.

At the very least, you'll have a couple of basic customization options available in the **Properties** panel. Some transitions have several. You may need to scroll down in the panel to see all of the options available.

At **Alignment**, you can select whether the transition overlaps one or the other, or both, clips evenly.

## Customizing a transition in the Properties panel

To open a transition's properties, double-click on it in your project's timeline or sceneline, or click to select it, and click Edit Transition in the Transitions panel.

Each transition has its own set of customizable properties, but virtually all include the options to set where the transition centers and how long the transition lasts, as well as the option to reverse the transition's animation.

You can check the option to **reverse** the transition so that, for instance, it replaces the old clip with the new in a movement from left to right, rather than from right to left.

Many transitions include other options, and you can preview the transition, even with the actual source clips (check the **Show Actual Sources** box), right there in the **Properties** panel before you commit.

## Set the Default Transition

If you use the **Create Slideshow** feature in Premiere Elements (see **Create Slideshow** on page 58 of **Chapter 4, Explore the Project Media Panel**) you'll note that it offers you the option of applying the **Default Transition** between all of your slides.

By default, that transition is a **Cross-Dissolve**. However, you can designate any transition in the **Transitions** panel as the **Default Transition**.

To designate a transition as your default, **right-click** on the selected transition in the **Transitions** panel (**Ctrl-click** on a Mac) and select the **Set Selected as Default Transition** option.

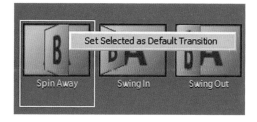

## How transitions work

To create the transitional sequence, the transition must "borrow" extra footage – from beyond the out point of clip 1 and from beyond the in point of clip 2, sometimes resulting in the transition showing frames you've trimmed away.

Out point of clip 1
"Head material" beyond the in point of clip 1
Transitional segment
"Tail material" beyond the out point of clip 2
In point of clip 2

Sometimes transitions seem to behave in mysterious ways. They may show frames of video you've trimmed away – or they may show a freeze frame of your video during the transition. However, once you understand what's actually going on, you may find it easier to work with the process to resolve these issues.

**1** In order to create the transitional segment – the segment during which both clips are displayed – the transition that you've added needs *a few extra frames*, beyond one clip's end and the next clip's beginning, as illustrated above.

Officially these extra frames are called "**head**" and "**tail**" material.

Unfortunately, this sometimes means that frames you've trimmed away from the end or beginning of a clip will appear during this transitional segment!

If this happens, you may need to trim a few more frames from the beginning or end of the clip so that, even amidst the transition, these unwanted frames are not displayed.

**2** If there are no extra frames beyond the beginning or end of your clips for the program to use to create its transition, the program will create a **freeze frame** of the last available video frame for the clip and use that for the transitional material.

This, too, can be a bit annoying if you're not aware of why it's happening. Once again, the solution is to trim back the clip so that the transition has at least a second of "head" or "tail" material to work with.

**3** You may also find, sometimes, that the transition will not sit evenly between two clips on your timeline but, rather, seems to be entirely over one or the other clip.

This is because the transition was not able to find the necessary head or tail material on at least one of the clips – so it has positioned itself over the clip which offers the most available transitional footage.

If this is not what you want, you can go to the **Transition Properties** panel, as described above, and set the transition's **Alignment** so that it sits evenly over both clips. However, you may find that this also creates an undesirable effect (such as a freeze frame in the head or tail material of one clip).

So weigh your options carefully. The default point at which the transition lands is usually the best available position for it.

**4** If you're using transitions between several photos (as in a slideshow) or even titles, you may find that the transition regularly rests over one or the other clip entirely. In this case, it's best not to bother to tweak its position since, with a still image, head, tail and freeze frames all look the same.

The Gradient Wipe transition creates a wipe in any shape you create, by following the pattern from black to white.

To load a custom pattern, click the Custom button in the Transition Properties panel, then click Select Image in the Gradient Wipe Settings and browse to your image.

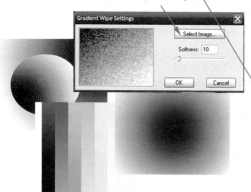

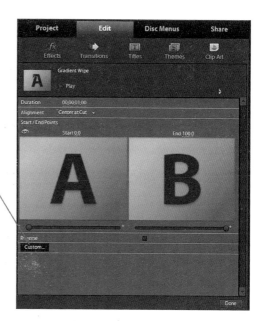

## Create custom transitions with the Gradient Wipe

One of the most versatile **Video Transitions** available in Premiere Elements is the **Gradient Wipe**.

The **Gradient Wipe** will create a *custom* wipe from one clip to another based on any gradient (black to gray to white) pattern you provide!

Once you drag the **Gradient Wipe** onto a point between two clips, open the **Properties** panel by double-clicking on the transition on your timeline, or by selecting the transition on your sceneline, and clicking on the **Edit Transitions** button on the **Transitions** panel.

At the bottom of the options listing for the **Gradient Wipe** in the **Transition Properties** panel, you'll see a button labeled **Custom**.

Click on the **Custom** button to open the **Gradient Wipe Settings** panel. This panel will display a default gradient pattern along with a slider to adjust its softness.

Click on **Select Image,** and you'll find the option to browse to any gradient image on your computer – or any photo or graphics file at all, in fact – and select it as a pattern for the wipe.

The **Gradient Wipe** will base its wipe pattern on a movement from the blackest to the whitest area in the graphics file or on a pattern you've provided.

In other words, by using a grayscale image you've created in Photoshop Elements, you can design virtually any transitional wipe pattern you can imagine!

For more information on the **Gradient Wipe** and how to use it – plus a free pack of several gradient patterns – see my *Steve's Tips* article "The Gradient Wipe" and the free "Gradient Wipe Pack" on the products page at Muvipix.com.

**Open the Properties Panel**
**Default Clip Properties**
**Adjust Effects**
**Paste Attributes**

Chapter 13
# Customize Effects in the Properties Panel
## Adjusting your effects settings

The Properties panel is second only to the Timeline/Sceneline panel as the most powerful and important workspace in Premiere Elements.

The Timeline/Sceneline panel may be where you assemble, trim and order your clips, but the Properties panel is where you make the movie magic happen!

It's where the effects are added, adjusted and removed. It's where motion paths and many special effects are created.

Four ways to
open the
Properties panel

Select Properties
from the Window
drop-down menu.

Click Edit Effects
in the Effects
panel.

Click on the
Properties (list)
icon on the
timeline or
sceneline.

Right-click on a
clip (Ctrl-click on a Mac)
on your project's
timeline or sceneline
and select
Show Properties.

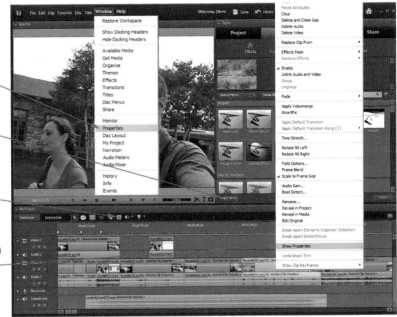

## Open the Properties panel

When an effect is added to a clip, it is also added to that clip's list of properties. The effect can then be adjusted, removed or keyframed in that clip's **Properties** panel.

You can launch the **Properties** panel workspace for any clip on your timeline or sceneline in a number of ways:

- **Click on the Properties button** on the **Timeline/Sceneline** panel. You'll need to then click on a clip on your sceneline or timeline to see its properties and effects;

- **Right-click on a clip** on your timeline or sceneline (**Ctrl-click** on a Mac) and select **Show Propertie**s;

- Click to select a clip on your timeline or sceneline and, in the **Effects** panel, click the **Edit Effects button**; or

- Select **Properties** from the **Window** drop-down menu

Every clip has its own **Properties** panel, and when you select a clip and open the panel, you'll see the properties for as well as any effects added to that particular clip.

**Keyframing** is the process of creating motion paths or effects that change settings over time (such as a **Crop** effect with an animated cropping movement or a **Ripple** effect that shows actual, moving ripples across your clip). For a more detailed discussion of making magic by keyframing, see **Chapter 14, Keyframing**.

## The Properties panel

The Properties panel lists all effects applied to a clip, including certain default properties.

The default video properties are Motion and Opacity.

The default Audio properties are Volume and Balance.

Click triangle to open settings for your effects and properties.

Enable/disable effect or property.

Reset selected effect to default.

Loop audio playback for this clip.

Play audio for this clip.

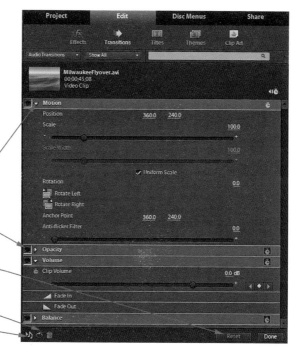

# Default clip properties

There are some properties that are attached to every clip by default. Which of these appear in that clip's **Properties** panel depends on whether the clip is video only, audio only or both.

To see the individual settings for any effect or property, or to make an adjustment to a property or effect, click on the little, white triangle to the left of the property's listing. This will open the property and display its individual settings, as in the illustration above.

**The default properties for every video clip or still are:**

> **Motion.** Includes the properties of **Position, Scale** and **Rotation** – the settings used to keyframe motion paths. (See **Chapter 14, Keyframing** for detailed information on how to create motion paths using these properties.)
>
> **Position** is the position of the center of a clip in a video frame, measured in pixels.
>
> **Scale** is the size or resizing measurement of your clip, listed as a percentage.
>
> **Rotation's** setting is a measure of degrees of angle imposed on your video image.
>
> The settings for the **Motion** properties can be changed numerically or, more intuitively, by clicking on the video image in the **Monitor** panel and dragging it or its corner angles to change its position, size or rotation.
>
> **Opacity. Opacity** is the transparency level of a clip. (Well, technically opacity is the *non-transparency* level of a clip.)
>
> The fading in or out of a clip (added to a video clip by **right-clicking** and selecting **Fade In** or **Fade Out**, as discussed on page 141) is actually a function of **Opacity**, using keyframing to bring it from 0% opacity to 100% or vice versa.

**The default properties for every audio clip are:**

Volume. The sound level on an audio clip.

This effect is one of the most common to keyframe, so that levels can be set for specific points on a clip. The easiest way to keyframe the audio levels for a clip is right on the **Timeline** (as discussed in **Adjust the audio levels at specific points in your video** in **Chapter 7, Edit Audio on the Timeline**).

Balance. **Balance** affects the audio levels for left and right stereo audio channels relative to each other.

As effects are added to a clip, they are added to the list of effects and properties in that clip's **Properties** panel.

Many effects can be added to a single clip, and you can even add multiples of the *same* effect to increase its intensity.

To increase the audio level of a particularly quiet clip, for instance, you can add several **Volume** effects to it and adjust the slider in the **Properties** panel for each to its maximum setting (as in **Adjust an effect or property**, below) until the clip's audio is at an acceptable level.

(For more information on adding effects, see **Finding and applying an effect** on page 124 of **Chapter 11, Add Video and Audio Effects.**)

Many effects, when first applied, may not show a significant change in your clip at their default settings. You may need to adjust the effect's settings in the **Properties** panel to see any real change.

## Adjust an effect or property

Once you've opened the **Properties** panel for a clip, you'll see a list of all of the effects added to that clip as well as the default properties of **Image Control, Motion, Opacity, Volume** and **Balance,** as applicable.

Click the little white triangle to the left of any effect or property listing to display its settings controls.

Some effects (such as **Lightning**) offer dozens of settings for customizing the effect. Others (such as **Posterize**) may offer only a few – or even a single "intensity adjustment" slider.

Many effects (**Spherize**, for instance) will show almost no effect when applied to your clip *until* you adjust their settings.

In nearly every case, once you've applied an effect to a clip, you'll need to change the settings to see any significant change to your audio or video. (A few effects, such as the **Black & White** effect, have no settings at all. They are either on or off.)

There are always several ways to adjust the settings for an effect.

## Adjusting effects in the Properties panel

Open the effect's properties to adjust using numbers or the sliders.

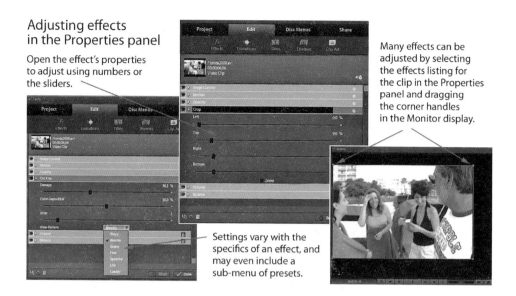

Many effects can be adjusted by selecting the effects listing for the clip in the Properties panel and dragging the corner handles in the Monitor display.

Settings vary with the specifics of an effect, and may even include a sub-menu of presets.

**Numbers** – The numbers that represent an effect can, depending on the effect, represent the effect's **Position** (measured in pixels across the frame), percentage (as in **Opacity**) or intensity. To change a number, click on it and type in a new amount.

Alternatively, you can click and drag right and left over a number to increase or decrease its level.

**Sliders** – The intensity or percentage for a large number of effects settings can be increased or decreased by moving sliders back and forth in the **Properties** panel.

**On the Monitor** – The most intuitive way to adjust many effects is to click to highlight the effect in the **Properties** panel and then make your adjustments right on the video displayed in the **Monitor**.

When the effect listing is selected in the **Properties** panel, a position marker or corner handles for many effects will appear on the clip in the **Monitor**, as illustrated above. You can then click on this marker or corner handles and drag them into your desired positions.

For effects that involve motion (such as repositioning, rotating or resizing the video image) dragging the corner handles in the monitor will move, turn or resize the image.

For effects that involve shaping or sizing (such as scaling, cropping or using one of the garbage mattes) dragging the corner handles will reshape the image or affected area.

Once you start adjusting the settings, the changes will be immediately displayed in your **Monitor** panel. (If they're not, it's because the **CTI** playhead isn't positioned over the clip you're adjusting on your timeline.) The exception is the **Lightning** effect, which is so intensive and erratic that you'll need to play back the clip to see how your adjusted settings have affected the clip.

## Disable or remove an effect

Once you've adjusted the settings for an effect, you can do a before-and-after comparison by temporarily turning off – or disabling – the effect.

To temporarily turn off the effect, click on the eyeball icon to the left of the effect or property listing in the **Properties** panel.

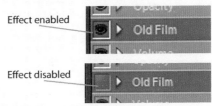

Effect enabled

Effect disabled

The eyeball will disappear and so will the effect's change on your video image.

To turn the effect back on, click on the same spot. The eyeball icon will return and the effect will once again be enabled.

To remove an effect from a clip, **right-click** on the effect's listing in the **Properties** panel (**Ctrl-click** on a Mac) and select **Delete Selected Effect**. Alternatively, you can click to select the effect and click the trashcan icon at the bottom of the panel.

### Types of effects settings

Just as there is a wide variety of effects (some that shift colors, some that create transparency [see **Chroma Key** and **Videomerge** in **Chapter 11, Add Video and Audio Effects**], some that reshape or distort your video image), there is a wide variety of ways to change the *settings* for these effects.

Some settings increase the intensity of an effect. Some add optional elements to the effect. Other settings, depending on the effect, may shift color or define which areas on your video image are affected.

The **Crop** effect is an example. The settings for the crop effect define the percentage of the video image that will be cropped from each side. Dragging a slider representing any side's settings (or clicking to select the effect listing in the **Properties** panel and then dragging on the corner handles that become activated on the video image in the **Monitor**) crops away the clip's sides.

Additionally, any effect's settings can be set to change as the clip plays, creating an animated change, using **keyframes**.

- The **Basic 3D** effect, for instance, can be keyframed to create the illusion that your video image is tumbling back into space.
- The **Crop** effect can be animated using keyframes so that the amount of the video image that is cut away changes over the course of the clip.

For more information on how to create these types of motion paths and animated effects, see **Chapter 14, Keyframing** .

# Save a custom Preset

Once you've adjusted, or even keyframed an effect or property, you can save it as a **Preset** so that you can use it on another clip, even in another project. (To learn more about keyframing and creating motion paths, see **Chapter 14, Keyframing.**)

To save your effect setting or keyframed effect as a **Preset**, **right-click** on the effect's listing in the **Properties** panel (**Ctrl-click** on a Mac) and select **Save Preset**.

The option screen will then prompt you to name your preset.

If your effect includes a keyframed motion, the screen will ask you if you'd like to set this animation to appear at the beginning or end of the clip it is applied to.

You can also include a description of the effect, if you'd like.

Click **OK** to save the **Preset**.

The new Preset will be available under **My Presets**, on the drop-down menu in the **Effects** panel. (See  page 131 of **Chapter 11, Add Video and Audio Effects,** for more information.) You can apply this preset to any clip, just as you would apply any effect or any of the default presets, by dragging it onto a clip or by selecting the clip and clicking the **Effects** panel's **Apply** button.

Applying the preset to a clip automatically applies the motion path or effect, at the settings you initially customized, including any keyframed motion you've added to it.

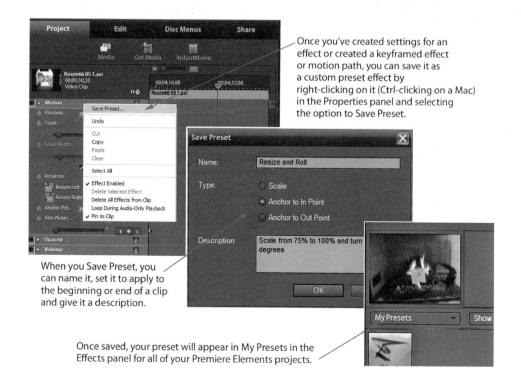

Once you've created settings for an effect or created a keyframed effect or motion path, you can save it as a custom preset effect by right-clicking on it (Ctrl-clicking on a Mac) in the Properties panel and selecting the option to Save Preset.

When you Save Preset, you can name it, set it to apply to the beginning or end of a clip and give it a description.

Once saved, your preset will appear in My Presets in the Effects panel for all of your Premiere Elements projects.

## Paste Attributes

If you've created an effect – even one that includes keyframed motion – for one clip, you can easily apply it to several other clips in just a few clicks using **Paste Attributes**.

**Right-click** on a clip on your timeline to which you've added your effect or keyframes (**Ctrl-click** on a Mac) and select **Copy** from the context menu.

Then select another clip – or even a group of clips – **right-click** (or **Ctrl-click**) and select **Paste Attributes**.

All of the original clip's effects, adjustments and keyframed actions will automatically be applied to your selected clips!

**Basic Keyframing**
**Create a Motion Path Pan & Zoom**
**Advanced Keyframing Effects**

Chapter 14
# Keyframing
## Animating effects and creating motion paths

Keyframing is the system that Premiere Elements uses to create motion paths, and to create and control effects that change their settings over time.

With keyframing, you can control the level of an effect or the scale and/or position of a clip at precise points throughout the duration of the clip.

You can raise and lower the audio level at precise points; you can create panning and zooming around a photo; you can even animate, at precise points in any clip, the intensity or movement of a video effect.

The principle is a simple one: You indicate which two or more points (**keyframes**) on your clip represent settings for a position, scale, effect or level of an effect and the program automatically generates the transitional frames between those points.

You can, for instance, using **Scale** and **Position** settings, set one keyframe point to display a close-up of one corner of a still photo in your video frame, and then set the **Scale** and **Position** of the next keyframe point to display the entire photo. Premiere Elements will then automatically create the smooth motion path between those two positions, seeming to zoom out from the corner to a view of the entire photo.

With Premiere Elements, you can add any number of keyframes to a clip, creating as much motion or as many variations in your effects' settings as you'd like.

But the real power of this tool is in how easy it is to revise and adjust those positions and settings, giving you, the user, the ability to fine tune your path or effect until it is precisely the effect you want to achieve.

Although there are other workspaces in which you can create and edit keyframes (See **Adjust the audio levels at specific points in your video**, on page 88 of **Chapter 7, Edit Audio on the Timeline**), most of your keyframing work will likely be done on the **Properties** panel.

## Keyframing vs. overall adjusting an effect

Until you begin a keyframing session (by clicking **Toggle Animation**, as described below), any positioning, scaling or settings you make for an effect or property in the **Properties** panel will apply to the *entire* clip.

In other words, if you change the **Scale** to 50%, your entire clip will appear at 50% of its size.

However, once you click **Toggle Animation** (the little stopwatch icon) and turn on keyframing, every change to the effect or property you make will generate a **keyframe point** at the position of the **CTI** (Current Time Indicator) on your timeline.

It becomes a sort of "waypoint" for your effect or motion path.

When you create another keyframe point later in the clip and apply new settings to the effect or property, the program will create a path of motion, animation or transition between the two points.

Keyframing is about creating animated effects or motion paths using points representing different position or effect settings.

Premiere Elements creates a smooth, animated transition between these "keyframes."

A motion path between Position and Scale settings on a photograph is called a motion path or a Pan & Zoom – or, commonly, a Ken Burns effect.

You can open the **Properties** panel for any clip by:

- **Clicking on the Properties button** on the **Timeline/Sceneline** panel. You'll need to then click on a clip on your sceneline or timeline to see its properties and effects;

- **Right-clicking on a clip** on timeline or sceneline (**Ctrl-clicking** on a Mac) and selecting **Show Properties**;

- Clicking to select a clip on your timeline or sceneline and, on the **Effects** panel, clicking the **Edit Effects button**; or

- Selecting **Properties** from the **Window** drop-down on the Menu Bar.

(For more information about opening the **Properties** panel for a clip and adjusting effects, see **Chapter 13, Customize Effect in the Properties Panel**.)

CHAPTER 14

Accessing and understanding the Properties panel and the keyframing workspace

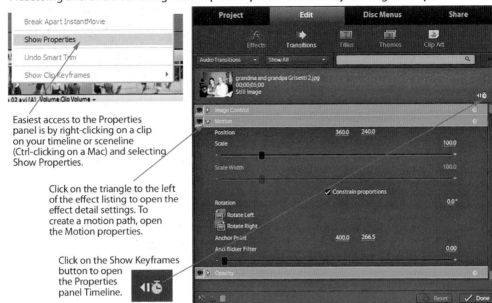

Easiest access to the Properties panel is by right-clicking on a clip on your timeline or sceneline (Ctrl-clicking on a Mac) and selecting Show Properties.

Click on the triangle to the left of the effect listing to open the effect detail settings. To create a motion path, open the Motion properties.

Click on the Show Keyframes button to open the Properties panel Timeline.

## Open a keyframing session

When you first open the **Properties** panel for a clip, the keyframing workspace is hidden.

To reveal this workspace (the **Properties panel timeline**), click on the **Show Keyframes** button (the stopwatch icon with the arrow pointing left) in the upper right of the panel, as illustrated on the following page.

You can widen the display of this timeline by dragging on the edge between the timeline area and the effects and properties listings.

The **Properties panel timeline** (illustrated on the facing page) is your workspace for creating, adjusting and editing your keyframes.

The time positions on this timeline represent positions, in time, on the clip itself. In fact, if you're editing in timeline mode, you'll notice that, as you move the **CTI** on the **Properties panel timeline,** the **CTI** on your project's main timeline will move in sync with it.

## Create a simple motion path using keyframes

To demonstrate how to use keyframes, we'll create a simple motion path – a pan and zoom from the middle of a photo.

1   With the **Properties** panel open and a still photo clip selected on your timeline or sceneline, click on the triangle to the left of the **Motion** property listing to reveal the settings for **Motion** – **Position**, **Scale** and **Rotation**.

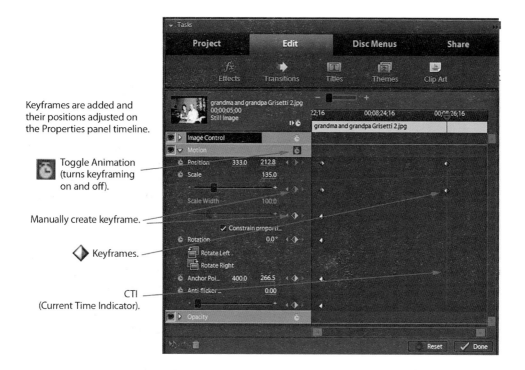

Keyframes are added and
their positions adjusted on
the Properties panel timeline.

Toggle Animation
(turns keyframing
on and off).

Manually create keyframe.

Keyframes.

CTI
(Current Time Indicator).

2    Turn on keyframing for the **Motion** property by clicking on the
     **Toggle Animation** button (the stopwatch at the right end of the
     effect or property listing, as illustrated above).

     When you click the **Toggle Animation** button, a keyframe point – or
     set of keyframe points – is automatically created at the position of
     the **CTI** representing the current settings for that effect.

3    Move the **CTI** to a new position, a few seconds to the right, on the
     clip's **Properties panel timeline.** Then change the **Position** and **Scale**
     settings, by changing the setting numbers or by clicking on the clip
     in the **Monitor** panel and either dragging the screen image to a new
     position or dragging on its corner handles to resize it.

## The Pan and Zoom Tool

In addition to its traditional keyframing workspace, Premiere Elements 10
includes a very intuitive workspace for creating pan and zoom motion paths
over your photos, accessible by way of a button along the top left of the **Timeline** panel.

For more information on this new **Pan and Zoom** workspace, see **Create a Pan and
Zoom motion path** on page 84 of **Chapter 6, Edit Your Video in Timeline Mode.**

## A Simple Motion Path Created with Keyframes

CTI at the beginning of the clip.

Clicking Toggle Animation creates keyframe points for all settings for the effect or property.

When the CTI is in a new position, any changes to any setting automatically creates new keyframe points.

A line on the Monitor represents the path of motion in pan & zoom.

Details of Properties panel Motion settings.

Toggle Animation button.

Position is the location of the clip's Anchor Point relative to the center of the frame, measured in pixels.

Scale is the percentage the clip has been increased or decreased in size.

Jump CTI to previous keyframe point on timeline.

Create new keyframe point at CTI's current position.

Jump to next keyframe point on timeline.

As with most effects, Motion's Position and Scale settings can be changed numerically here, or by clicking on the image in the Monitor and either dragging it to a new position or resizing it by dragging on the corner points.

As you change the settings at this new **CTI** position, new keyframe points will automatically be generated on the **Properties panel timeline**. (Note that you can also manually create new keyframes by clicking on the diamond-shaped **Make Keyframe** buttons to the right of each effect's setting.)

You have just created a simple motion path!

If you play back the clip, you can see how the program creates the movement between your two sets of keyframe points, using your keyframed settings to define the path.

## Edit your keyframes

The beauty of the keyframing tool is that any motion path or effects transition is infinitely adjustable.

By dragging the keyframe points closer together or further apart on the **Properties panel timeline**, you can control the speed at which the motion occurs. (The closer the keyframes are to each other, the faster the animation.)

You can add more keyframe points and/or delete the ones you don't want. And, if you really want to go deep, by **right-clicking** on any keyframe point (**Ctrl-clicking** on a Mac) you can select the option to interpolate the animation movement or use **Bezier** control handles to change the shape of the motion path or vary the speed of the motion.

## Many applications for keyframing

Keyframing is used to control audio volume levels at precise points in your video project. (For more on controlling audio levels with keyframes, see **Adjust the audio levels at specific points in your video** on page 88 of **Chapter 7, Edit Audio on Your Timeline**.)

With keyframing, you can also control effects, such as **Crop**, so that the area of your image that's cropped widens, narrows or changes position as the clip plays, as illustrated on page 164.

Or you can very precisely increase or decrease the intensity of an effect on a clip or animate a **Picture-in-Picture** effect. (See **Use L-cuts, J-cuts and multiple tracks** on page 78 of **Chapter 6, Edit Your Video in Timeline Mode**.)

You can even use keyframes to create an animated 3D movement for your video image using the **Camera View** or **Basic 3D** effect so that your video images seems to tumble head over heels in space.

Indeed, mastering the keyframing tool is the key to getting to the deeper aspects of Premiere Elements. (It also plays a major role in Adobe After Effects and Apple's Final Cut programs.)

It may not seem intuitive at first. But, once you develop a feel for how it works, you'll soon find yourself able to see all kinds of applications for it in creating and refining all manner of visual and audio effects.

For more information on some of the deeper aspects of keyframing and their applications, see my *Steve's Tips* articles "Advanced Keyframing: Editing on the Properties Panel Timeline" and "Advanced Keyframing 2: Keyframing Effects," available on the products page at Muvipix.com.

There is practically no limit to the special video and audio effects you can create with Premiere Elements.

If you'd like to learn some advanced tricks with keyframing– like creating explosions in the sky or having a person confront his identical twin, making your photos look three-dimensional or creating amazing titling effects – check out our book *Cool Tricks & Hot Tips for Adobe Premiere Elements*.

## Using Keyframes to create animated effects

Using Basic 3D effect with keyframes to animate screen image to spin in 3D.

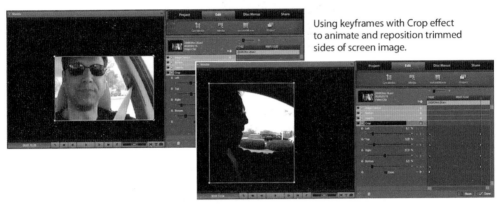

Using keyframes with Crop effect to animate and reposition trimmed sides of screen image.

Using keyframes to change endpoints of Lightning over time so that the effect "follows" an image across the screen.

Full of bright, colorful illustrations and step-by-step instructions for creating 50 very cool special effects – with dozens of helpful "Hot Tips" thrown in for good measure – it's a book that will show you the amazing potential of this simple, inexpensive program.

The book is available through major book stores online as well as at the Muvipix.com store. For more information as well as examples of some of the effects you'll learn to create, see Muvipix.com/CoolTricks.

**File Management with the Organizer**

**The Media Browser**

**Keyword Tags and Metadata**

**Smart Tags and the Media Analyzer**

**Albums**

**Stacks**

**Fix, Create and Share**

Chapter 15
# The Elements Organizer
## Managing your media files

The Elements Organizer, which comes bundled with both Photoshop Elements and Premiere Elements, is Adobe's media file management tool.

It's a way to organize, to search and to create search criteria for your audio, video and photo files.

It also includes a number of great tools for creating everything from slideshows to postage stamps from your media files!

The Media Browser     Search bar     Photoshop.com logon     Keyword Tags     Albums     Media Browser Display Options

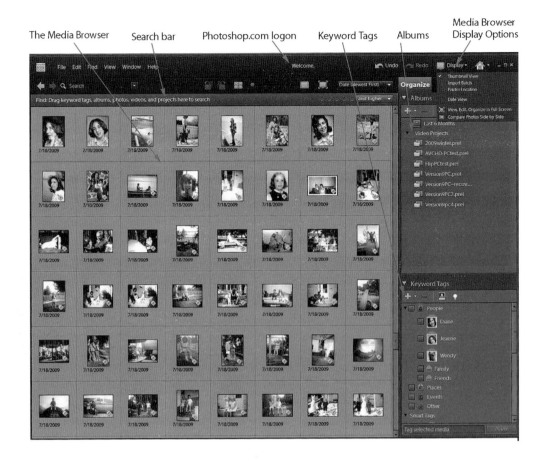

The Organizer is the "Elements" consumer version of Adobe's professional-level **Bridge** file management software (a standard feature of Adobe's Creative Suites).

It's not quite as powerful or as elegant as **Bridge**, of course. But the Elements Organizer offers some terrific tools for organizing, searching, cataloging and managing your media files.

Additionally, the Organizer includes a number of tools for working with your still pictures to create photo projects, like calendars, scrap books and online or video slideshows, as we discuss in **Fix, Create and Share** on page 178.

The Elements Organizer links directly to both Premiere Elements and Photoshop Elements and it can be launched from the **Welcome Screens** or by clicking the **Organizer** button in the editing workspaces of either program. Most media files can be sent to Photoshop Elements or Premiere Elements by **right-clicking** on them and selecting the **Edit** option from the context menu.

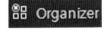

Think of your Elements Organizer as a giant search engine that can be programmed to store and retrieve the audio, video and still photo files on your computer, based on a wide variety of criteria – some of which you can assign and some of which are inherently a part of your photo, sound and video files when they're created.

These search criteria aren't limited to obvious details – such as the type of media or the date it was saved to your computer.

Search criteria can include **Keyword Tags** – or it can be minute technical details, such as the type of camera that was used to shoot a photo or whether the photo was shot with a flash or natural light.

Furthermore, the Organizer includes features that support other tools and functions in both Premiere Elements and Photoshop Elements. (The **Smart Tags Media Analyzer**, discussed on page 172, for instance, preps your video files for use with a number of new tools in Premiere Elements.)

Your Elements Organizer's media files can also be stored in **Albums**, which have both a filtering function and play a role in the Organizer's online file back-up system (as we discuss in **Designate an Album for online back-up** on page 177).

## The Media Browser area

Video file

The main area of the Organizer's interface, in which your media files are displayed as thumbnails and which dominates the Organizer workspace, is called the **Media Browser**.

There are several types of media files, and they are each represented by slightly different thumbnail images in the **Media Browser**, as illustrated to the right:

Photo file

**Video files** are represented as image thumbnails with a filmstrip icon on the upper right corner.

**Photo files** are represented by a plain thumbnail of the image file.

**Audio files** are represented by blue thumbnails with a speaker icon on them.

The size of these thumbnail images in the **Media Browser** is controlled by the slider at the top of the interface.

Under the **View** drop-down on the Organizer menu bar, in the **Media Types** sub-menu, you can filter which file types are displayed in the **Media Browser** (as illustrated on page 172).

Audio file

## The Search Bar

A quick and easy way to search your media files is to drag an **Album** or **Keyword Tag** onto the **Search Bar** that runs along the top of the **Media Browser**. The Browser will then display only the media files that are included in this **Album** or to which those **Keyword Tags** apply.

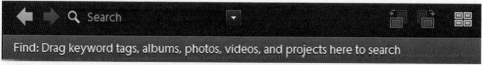

You can search your media files by using the Search Box or by dragging a Keyword Tag or Album onto the Search Bar.

## The Organizer Catalog

The media files that the Organizer manages and displays, as well as the metadata that defines them, are said to be in the Organizer's **Catalog**. Some files are added to this **Catalog** automatically, while others may be added to the **Catalog** manually.

All of the video clips or photo files that you edit with Premiere Elements or Photoshop Elements are automatically added to your Elements Organizer **Catalog**. If you download or capture video or photos to your computer using any of the tools in Premiere Elements or Photoshop Elements, they too are automatically added to your Organizer's **Catalog**.

## Manually add to and update your Organizer Catalog

The first time you launch the Elements Organizer, it will offer to search your computer for media files to add to the **Catalog**. (If you've had a previous version of the Organizer installed, the program will offer to simply update your existing **Catalog**.)

### Get Photos and Video

You can manually add additional files to your **Catalog** using the **Get Media** tool, under the Organizer's **File** menu, illustrated above.

- To manually add files and folders full of files to your Organizer's **Catalog**, select **Get Photos and Videos**, then, from the sub-menu, select **From Files and Folders**. Browse to the files you would like to add – or to the folder of files – and click **Get Media**.

- Media files can also be *automatically* added to your Catalog by selecting **Get Photos and Video** then, from the sub-menu, **By Searching**.

- Additionally, this menu offers to activate your scanner or download photos from your camera or card reader. As you scan or download your photos, they are automatically added your **Catalog**.

### Import files from your iPhoto catalog

If you're running the Elements programs on a Mac, you can easily import your catalog of photo files from your iPhoto catalog into the Organizer **Catalog**.

To do so, select, from the Elements Organizer's **File** menu, **Get Photos and Videos** and, from the sub-menu, **From iPhoto**.

### Set up Managed and Watched Folders

Media can also be added to your Organizer Catalog be designating folders on your computer as **Managed Files** or **Watched Folders**. More information on this method of maintaining your **Catalog** are discussed on page 170.

### Resync an out-of-sync Catalog

If you move, delete or change files using Windows Explorer or a program other than one of the Elements programs, you may find your Organizer's **Media Browser** will display some media thumbnails with broken or outdated links.

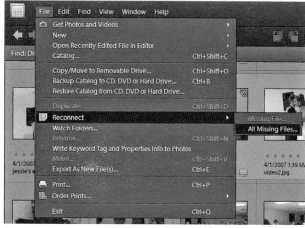

To update these connections manually or to remove the thumbnail of a deleted file from the Organizer **Catalog**, go to the **File** menu and select the option to **Reconnect/All Missing Files**.

Reconnecting thumbnails to files – and deleting dead links.

The Organizer will update your links and indicate for you all of the thumbnails in the **Media Browser** that do not have files linked to them, offering you the option of deleting these dead thumbnails.

To avoid the program's losing track of the links to your media, it's best to use the Elements Organizer to move or remove files from your computer:

* To delete a file using the Organizer, **right-click** (**Ctrl-click** on a Mac) on the file(s) and select **Delete from Catalog**. You will then be given the option of merely removing the file from the **Catalog** or removing it completely from your hard drive.

* To move a file to a new location on your computer using the Organizer, click to select the file(s) and, from the **File** drop-down, select the option to **Move** and then browse to the new location.

## Switch to Folder View

By default, the **Media Browser** displays your files according to the dates they were saved, from most recent to oldest. However, you can change this workspace so that your media files are displayed in whatever view you find most intuitive – and sorted by date is by no means the only way to view your files.

The **Display** button – in the upper right corner of Elements' Organizer interface – offers a variety of options for displaying your media files.

Select the **Folder Location View** from the **Display** drop-down and the Organizer becomes a means of browsing the contents of your computer drive(s) by folder, with all the media files represented as previewable thumbnails.

An advantage of the **Folder Location View** is that it gives you access to even more tools for managing your Organizer's **Catalog**.

To add a folder's files to the **Catalog** in **Folder Location View**, **right-click** on the folder displayed along the left side of the **Media Browser** (**Ctrl-click** on a Mac), and select one of the following options:

An Unamanaged folder
(Files not included in catalog)

A Managed Folder
(Files added to catalog)

A Watched Folder
(Catalog auto-updates files)

Add to Watched Folders creates a dynamic link to the Organizer. Any media files you add to or remove from this folder will automatically be updated to the Organizer's **Catalog**.

Add Unmanaged Files to Catalog immediately adds whatever media files are in the folder to the Organizer's **Catalog**.

The changed status of the folder is reflected in the folder's icon, as illustrated on the left. (The **Managed Folder** icon indicates that the folder's files have already been added to the Elements Organizer's **Catalog**.)

## What is metadata?

Metadata is the hidden information embedded in virtually every computer file, including when the file was saved, who modified it last, what program created the file, etc.

The Elements Organizer uses metadata to manage, order and search your media files.

By default, all of your media files carry certain metadata. When you first open the Organizer, for instance, in the default **Thumbnail View**, you'll immediately notice that the files are categorized according to the date they were saved to your computer's drive.

If you've poked around in the Organizer at all, you've probably noted that you can display these files from most recent to oldest or oldest to most recent.

"**Date saved**" is the simplest display of metadata and the most basic way to search through your media files – but it's far from the only way to search your files.

You can also isolate your files by type of media so that the **Media Browser** displays only video, photo and/or audio files. Or, by using the Organizer's **Timeline** (which is activated under the **Window** drop-down on the Organizer's Menu Bar), you can quickly browse to media for any specific date.

In fact, you'd probably be surprised to learn how much metadata a typical photo file actually contains! **Right-click** on any photo file that you've downloaded from a digital camera in the **Media Browser**, for instance, and then select **Show Properties**. This will open the Organizer's **Properties** panel.

Now click on the **Metadata** button (the little "**i**" icon inside the blue circle) on the **Properties** panel.

If you've selected the option to view the **Complete** data, you'll find a couple dozen lines of detailed information about your photo.

Called **EXIF data**, this is information your digital camera writes to all of your photos, and it can include the date and time the photo was shot, the photo dimensions, the make, model and serial number of camera that was used to take the photo, the shutter speed, if a flash was used, what settings and F-stop setting was used, if it was shot with manual or automatic focus and so on.

All of this is metadata. And it can be used – along with any additional metadata you assign manually – as search criteria in the Elements Organizer.

To search by metadata, go to the **Find** drop-down on the Organizer Menu Bar and select the option to **Find by Details (Metadata)** as illustrated below right.

In the option screen that opens, you can set up a search to find, for instance, all photos shot on a specific date or at a specific time, at certain camera settings – in fact, you can search by pretty much any of the metadata attached to your photo or other media file!

Also under this **Find** drop-down menu, you'll find many more search methods for your files. One of the most amazing search functions, in my opinion, is the Organizer's ability to locate files that contain **Visual Similarity with Selected Photo(s) and Video(s)**.

That's right: If you have a picture of the beach or the mountains or even of an individual, the Organizer will find for you all of the other photos in your collection that have similar color schemes and visual details!

It's not magic, of course. I set it to search for photos similar to a bride in her gown and my hits included a photo of a hamburger, wrapped in waxed paper. But it's still pretty amazing that it does work to some extent.

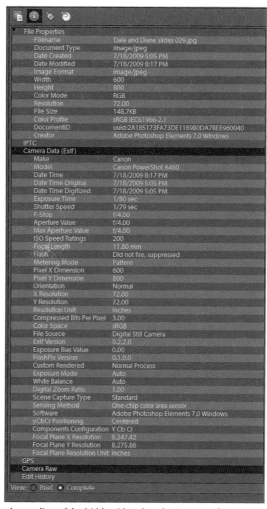

A sampling of the hidden Metadata that's a part of every digital photo's data

Searching photo files using Metadata.

## Metadata in different views

There are a number of ways to add searchable metadata to your media files. You can, for instance:

- Place your media in **Albums** (as discussed on page 175).

- Add **Keyword Tags** (as discussed on page 173) or identify individuals in your photos with the **People Recognition Tool** (as discussed on page 176).

The View menu offers a number of options for viewing and filtering the files displayed in the Media Browser.

- Add **Smart Tags** (as on the facing page) or use **Smart Tags** to automatically add your media to **Smart Albums** (as discussed on page 175).

- Apply one to five star ratings to your clips (by right-clicking on the thumbnail in the **Media Browser** and selecting the option).

When the Display mode is set to Date View, your media is catalogued by date on a calendar interface.

Your media clips are automatically tagged with metadata based on the date they were created or added to your computer. Naturally, you can display them according to the date saved (most recent-to-oldest, by default, or vice versa). Or, from the **Display** menu, you can choose **Date View,** which will display your files by date in a calendar interface.

## The Smart Tags Media Analyzer

**Smart Tags** are **Keyword Tag** metadata (see page 174) that the Elements Organizer automatically adds to your media files after analyzing them.

Depending on how you have it set up in the Organizer's preferences, the **Media Analyzer** will manually *or automatically* scan your video, audio and photo files and then tag them with metadata based on their audio qualities, brightness and contrast, motion, shake, blur, face presence and object motion.

These results are then automatically added as **Smart Tags** in the **Keyword Tags** panel (as illustrated on the facing page) and can be used for filtering your **Media Browser** searches or for preparing your files for later use in a Premiere Elements project.

Whether you set the **Media Analyzer** up to run automatically, in the background as you work, or you use it manually as needed on specific files depends on how much you value these **Smart Tags** – and how much the automatic **Media Analyzer** impacts your computer's performance while you're trying to do other things.

It is purely a personal preference.

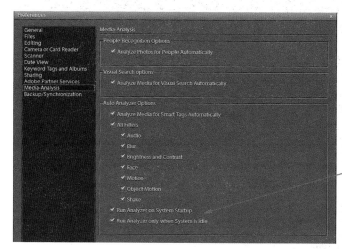

Media Analyzer settings in the Organizer's Preferences (under the Edit menu).

The Analyzer can be set to run "silently" in the background, Smart Tagging your clips automatically.

The **Media Analyzer's** auto-run preferences are found under the Organizer's **Edit** menu.

**Smart Tags** play a role in the functionality of a couple of tools in Premiere Elements. And disabling the **Media Analyzer's** auto-run function can mean that these tools will perform more slowly on certain clips or may not function at all. (Details on how these tools work can be found in **Chapter 6, Edit Your Video in Timeline Mode**):

- Both **Smart Trim** (page 74) and **Motion Tracking** (page 82) use information gathered by the **Media Analyzer** as part of their functionality. If you have not pre-analyzed a clip before you apply either of these tools to it, the program will offer to run the **Media Analyzer** on the clips before launching the tool.

- The **Smart Fix** tool in Premiere Elements (page 70) will *only* function for clips that have been **Media Analyzed** and **Smart Tagged** by the Organizer prior to your adding them to your timeline. In other words, if you have disabled the **Media Analyzer** and you have not generated **Smart Tags** for the clips that you are adding to your project, Premiere Elements will *not even offer* to **Smart Fix** them and you will not be able to manually **Auto Enhance** them.

Even if you've disabled the automatic **Media-Analyzer**, you can *manually* run it on clips in either the Elements Organizer's **Media Browser** or in the Premiere Elements **Project** panel. To do this, **right-click** on a clip or clips (**Ctrl-click** on the Mac) in the Organizer's **Media Browser** or the Premiere Elements **Media** panel and select **Run Media Analyzer** from the context menu.

Smart Tags are Keyword metadata that the Organizer automatically generates based on its Auto Analysis of clips. These Smart Tags can not only be used to filter searches but also play a role in the function of several of Premiere Elements' tools.

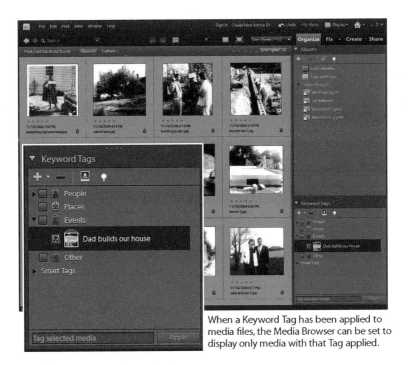

When a Keyword Tag has been applied to media files, the Media Browser can be set to display only media with that Tag applied.

## Assign and search with Keyword Tags

**Tagging** is a way to manually add custom metadata to your media files.

In the **Keyword Tags** palette, you'll see a handful of basic **Categories** – People, Places, Events, Other.

Creating a new **Tag** is as simple as clicking on the **+** symbol on this palette. You can create as many **Tags** and as many **Categories** – and **Sub-Categories** under them – as you'd like. You can, for instance, create a **Sub-Category** under Places and name it France. Then, within that **Sub-Category**, create **Tags** for Cousin Pierre, Landmarks, The Louvre, etc. (You can even drag your **Keyword** sub-categories in an out of categories on the **Keyword Tags** panel!)

Assigning a **Tag** to a media file is as simple as dragging the **Tag** from the **Keyword Tags** palette onto the selected file or files in the **Media Browser**. (You'll notice that, once you do, a little, brightly-colored **Tag** icon will appear on the lower right of the file.)

You can assign as many **Tags** as you'd like to a file. And you can assign the same **Tag** to as many files as you'd like.

Adding **Keyword Tags** to hundreds of accumulated digital photos may seem at first like a lot of housekeeping – but the payoff is great!

When you next want to locate the files for a particular **Tag**, you simply click on the **Tag's** listing in the **Keyword Tags** palette to toggle it on. A little pair of binoculars will appear next to the selected **Tag**. Only media files that have been assigned to that **Tag** will appear in the **Media Browser** area.

If you click on a major category, all of the files assigned to all of that category's sub-categories of **Tags** will appear. As you narrow your **Tag** search, only the files assigned to the **Tag** will be displayed.

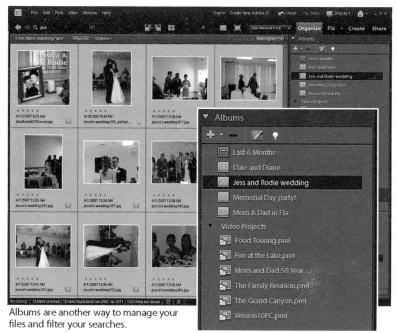

Albums are another way to manage your
files and filter your searches.

## Assign and search with Albums

Just as you can add **Tags** to a file, you can catalog your media files into **Albums** for easier
searching and filtering.

As with **Tags**, you click on the **+** icon in the **Album** panel to create an **Album**. And, as with **Tags**,
to assign a file to an **Album**, you simply drag the **Album** from the **Albums** palette onto the media
file or files in the **Media Browser**. A little green icon will appear in the lower right of each file.

In addition, the Organizer automatically creates a new **Album** whenever you create a new Premiere
Elements **Video Project** and assigns all of the media for that project to it. (These **Albums** will appear
as yellow icons rather than green, as illustrated above.)

To locate the media files assigned to a particular **Album**, click to select that **Album's** listing in the
**Albums** panel. Only the files assigned to that **Album** will appear in the Organizer's **Media Browser**.

Any **Album**, including a **Video Project Album**, can be removed by **right-clicking** on it and selecting
the **Delete** option.

## Create a Smart Album

An interesting feature of the **Album** palette is its ability to create **Smart Albums**. (You'll find the
option under the **+** button in the **Albums** palette.)

When you create a **Smart Album**, you merely set up the
criteria, based on metadata or **Tags**, and the Organizer will
automatically assign your media files to that **Album** based on
that criteria. You can, for instance, create a **Smart Album** that
searches for files you've assigned five-star ratings to. As you
rate and re-rate your media files, the **Smart Album** feature will
automatically update its file collection for that  **Smart Album**.

## People Recognition Keyword Tags

**People Recognition** is a way to identify people in your photos, and to include that identification metadata as **Keyword Tags**.

Amazingly, the tool Adobe has designed for this task is so intuitive that, as you use it, it will begin to identify people it recognizes on its own!

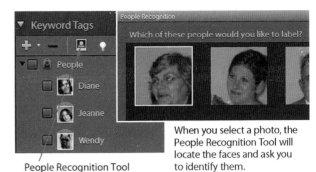

People Recognition Tool

When you select a photo, the People Recognition Tool will locate the faces and ask you to identify them.

1. Select one or more photos in the Organizer's **Media Browser** workspace and click the **People Recognition** button on the **Keyword Tags** palette, as illustrated above. (**People Recognition** does not work with video clips.)

   The tool will display thumbnail images of the faces of people in your selected photos and ask you "**Which of these people would you like to label?**"

2. Identify the people in the picture. Once you've typed in his or her name, it will appear as a **Keyword Tag** under the **People** category, linking to your photo.

3. As you continue to identify people, the program will build a database of features and will soon begin guessing at people's names. Sometimes this guess will appear as one of three possibilities. Other times it will ask simply, "**Is this –?**"

4. Occasionally the tool will try to identify something in your photo that's not a face at all. In that case, just click the **X** above the thumbnail. Other times it may not identify a face in a scene. In that case you can ID the face manually.

To manually add a **People Recognition** tag to a photo, **double-click** on the photo in the **Media Browser**. The photo will zoom in to full-screen view.

Click the **Add a Missing Person** button (in the lower right of the photo space). An identification box will appear in the upper left corner of your photo. Drag it into position over the person you want to ID and type in the person's name in the space provided.

As you identify people, they will appear as **Tags** listed under the **People** category of **Keyword Tags**.

Once **People Recognition** tags have been applied, you can locate all photos in which a given person appears by clicking on his or her name in the **Keyword Tags** palette.

## What are Stacks?

Another way to bring order to the many files in your **Media Browser** is to store them in **Stacks**. **Stacks** are essentially groups of photos that you create – usually of similar photos, but that's up to you.

When you create a **Stack**, only one file in the stack is displayed in the **Media Browser** (with a **Stack** icon on it). The rest of the files in the stack are hidden "behind" it – as if they were in a stack.

To create a **Stack**, select several files (by dragging across them, by holding the **Shift** key as you select the first and last in a series or by holding the **Ctrl** key and selecting one at a time) and then, from the **Edit** menu, select **Stack/Stack Selected Photos** (or press **Ctrl+Alt+s** in Windows or ⌘+**Opt+s** on a Mac).

A Stack is a set of photo files stored under the same thumbnail in the Photo Browser.

The arrow link unstacks the set.

When Organizer Fixes are applied to a photo file, the changed and unchanged versions are saved as a Stack.

## Designate an Album for online back-up

**Albums** play a role in **Photoshop.com's** online file back-up service. Once a media file has been assigned to an **Album**, it can be designated for online backup.

When you create a new **Album** (by clicking the green **+** button) or edit an existing **Album** (by **right-clicking** on it), the **Album** panel will display the option to **Backup/ Synchronize** the contents of the **Album** online.

When you manually create or edit an Album in the Organizer, you'll have the option of setting it to backup online automatically.

On the **Backup/Synchronization** page of the Organizer's **Preferences** (located under the **Edit** drop-down menu) you can see a list of all of the **Albums** that have been designated for online backup as well as an indicator of how much free space you have in your **Photoshop.com** account. For more information on using this service, see **Back your files up online** on page 189 of **Chapter 16, Photoshop.com** )

Stacks are also created automatically when you apply an Organizer **Quick Fix** to a photo. Within this **Stack** is both the cleaned-up and original photo.

To reveal all the files in a **Stack**, click on the unstack arrow button on the right side of the **Stack** thumbnail, as illustrated on the previous page.

To open all **Stacks**, go to the **View** drop-down on the Organizer menu bar and select the option to **Expand All Stacks**.

## Fix, Create and Share

In addition to its media file management system, the Elements Organizer includes a number of tools for producing a wide range of projects under its **Fix, Create** and **Share** tabs.

Most of these are guided tools that walk you through the process of fixing, creating and/or sharing your various files and projects.

### Fix tools

Under the **Fix** tab, the Elements Organizer includes a number of basic **Photo Fix** tools, which can be applied to any photos you've got selected in the Organizer's **Media Browser** area. Once you apply one of these **Photo Fixes** to a photo, the Organizer **Media Browser** will display the photo as a **Stack** that includes both the fixed photo and the original version.

Additionally, if you click on the little white arrow on the right side of the **Fix** tab, you'll find options for **Full Photo Edit, Quick Photo Edit** and **Guided Photo Edit** – tools that launch the full editor workspace of Photoshop Elements, if you have that program installed on your system.

### Create projects

Under the **Create** tab, you'll find tools for creating several photo projects, many of which can be printed on your home printer or output professionally:

> **Photo Prints** that you can either send to your home printer or order produced by **Shutterfly** or **KodakGallery.com**.
>
> Custom **Greeting Cards**.

A **Photo Book** or **Photo Collage** – scrapbook-like layouts for your photos which can be professionally produced by **Shutterfly** or **KodakGallery.com**.

A **Photo Calendar.**

A **Slide Show,** which you can then either output as a WMV file for displaying on a Web site or forward to Premiere Elements for production as a video. (This feature is not available in the Mac version.)

An **InstantMovie** or **DVD with Menu** (options which launch your selected media in the Premiere Elements workspace).

Custom **Photo Stamps,** which can then be used as legal U.S. postage.

Templates for creating a jewel box-style **CD Jacket** (Two 4³/₄"x4³/₄" faces with a ¹/₂" spine), a larger format **DVD Jacket** (two 5¹/₈"x7¹/₄" faces with a ³/₄" spine) and a **CD/DVD label.**

A **VCD with Menu** for output to DVD or CD. (This feature is not available in the Mac version.)

A **Flipbook** animation. (This feature is not available in the Mac version.)

### Share options

Under the **Share** tab, you'll find tools for outputting the still photos and videos you have selected in your Organizer **Media Browser** as:

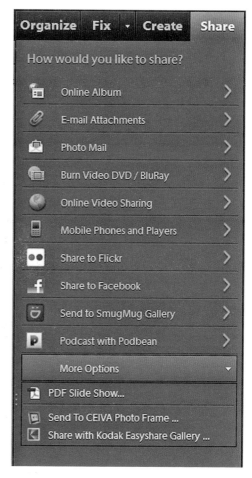

An **Online Album**. (For more information on creating an **Online Album**, see page 187 of **Chapter 16, Photoshop.com**.)

**E-mail Attachments** or HMTL-based **Photomail,** which can be e-mailed directly from the Organizer to people selected from your **Contact Book** (as created in the Organizer's **Preferences)**.

A **Video DVD/BluRay** (an option which launches Premiere Elements).

Output to **Mobile Phones or Players** (another option which launches Premiere Elements).

Uploads to your **Flickr, Facebook** or **YouTube** account or to an online **SmugMug Gallery.**

A podcast to **Podbean,** via Premiere Elements. (For more information, see **Chapter 18, Share Your Movie**.)

A **PDF Slideshow.**

Photo files delivered, via the Internet, to a designated **CEIVA Digital Photo Frame** anywhere in the world.

Uploads to your **Kodak Easyshare Gallery.**

**Your Photoshop.com Account**
**Display Your Photos Online**
**Create an Online Album Slideshow**
**Back Up Your Media Files Online**
**Photoshop Express**
**The Inspiration Browser**

Chapter 16
# Photoshop.com
## Your online connection

If you've used online photo-sharing sites like Flickr, Facebook and Picasa, you'll likely feel right at home with many of the features on Photoshop.com.

But Photoshop.com adds a number of additional features – tools for editing and managing your photo files as well as tutorials, supplemental templates and tools for both Premiere Elements and Photoshop Elements.

In fact, it offers an awful lot for a free service. And even more for its premium package.

The Photoshop.com Library    The Media Browser    Upload tools for photo and video    Selected clip's properties

Albums can be designated as public or private.

Photo editing and download tools

Photoshop.com is Adobe's online connection for Photoshop Elements and Premiere Elements.

Photoshop.com is an online service, included as a bonus feature with Premiere Elements and Photoshop Elements, which incorporates a number of tools for photo and video sharing and management. Although you don't need either of these programs to access the site, both Photoshop Elements and Premiere Elements include functions that take particular advantage of the site's features.

Photoshop.com includes five categories of services:

**A photo sharing and display area**, which includes tools for managing and organizing your online photo and video files as well as accessing your other online galleries (page 185);

**Online file back-up** and storage space (page 189);

**A basic photo editing tool set** – online touch-up, fix and special effects tools for photos you've uploaded to the site (page 190);

**An Inspiration Browser**, including tutorials and other training materials for Adobe products (page 191);

**Additional templates and themes** for Premiere Elements and Photoshop Elements (page 192).

Like the Organizer, it's difficult to do the entire product justice with one short chapter. However, we'll try to give you a general overview of its key features and hopefully they will inspire you to explore it further.

At the writing of this book, this service is available only to US residents. However, Adobe does have plans to expand the service worldwide as it continues to grow.

## Create an account and log in

Anyone can create an account on Photoshop.com. But, if you've got Photoshop Elements or Premiere Elements, your logon gives you a live link-up to the site any time you're working in either program. This becomes a real bonus if you plan to take advantage of the free tutorials or the premium themes and templates, as we'll discuss later.

You can create your account by going to **www.photoshop.com** – or you can do it right from the Premiere Elements or Photoshop Elements start-up screens (or even from within either program's working interface).

When you create an account from Photoshop Elements or Premiere Elements, you'll be logged in automatically whenever you launch one of the programs.

Once you've created an account and logged in from within these programs, you'll be automatically logged in to the site any time you launch either program. (You must have an always-on Internet connection in order to have a live connection with **Photoshop.com**.)

Both programs send and receive data, to some extent, from **Photoshop.com** on a regular basis. Both also include features for sharing directly to the site.

In order to fully use **Photoshop.com's** services, you'll need to load the **Adobe Air Uploader**, a program for interfacing with the site and syncing its library with the media on your computer. You'll be prompted to load this program when you create a **Photoshop.com** account or when you access the content on the site.

## Your Photoshop.com

If you go to **Photoshop.com** through your Internet browser, log into the site by clicking on the **Sign In** link in the upper right of the Web page and signing in with your **Adobe ID** (an e-mail address) and password. This will bring you to the My Photoshop.com **Welcome Page**. From this page, you can link to friends or send them notifications, update your profile or access your **Gallery**.

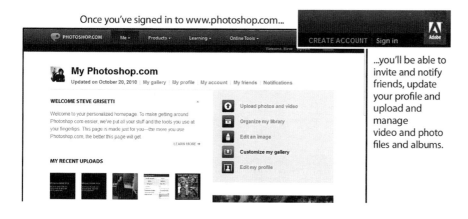

Once you've signed in to www.photoshop.com...

...you'll be able to invite and notify friends, update your profile and upload and manage video and photo files and albums.

## The Gallery

The **Gallery** displays all of the **Albums** that you've created from your **Library** of media files.

Your **Albums** are either public – in which case anyone can view them – or private – in which case only those you've invited can access them. You can set whether any given **Album** is public or private when you upload your media files (as discussed on the facing page) or at any time, as you manage your **Library**, as discussed below.

## Friends

Photoshop.com also includes many elements of a social media Web site.

To build a **Friends** list, click on the **My Friends** link on any Photoshop.com Web page and then, on the **My Friends** page, click the **Find Friends** button.

You can invite others to join your Photoshop.com **Friends** by tapping into your Yahoo, Gmail or Hotmail contact lists or by simply typing in their e-mail addresses in the space provided.

## The Library

**The Library** includes every photo or media file you have stored on the site, including those you are backing up from your computer. Your **Library** is where you manage your online media files and where you designate which are displayed and how.

In addition, your Photoshop.com **Library** can include photos and video you've posted to Facebook, Flickr, Photobucket and Picasa, as described in **Link to other Sites** on page 188.

To access your **Library**, go to the **Me** drop-down menu at the top of the Photoshop.com Web page and select **My Library**, as illustrated on the right.

Display your video and photo Albums on the Gallery page.

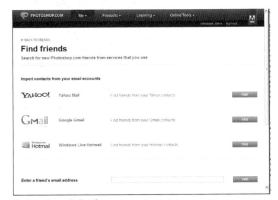

Build a Friends list from your contacts.

Upload, manage, edit and order your video and photo files in the Photoshop Express Organizer on the Library page.

The **Library** displays all of the media files that you've loaded to Photoshop.com, including files you are backing up on online (page 189) and photo and video files you are linking to on other sites (page 188).

In the **Library**, your media files are displayed as thumbnails in the **Media Browser**, a workspace very similar to the **Media Browser** in the Elements Organizer (**Chapter 15**).

And, like the Elements Organizer, the media files you've loaded to Photoshop.com are stored in **Albums** (listed along the left side of the web page). As in the Elements Organizer, when you click to select an **Album** in this list, the **Media Browser** displays only the media files assigned to that **Album**.

These **Albums** correspond to the **Albums** displayed on your Gallery page (as illustrated at the top of the facing page). You can designate in the **Library** which of these **Albums** are open to the public and which can be viewed only by people you invite to view them. To access an **Album's Public** or **Private** settings, **double-click** on its listing on the left column of the **Library** Web page.

## Upload photos and video to Photoshop.com

To upload photos or videos to your **Library**:

1   Click the **Upload** button in the upper right of the **Library** page.

An Explorer or Finder browse window will open on your computer. Browse to the photos or videos you'd like to upload. (By holding down the **Shift** or **Ctrl** key as you click to select your photos, you can choose several in one swoop.)

When you've gathered your entire set, click **Open**.

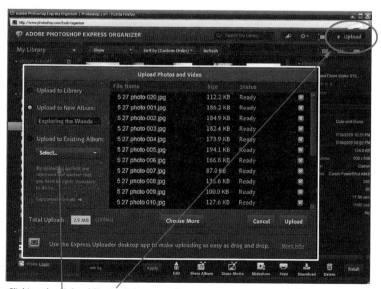

Clicking the Upload Photos link opens a browser to your computer's files. Once you've selected your photo or photo set, you'll be prompted to save the files to a new or existing Album.

Once you've uploaded your photos to an Album, Photoshop.com will offer to display them using one of its basic or Plus Membership slideshow templates.

**2**  Assign your media files to an **Album**.

As illustrated on page 185, you may send your files to an existing **Album** or select the option to **Upload to a New Album**.

Click **Upload**.

Your files will load to Photoshop.com.

**3**  Share or create a **Slideshow**.

Once your media files have uploaded to the site, the site will offer you the option of **Sharing** your files or creating a **Slideshow**.

**If you select Share,** the site will generate an e-mail inviting your guests to view media as a slideshow or as a web page.

**If you select Slideshow,** the site will invite you to select a slideshow template. Once you've selected a template and clicked **Finish**, your slideshow will be available for viewing in your **Gallery**.

Although you can load your photo and video files using the site's tools, both Premiere Elements and the Elements Organizer also include tools for loading slideshows, photos and media to Photoshop.com directly from the programs.

Premiere Elements' tools are described on page 212 of **Chapter 18, Share Your Movie**.

One of the Organizer's **Share** tools is described on the facing page.

## Create an Online Album with the Elements Organizer

An **Online Album**, created in the Elements Organizer, can be a very cool way to display your photos.

I've used them to create some very attractive, professional-quality online portfolios of my design work.

To create and load an **Online Album** from the Organizer, select **Online Album** from the *What would you like to share?* options under the **Share** tab, as illustrated on the following page.

1   The first screen will offer you the option of selecting an existing **Album** from your Organizer's catalog or creating a new **Album**.

If you have photos selected in your **Media Browser** when you launch this tool, they will automatically be added to your new **Album**.

To send your slides to Photoshop.com, select the **Share To** option, as illustrated on the right. Click **Next**.

2   A new screen will appear displaying a preview of your **Online Album** slideshow, using one of the program's very cool online templates. If you'd like to assign another template to your slideshow, you can browse through nearly 30 options.

When you're happy with the slideshow template you've applied, click the **Done** button at the bottom of the panel.

The slideshow and photos will be uploaded to your **Photoshop.com Gallery**.

The Share Online Album button under the Organizer's Create tab launches a wizard for creating an online slideshow.

You may gather your slideshow photos by selecting an existing Album or, if you've selected photos in your Media Browser prior to starting this Share tool, you may create a new Album.

Select the option to Share to Photoshop.com and click Next.

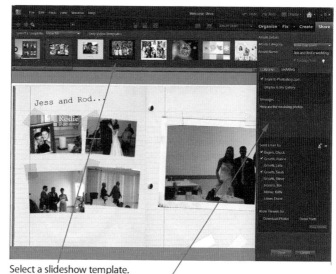

Select a slideshow template.

Type a message and send an e-mail to your contacts.

## Remove photos and Albums

**Albums** and individual media files can be easily deleted from your Photoshop.com **Library**.

> **To remove individual media files**, click to select the photo or video file in the Photoshop.com **Library Media Browser** (or select several by holding down the **Ctrl** or **Shift** key as you click) and either click the **Delete** button in the lower right of the Web page or **right-click** and select **Remove from Library**.

> **To remove an Album**, click to select the **Album** from the listing along the right side of the Photoshop.com Library Web page and then click the **X** to the right of the listing, as in the illustration.

Delete individual media files by right-clicking on them or by selecting them and clicking the Delete button along the bottom of the Library Web page.

An option screen will appear. Checking the option to **Also permanently delete all items in this album from the library** will remove both the album and the media files inside it.

If you do not check this option, the **Album** will be removed but the media files will remain in your Photoshop.com **Library**.

When you delete an Album, you have the option of removing the media also or leaving it in your Library.

## Link to photos on other sites

A very cool feature on Photoshop.com is its ability to link its **Library** with other sites on which you have photo galleries.

To link to these other sites, click on the **My Library** link at the top of the Photoshop.com interface.

The **Other Sites** you can link to, listed along the bottom left of the interface, are **Facebook**, **Flickr**, **Photobucket** and **Picasa**.

Clicking the **Login** link for each of these sites, and agreeing to the required permissions, will make the photos you have posted to any of these sites visible in your **Photoshop.com** photo browser.

You can even use the **Photoshop Express** tools (page 190) to touch up these photos.

Your Photoshop.com Library can include photos ported in from your other gallery sites.

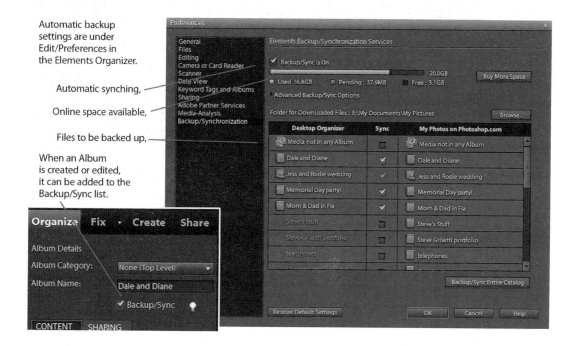

Automatic backup settings are under Edit/Preferences in the Elements Organizer.

Automatic synching,

Online space available,

Files to be backed up,

When an Album is created or edited, it can be added to the Backup/Sync list.

## Back your files up online

A key function of the Organizer is its role in backing your files up to **Photoshop.com**. The options and settings for this back-up tool can be found in the Organizer's **Preferences**, under the **Edit** drop-down on the Menu Bar, under **Back-up/ Synchronization**.

This **Back-up Synchronization** option screen will list the **Albums** you have designated for back-up as well as the option to back-up your media files not included in any **Albums**.

When the **Backup/Sync Is On** option is checked, at the top of the panel, the program will automatically store a copy of all of the media files you've indicated to your Photoshop.com account, usually backing up your files when your computer is idle.

Your free Photoshop.com account includes 2 gigabytes of storage space. A **Plus** account ($49.99 per year) increases your storage space to 20 gigabytes. Additional premium plans offer up to 500 gigabytes of online storage space. You can find the option to upgrade your account under the **My Account** link in the Elements programs and by clicking the **Buy More Space** button on this preferences panel.

Whenever you create a new **Album** (by clicking the green **+** button at the top of the **Albums** panel), you will be given the option to set it to **Backup/Synchronize** to **Photoshop.com**, as in the illustration above. This **Album** will then automatically be added to your Organizer's **Backup/Synchronization** list. (See **Designate an Album for online back-up** on page 177.)

For more information on creating **Albums** and storing media in them, see **Assign and search with Albums** on page 175 of **Chapter 15, The Elements Organizer.**

## Touch up your photos with Photoshop Express

When you select a photo in the Media Browser and click the Edit button at the bottom of the Web page, the selected photo will open in Photoshop Express, a set of simple tools for touching up or playing with your photos.

**Photoshop Express** is an online set of basic tools built into Photoshop.com for cleaning up and touching up your photos.

To access this tool kit, click to select a photo in the Photoshop.com **Photo Browser** from either the **Library** or an **Album**.

Along the bottom of the **Photoshop.com** interface you'll see a listing of actions, as illustrated at the top left. Click on the **Edit** button to open Photoshop Express.

The photo you've selected will open in an editor workspace.

Along the left side of this workspace will be displayed a kit of basic touch-up tools – many of which you'll recognize from the similar tools in Photoshop Elements.

When you select any tool, its potential effects will be displayed as thumbnails along the bottom of the interface, as illustrated above.

To apply the effect, just select the thumbnail that best represents the change you're looking for

After editing your photo, you can then select, from the panel on the lower right of the interface, the option to **Reset** the photo, **Cancel** all changes and return to the **Photo Browser** or **Finish** and save the changes.

Photoshop.com

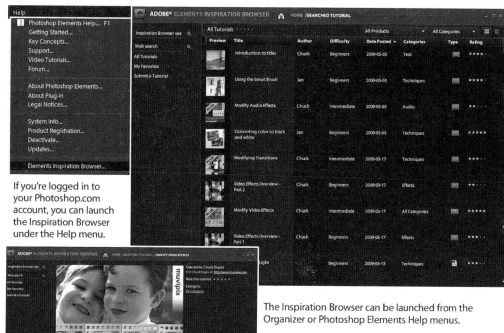

If you're logged in to your Photoshop.com account, you can launch the Inspiration Browser under the Help menu.

The Inspiration Browser can be launched from the Organizer or Photoshop Elements Help menus.

It offers a number of video tutorials and articles by some of the world's top training sites, including Muvipix.com, as well as tutorials contributed by individual users.

## Access the Inspiration Browser

Your **Photoshop.com** account includes links to an ever-growing library of tutorials and articles for making the most of the site as well as for using Premiere Elements and Photoshop Elements.

These tutorials have been created by Adobe and by several of the world's top trainers, including **Muvipix.com**.

Basic tutorials for using the **Photoshop.com** site can be found by selecting the **Tutorials** link from under the **Help** button in the upper right of your **Photoshop.com** home page.

These video tutorials will show you how to create a **Photoshop.com** account, how to share your photos and how to use the photo touch-up tools available on the site.

A much larger library of tutorials for a number of Adobe products is available through the **Inspiration Browser**, an area of **Photoshop.com** that's only accessible from within Adobe's products.

You can reach the **Inspiration Browser** one of two ways from Photoshop Elements, Premiere Elements and/or the Elements Organizer:

From the **Welcome Screen for Photoshop Elements or Premiere Elements**, click on the **Tips & Tricks** link;

From within Photoshop Elements or the Elements Organizer programs, select the **Inspiration Browser** option from the **Help** menu.

Once you're in the **Inspiration Browser**, you can search or browse the entire library of tutorials for Adobe products, either by clicking the **All Tutorials** link or by typing a subject in the **Quick Search** window.

Clicking **All Tutorials** displays a listing of the entire library of animated tutorials and articles. The two drop-down menus on the upper right of the interface will filter the list by product and/or by subject.

By clicking on the appropriate column header, the tutorials can also be sorted by Rating, Difficulty, Author, etc.

If you feel so inspired, you can even contribute a tutorial of your own to this site (in either PDF or FLV format).

Adobe reserves the right to edit your submission, and you'll receive no monetary compensation for your contribution – but you will have the privilege of knowing you've contributed to a growing library of accumulated knowledge.

## Access additional Plus Members Only content and templates

Finally, subscribing to **Photoshop.com** as a **Plus Member** gives you access to additional templates, themes and effects for both Photoshop Elements and Premiere Elements. (**Plus Memberships** start at $49 per year.)

This additional content is integrated into each program and loaded automatically. And, as long as you've got an always-on Internet connection and you're signed on to **Photoshop.com** when your program launches, this content will appear in programs automatically as you work. The templates and effects are identified by a yellow or blue banner that appears over the upper right corner, as illustrated on the facing page.

The drop-down menus under Effects, Transitions, Titles, Themes, Clip Art and Disc Templates include links to additional online Photoshop.Com Plus Member content.

Links to this additional content can be found under **Themes**, **Transitions**, **Effects**, **Titles**, **Clip Art** and **Disc Templates**.

Similarly, under the **Share** tab on the Elements Organizer, if you select the option to create an **Online Album** (as described in **Create an Online Album with the Organizer**), you will find listed, among the **Album Template** categories, a link to **Photoshop.com Plus Members Only**.

In Photoshop Elements, this additional content can be found among some of the templates listed under the various tasks under the **Create** tab.

For instance, click on the **Create** tab in the **Editor** workspace and then select a **Project** (a **Photobook**, for instance). Click on the **Artwork** button.

Among the options in the drop-down menu on the **Content** palette, you'll find a listing for additional Photoshop.com artwork for **Plus Members Only.**

Once you apply a theme, template, effect or transition from **Photoshop.com**, you'll need to wait a few moments for it to download from the site to your computer. But, once it downloads, it should perform just as the themes, templates, effects and transitions that were included with the program.

Plus Member Only templates, transitions and effects are indicated with a banner over the upper right corner.

**Add Menu Markers**

**Select a Menu Template**

**Customize Your Menu's Background and Music**

**Customize Your Menu's Text**

**Add Media to a Menu's "Drop Zone"**

Chapter 17

# Create Disc Menus

## Authoring your DVDs and BluRay discs

Once you've finished your Premiere Elements video project, you'll want to share it in the most attractive package possible.

Premiere Elements includes over 60 templates for creating DVD and BluRay disc menus for your videos. And it includes tools for customizing them in a variety of ways!

Although the DVD and BluRay menu authoring system in Premiere Elements isn't as advanced as it is in many standalone disc menu authoring programs (like Adobe's Encore), you can do a surprising amount to personalize your disc menus just by using Premiere Elements' library of disc menu templates and basic menu customization features.

Once you've applied and customized your disc menus, you can then create a DVD or BluRay disc using the options under the **Share** tab, as described in **Output a DVD or BluRay Disc** on page 209 of **Chapter 18, Share Your Movie.**

## Add Menu Markers to your movie project

The **Set Menu Marker** tool is a very important part of the DVD and BluRay disc authoring process in Premiere Elements.

The **Menu Markers** you place on your timeline or sceneline will link to scene buttons on your disc's menu pages.

Selecting **Set Menu Marker** from the blue **Markers** drop-down menu (as in the illustration above) on the **Timeline/Sceneline** panel creates a **Menu Marker** on your timeline or sceneline at the position of the **CTI** (Current Time Indicator) playhead. You can later drag this marker to any other position on the timeline if you'd like.

When this **Menu Marker** is first created, a **Menu Marker** option screen will open. (You can reopen it at any time by double-clicking on the menu marker on your timeline or by **right-clicking** on your clip on the sceneline (**Ctrl+clicking** on a Mac) and selecting the **Set Menu Marker** option.) This screen includes a number of options for creating your marker.

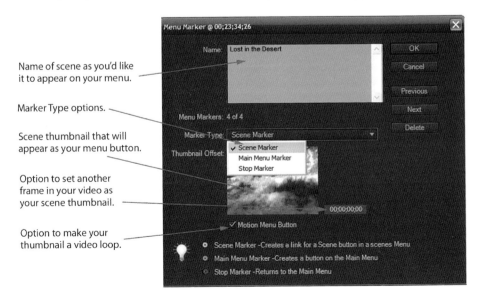

Name of scene as you'd like it to appear on your menu.

Marker Type options.

Scene thumbnail that will appear as your menu button.

Option to set another frame in your video as your scene thumbnail.

Option to make your thumbnail a video loop.

As indicated at the bottom of the **Menu Marker** option screen, there are three different types of **Menu Markers** (as selected under the **Marker Type** drop-down), each with its own unique function.

Green Scene Menu Markers will be linked to buttons on your DVD or BluRay disc's **Scene Menu** page(s).

Blue Main Menu Markers will be linked to buttons on your DVD or BluRay disc's **Main Menu** page(s).

Red Stop Markers stop your movie's playback and return your viewer to your disc's **Main Menu** page. By using these **Stop Markers**, you can create a disc with a number of short movies on it, your viewer returning to the main menu at the end of each.

Type a name for your marker in the space provided. This name will automatically appear as the name of the linked button on your disc's main or scene menu.

The image from your movie displayed in the **Thumbnail Offset** is what will appear as your menu button on your menu page.

Changing the timecode that appears to the right of this thumbnail – either by typing in new numbers or by clicking and dragging across the numbers – will change which frame from your video is displayed as the button link. (Changing this thumbnail image will *not* affect the location of the marker itself on your project's timeline.)

Checking the **Motion Menu Button** checkbox will cause your button to appear as a short video loop rather than a freeze frame from your video.

Clicking and dragging over the timecode for the Thumbnail Offset changes the thumbnail image that is displayed for the Menu Marker on your DVD or BluRay disc menu.

For more information on how to create and use **Menu Markers**, see my *Steve's Tips* article "DVD Markers," available on the products page at Muvipix.com.

## Add Menu Markers automatically

If you've not yet added menu markers to your project's timeline or sceneline, you will be prompted to create menu markers when you launch the **Templates** workspace. You can then opt to return to the **Edit** workspace and manually add menu markers – or you can select an option to automatically create markers.

- **If you choose to automatically create menu markers**, you'll be prompted with a number of options, including the option to set markers based on time, scene, etc.

- **If you choose not to include menu markers**, the program will generate a menu with a main menu page only and only a **Play** button linking to the beginning of your movie.

- **If you choose not to include menu markers at this time** and you later add a menu marker, a scene menu will automatically be generated for you at that time.

Premiere Elements offers dozens of high-quality, easily customizable menus for your DVDs and BluRay discs in a wide variety of categories.

## The basics of adding a Disc Menu template

Premiere Elements comes bundled with over 60 standard and hi-def disc templates, in categories from Entertainment to Travel to Sports to Kids to Birthdays and Weddings – from playful to serious to silly to artistic.

Many of these templates come complete with audio and/or video loops that add life to your menus. These menus are indicated with a little media icon on the upper right corner.

Also, many of these templates include a "drop zone," a designated area on the menu page into which you can place a video clip or still. (More about that on page 202.)

## Apply a DVD or BluRay disc menu template

To apply a disc menu template to your project, select the **Disc Menus** tab and click on the **Templates** button.

Premiere Elements includes a library of over 100 DVD and BluRay disc templates in 15 different categories.

If you have a **Plus** premium membership with **Photoshop.com** and an always-on Internet connection, you can find additional templates by selecting the **Plus Members Only** option from the drop-down menu in the **Templates** panel. (For more information on Photoshop.com Plus Membership, see page 192 of **Chapter 16, Photoshop.com**.)

When you initially launch this workspace, the **Monitor** will be replaced by the **Disc Layout** panel, and the Tasks panel will display the library of disc menu templates.

You can filter this list by selecting a category of templates from the panel's category drop-down menu. You can then browse the templates in the panel or go directly to a specific template by selecting it from the second drop-down menu (which displays **Show All** by default).

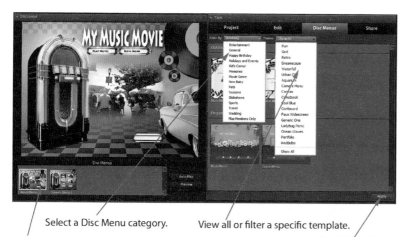

Select a Disc Menu category.  View all or filter a specific template.

The Disc Layout panel will display your applied template
with links to your Menu Markers automatically generated.

Apply template.

Once you've selected a template by clicking on it, click the **Apply** button in the lower right of the panel.

Once you've applied a template, the **Disc Layout** panel will display your entire menu set as thumbnails in the **Disc Menus** preview window at the bottom of the panel. The program will add as many extra pages as necessary to accommodate all of your scene and main menu markers.

The **Disc Layout** panel's main window will initially display your main menu, as illustrated above. If you click on any of the other menu page thumbnails in the panel running along the bottom of the **Disc Layout** window, that menu page will appear in the big **Disc Layout** window.

As mentioned in **Add Menu Markers**, on page 196, the names you give to your main and scene menu markers will appear as the names of the scene links and main menu links on your disc menus. (To change this text, **double-click** on a text box or scene link, as described at the bottom of page 201.)

To see your menu system in action and test drive the links embedded in it, click the **Preview** button.

An important note about this **Disc Layout Preview**: The purpose of the preview is to allow you to see a *representation* of how your menu elements will come together and to allow you to test the navigation buttons.

*It is not meant to be a representation of the **quality** of your final menu template*. And, in fact, you'll probably be a bit disappointed with the quality of the picture onscreen. **Preview** is merely an opportunity for you test your navigation buttons.

So don't panic. Once your project is rendered and encoded as a disc, the quality will be up to DVD or BluRay standards.

Click on background in Disc Layout panel to open background replacement options.

Click to replace background of menu with your own still or video loop.

Set at which point in clip to begin video loop.

Click to replace or add your own audio loop.

Set duration for video/audio loop (max of 30 seconds).

Background has been selected.

Menu previews.

Click Auto-Play to create a disc with no menus.

Click to play preview of menu

## Customize your menus

Adobe has made it very easy to customize your menu pages right in this **Disc Menus** workspace. As a matter of fact, once you've applied a template in the **Disc Menus** workspace, as described above, the Tasks panel will change from a view of the templates library to the menu customization workspace.

Which customization options are available in this panel depends on which elements you have selected on the **Disc Layout** panel.

- **If you have the menu background selected** in the **Disc Layout** panel, the **Tasks** panel will display options for replacing the menu background with a still, video and/or audio clip.

- **If you have a block of text selected** in the **Disc Layout** panel, the **Tasks** panel will display options for customizing the text's font, style and color.

- **If you have a menu button selected** that includes a thumbnail image selected in the **Disc Layout** panel, the **Tasks** panel will display options for replacing or customizing the thumbnail image as well as options for customizing the accompanying text's font, style and color.

## Customize a menu background

When you have the menu page background selected in the **Disc Layout** panel, the **Tasks** panel will display options for replacing the background with a still or video, and/or replacing or adding a music or audio clip, as illustrated at the top of this page.

To add or replace any of these elements, click the **Browse** button and browse to a video clip, photo or audio clip on your computer.

(Note that some menu templates include foreground graphics that will remain, even if you swap out the background, and may partially obscure your new background. If you'd prefer not to include these graphics in your menus, you may want to start with one of the Generic templates, such as the one in the General set.)

Above, a new background clip has replaced the template background. When a text block is selected, the customization menu changes to a font, style and text color selection option screen. (Double-click on a text block to customize the content.)

If you're using a video clip as your menu background:

- You can use the **In Point** timecode (either by dragging your mouse across the numbers or by playing to a particular point and then pausing) to set your video loop to begin at a specific point in the clip.

- You can set the **Duration** of the video loop for any length up to 30 seconds.

You can also add or swap out audio loops that play as your menus are displayed. And, likewise, you can set the **In Point** for your audio clip such that the audio loop begins playing at any point in the song or clip.

To revert back to your menu's default background, music or sound, click on the appropriate **Reset** button.

## Customize your text

Double-click on a text block to edit or replace the text.

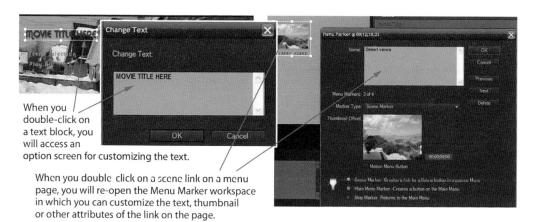

When you double-click on a text block, you will access an option screen for customizing the text.

When you double-click on a scene link on a menu page, you will re-open the Menu Marker workspace in which you can customize the text, thumbnail or other attributes of the link on the page.

Two Main Menu pages customized from the same Disc Menu template (Faux Widescreen).

## Customize your text styles

When you click to select a text block in the **Disc Layout** panel, the text customization workspace will display in the Tasks panel.

When a scene button or text block is selected, the Disc Menus panel will display options for customizing the text font, style and thumbnail with a still or video loop (motion menu).

Using this menu, you can change the font, font size and even color of the text.

The **Apply to All Text Items** button will apply your current font and text style to all of the text that appears on this menu page.

Once you've customized the look of your text, you can also customize its position on the menu page.

Click on the text block or button on the **Disc Layout** monitor and drag it to where you'd like it to appear.

## Add your media to a menu page "drop zone"

A number of disc menu templates include a "drop zone" – a designated area on the template into which you can drag your own pictures or videos.

You'll find examples of this in the Movie Genre/Fairytale template and the Wedding/Outdoor Wedding template.

To add a custom still or clip to one of these templates, click the **Organize** tab to open the Premiere Elements **Media** panel, then drag your clip or still from this panel onto the menu page in the **Disc Layout** panel, into the area labeled "**Add Your Media Here**."

(If the clip you want isn't displayed in the **Media** panel, click **Get Media** and browse to it first.)

Once you've placed your clip into the menu, drag the corner handles to resize and position it on the menu page.

The "**Add Your Media Here**" graphic is usually a guide for placement, based on the other graphics in the template. In most cases, you can size and place your new background clip wherever you'd like on the page.

An exception would be the General/Fun template, in which you'll need to size and position your clip pretty precisely in order for it to display in the template's provided picture box.

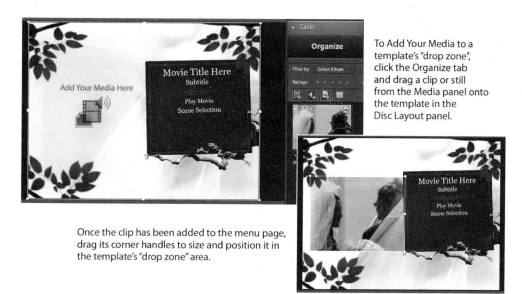

To Add Your Media to a template's "drop zone", click the Organize tab and drag a clip or still from the Media panel onto the template in the Disc Layout panel.

Once the clip has been added to the menu page, drag its corner handles to size and position it in the template's "drop zone" area.

**Share to a DVD or BluRay Disc**

**Share Your Movie Online**

**Share Your Movie as a Podcast**

**Share Your Movie as a Computer File**

**Share Your Movie to a Portable Device**

Chapter 18

# Share Your Movie
## Outputting from Premiere Elements 10

Once you've finished your video masterpiece and – if you're planning to output it to disc – you have applied and customized your disc's menus, you're ready to output your video so that you can share it with the world.

There are a number of ways to output from Premiere Elements, and a surprisingly large number of formats you can output to.

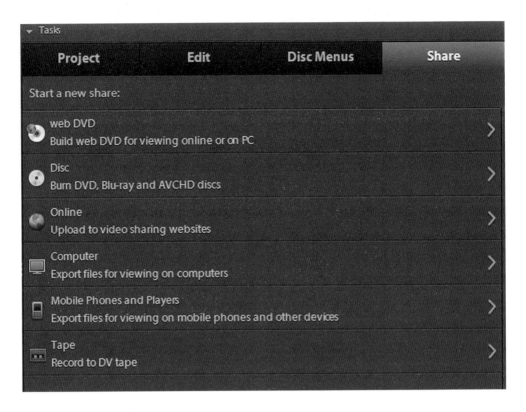

A click on the **Share** tab reveals a list of six output destinations for your video, each of which offers recommended formats and settings for your output as well as more advanced settings for more advanced users.

The **Share** destinations are:

**Web DVD** – Build a Web DVD for Viewing Online or on a PC (as discussed on page 208)

**Disc** – Burn DVD and BluRay Discs (as discussed on page 209)

**Online** – Upload to Video Sharing Websites (as discussed on page 212)

**Computer** – Export Files for Viewing on Computers (as discussed on page 214)

**Mobile Phones and Players** – Export Files for Viewing on Mobile Phones and Other Devices (as discussed on page 219)

**Tape** – Record to miniDV or HDV Tape (as discussed on page 220)

(If all six options don't show in this **Share** panel, you'll need to resize the panel by dragging on the boundaries between it and the adjoining panels.)

In most cases, these destination names do a pretty good job of leading you to the correct output settings. The exception is the **Computer** destination – which can create files that can be played on a computer, some portable devices and online and can be used to create video clips that can be used in other Premiere Elements projects.

## The file-sharing interfaces

No matter which destination and format you choose, there are basically four ways to share your files:

- Burn to a disc.
- Upload directly to a Web site.
- Output your file to your computer's hard drive.
- Output your video to an external device, like a phone or portable media player.

The **Upload to a Web site** options use a similar interface:

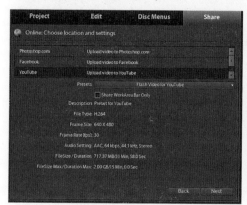 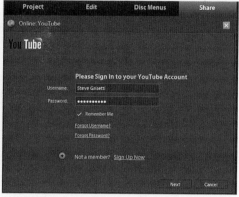

Select an online destination and preset. Click Next.   On the logon screen, sign in and then click Next.

Likewise, the options to **save a file to your Computer** and to **save for later uploading to another device** use a similar interface:

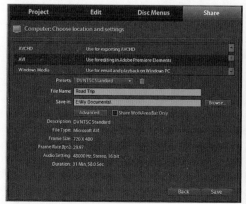 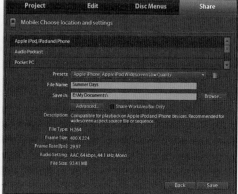

Select a preset, name your file and browse to a location. The saved files can then be moved to another device.

The methods for **burning to a disc** and **sharing to tape** are detailed in their respective sub chapters, later in this chapter.

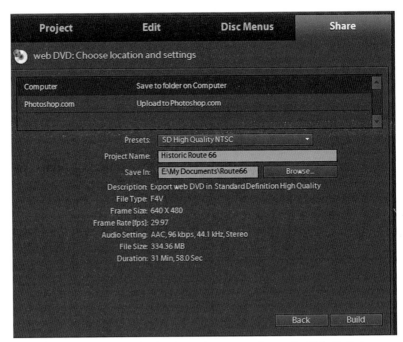

The WebDVD destination, under the Share tab, creates an interactive Web site that functions just like a DVD – complete with menus!

## Output to a Web DVD

**Web DVDs** are interactive FLV and HTML files that can be posted to a Web site or saved to a computer, but function like conventional DVDs – complete with main menus, scene menus and scene buttons!

**Web DVD** menus are created using **Menu Markers** and **Disc Menu** templates, as we describe in **Chapter 17, Author DVDs and BluRay Discs**. However, because of the way they are produced, **Web DVD** files play on a Web browser (Internet Explorer, Safari, etc.) rather than on a traditional DVD or BluRay disc player.

To create a **Web DVD**:

1   Select the **Web DVD** destination under the **Share** tab.

2   On the **Web DVD** option page, select the **Computer** or the **Photoshop.com** option.

3   Name your file and browse to select a **Save In** location or log in to Photoshop.com.

4   Click the **Make File** button.

A folder of files will be saved to the location you've selected.

Post this entire set of files to a Web site. The **Web DVD** is launched when a viewer goes to the site, connecting to the **Play_webDVD.html** file.

Likewise, to play the **Web DVD** on a computer, launch the **Index.html** file with your Internet browser.

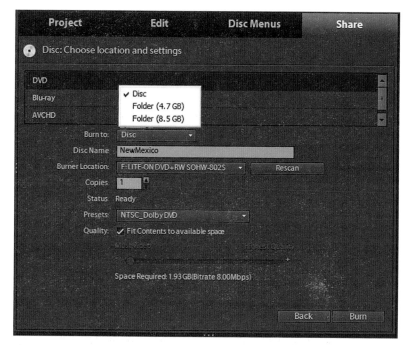

The Disc destination under the Share tab includes the options to burn directly to a disc or to save your DVD files to a folder on your hard drive.

## Output to a DVD or BluRay Disc

Probably the most common way to output a movie from your Premiere Elements project is to burn a DVD or high-definition BluRay disc.

Premiere Elements will burn to both single-layer and dual-layer discs and to both standard DVD and BluRay formats. (The program automatically scans your system to see which disc burner hardware you have and if you have a disc in the drive.)

Click to select the disc type you want to create from the listing at the top of the panel.

1    If you are burning a DVD, the **Burn To** drop-down menu will allow you to select the option to burn directly to a disc or to burn your DVD files to a folder on your hard drive for either a single-layer or dual-layer disk.

2    Type the name for your project in the space provided. (This is more important if you plan to burn your disc files to a folder on your hard drive for later burning to a disc, as described on page 210.)

3    Click the **Burn** button.

As a rule of thumb, you can fit about 70 minutes of full-quality video onto a standard (4.7 gigabyte) DVD at full video quality and about double that onto a dual layer disc.

A BluRay disc (which can store 25 gigabytes of data) can hold about two hours of hi-definition video, while a dual-layer BluRay disc can hold about twice that.

If you put more than these recommended capacities on a disc, Premiere Elements will automatically reduce the quality of the video as needed if you have the **Fit Contents** option checked. (This reduced quality may not be noticeable unless you try to squeeze considerably more content onto the disc than the optimal capacity.)

## Increase the odds for disc creation success

In a perfect world, outputting a disc from Premiere Elements would be as simple as selecting the options at this screen and hitting the **Burn** button.

Unfortunately, your computer's operating system is something of a living, continually evolving environment, with programs constantly at war for control over your hardware. And failures to burn directly to a disc with this program are somewhat common – which can be quite frustrating if you've waited hours for the program to encode your disc files, only to have it suddenly throw up an error code at the last minute.

If this is a problem for you (and you'll know because the operation will fail in its very last stages), the simplest solution is to go to the **Burn To** drop-down menu and select the option to burn your files to a **Folder** on your hard drive rather than directly to a disc.

Once these DVD or BluRay files are created, you can then easily use your computer's disc burning software (Nero, RecordNow, etc.) to burn the VIDEO_TS folder that the program creates to a DVD or BluRay disk. This process is detailed in **The "Burn Disc" Workaround** in the **Appendix**.

This may seem like an unnecessary workaround at first, but there are a number advantages to using this two-step method for creating discs and very few liabilities. (It certainly doesn't take any more time, and it only adds a few clicks to the process.)

If nothing else, it makes outputting several copies of your disc easier, since creating each will be a simple matter of burning this same VIDEO_TS folder to another disc (a process which takes only a few minutes).

## The challenge with home-burned DVDs

Although this is becoming less of an issue as home-burned DVDs and BluRay discs have grown in popularity, it's important to realize that not all DVD and BluRay players can play home-burned discs. This is because the process used to create commercial discs (pressing) is very different than the process you use to create discs on your computer (a chemical process).

Manufacturers have recognized the growing popularity of creating home-burned DVDs and BluRay discs and have been making their players more and more compatible with them. But be prepared for the occasional friend or client who simply can't play a disc you've created!

And, if for no other reason than because direct burns to disc can so commonly fail, we at Muvipix recommend regularly creating your DVDs with this two-step process. It really is worth the minimal extra effort to ensure the job gets done.

You can also increase the odds your disc burn will go smoothly and that your disc will be compatible with every possible DVD or BluRay player by using high-quality media.

Verbatim and Taiyo Yuden are two very reliable disc brands. Store brands, and even other popular name brands, can be a bit iffier. In our not-so-humble opinion, the little extra expense you'll incur by using one of these two quality brands will be more than offset by the knowledge that you'll get the best possible results and compatibility from them.

Also, *NEVER* stick a label onto your DVD or BluRay disc!

Labels can throw the spin and balance off when the discs are loaded into a player and the glue and label can damage the media itself. If you'd like to customize your discs, we recommend that you buy printable discs and use a good inkjet printer with disc printing capabilities. Epson and HP make very nice printers with this feature for under $100.

## Burn an AVCHD disc

A new feature in Premiere Elements 10 is the ability to burn an AVCHD disc.

AVCHD is an advanced compression format for high-definition video. Premiere Elements includes options for burning both 1920x1080 and 1440x1080 AVCHD formats. (As discussed on page 221, these two formats are essentially the same resolution – one using square and the other using anamorphic pixels to create their video images.)

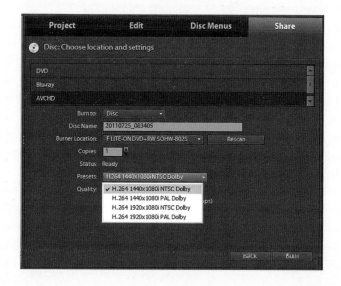

Many current BluRay disc players are capable of playing AVCHD video. However, before you distribute this format of disc, you should ensure your audience's disc players are AVCHD compatible.

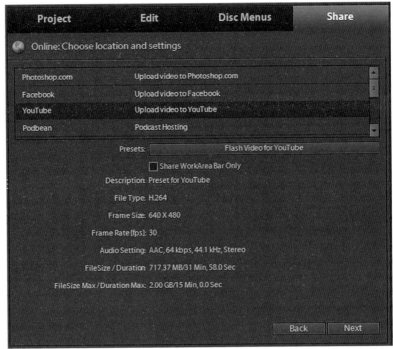

Online options let you load your video directly to a Web site, Photoshop.com, Facebook and YouTube – or to output a podcast to Podbean!

## Upload to a Web site or create a podcast

The **Online** output option is designed to transcode your video to another file format and upload it directly to a web site (including YouTube) in just a few easy steps.

1   Select the **Online** destination.

2   On the **Online** option page, select your online destination: **Photoshop.com, Facebook, YouTube** or **Podbean**.

   **Podbean.com** is a site for hosting podcasts – video or audio files that you post online on a regular basis and that your viewers can subscribe to and receive automatically.

   For more information on posting and subscribing to podcasts, see my *Steve's Tips* article "Podcasting with Premier Elements," on the products page of Muvipix.com.

3   Click the **Next** button.

4   Some output screens includes the option to automatically notify your friends that you've posted this video.

   Other site's output pages may require you to log on to your site or authorize Premiere Elements to access your account.

5   Click **Next** to post your video.

The **Presets** drop-down menu, by default, will display the optimal file format for uploading. You can also drop-down this menu and select another preset, if you'd like.

To export only the segment of your project defined by the **Work Area Bar**, check the **Share Work Area Bar Only** option. (For more information, see **Output a segment of your video using the Work Area Bar** on page 80 of **Chapter 6, Edit Your Video in Timeline Mode**.)

As with many automatic functions, this one may not always work as smoothly as it should. (This has less to do with Premiere Elements than with the fact that sites, like YouTube, are constantly changing the way they handle uploaded files.) And, if you have trouble getting your video directly to a site, you can click the **Back** button in the lower right corner of the panel and create your file using the **Computer** output option instead.

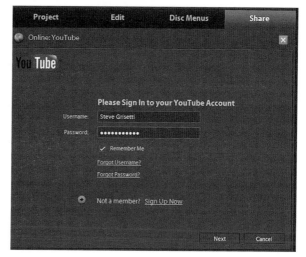

Once your video is created and saved to your hard drive (usually as a WMV, MOV or H.264/MP4 file) you can manually upload it to your site using the site's upload interface or using FTP utility software, such as the excellent, free FileZilla or the equally easy-to-use Easy FTP (as we discuss on page 230 of the **Appendix**).

Meantime, go the Premiere Elements's **Edit/Preferences/Web Sharing** and ensure that **Automatically Check for Services** is checked. (Or click **Manually Check for Services** for good measure.) This is one way of making sure that the Premiere Elements Web site interface is as up to date as possible.

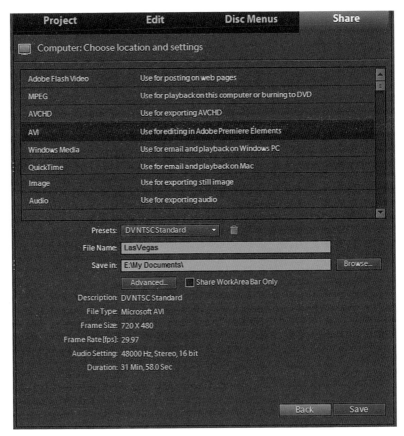

The most versatile output destination is Personal Computer, which allows you to save your video as a Flash, MPEG, AVCHD, DV-AVI, Windows Media, Quicktime (MOV) file, a still photo or an audio file.

## Output a file to your computer

The description following the option to share to a **Computer** is a little misleading.

With this option, you can not only create videos for viewing on a computer but you can use also save to any of the major video output formats or to a still or audio only file. In other words, you can not only output videos from this option for PC-based viewing, but you can also create videos that you can then post to web sites, send by e-mail, etc.

Also, this is where you'll find the option to output the all-important **DV-AVI** (full quality video) file (for PCs ) and **DV-MOV** (on Macs), as explained in **Exporting video to be used in another editing project** on page 215.

Next to each file format listing in this **Share** output category is a descriptor explaining the best use for that particular file format. You'll find a detailed discussion of each file format in detail in **Video output formats** on page 220. Once you've selected your output option, click the **Browse** button to select a location on your computer for your file to be saved.

To export only the segment of your project defined by the **Work Area Bar**, check the **Share Work Area Bar Only** option. (For more information, see **Output a segment of your video using the Work Area Bar** on page 80 of **Chapter 6, Edit Your Video in Timeline Mode**.)

## Output video for use in another video project

### For standard video

If you'd like to export your video project – or even a portion of your project – so that you can import it into another Premiere Elements standard video project on a Windows computer, your best **Share** format is the **DV-AVI**, available as a **Computer Share** output option.

The project you use this type of video file in should use the **DV project preset**, as we discuss in **Chapter 2, Start a New Project**.

The MacIntosh equivalent to the **DV-AVI** file is the **DV-MOV**. To output a **DV-MOV** file from your project, go to the **Share** tab and select the **Computer** destination. From the options listed, select **MOV** and, from the preset drop-down menu, select **DV**.

The file you output will have a **.mov** suffix.

### For high-definition video

If you'd like to export your video project – or a portion of your project – from a high-definition project for use in another high-definition project, your best **Share** option is the **MPEG** using the **1440x1080i** preset, available as a **Computer Share** output option.

The project you use this type of video file in should use the **HDV project preset**, as we discuss in **Chapter 2, Start a New Project**.

### Why these are the ideal Share options

The ideal source file for Premiere Elements and the universal language for PC-based video editors is the **DV-AVI**s. **DV-AVI**s maintain virtually all of the quality of your original source footage. Further, when used in a project using the **DV project preset**, your video will not need rendering until you apply an effect or transition to it.

For Premiere Elements, the ideal source format for high-definition video is the **HDV** format. When used in a project using the **HDV project preset**, this video will not need rendering until you apply an effect or transition to it.

### Working on a long project in short pieces

You'll often find a longer project much easier to work on in shorter pieces. Doing this can minimize system lugging and maximize program responsiveness as well as reduce the likelihood that you'll run into problems when you try to export your video as a DVD or BluRay disc.

Once your segments are completed and output to the appropriate format, open a new project – using the appropriate project preset – and combine the segments into a final mix.

To export only the segment of your project defined by the **Work Area Bar**, check the **Share Work Area Bar Only** option. (For more information, see **Output a segment of your video using the Work Area Bar** page 80 of **Chapter 6, Edit Your Video in Timeline Mode**.)

## Create Web video presets for WMVs and MOVs

For some strange reason, Adobe elected not to include output presets for creating Web quality versions of Windows Media and Quicktime files. Fortunately, if you need WMV or MOV files for use on your Web site or to stream over your company's intranet, creating your own Web quality presets is not terribly hard.

Video created using this method can be uploaded using FileZilla, as described on page 230 of our **Appendix**.

### Create a Web-ready WMV file

1   Go to **Share/Computer** and select the **Windows Media** output option with the **HD 720p 30** setting.

2   Click the **Advanced** button.

3   On the **Export Setting** screen that opens, set the following options:

**On the Video tab:**
**Codec:** Windows Media Video 9
**Encoding Passes:** One          **Bitrate Mode:** Constant
**Frame Width:** 320 pixels       **Frame Height:** 240 pixels

You may need to click on the chainlink button to un-constrain the proportions.
For widescreen video, set **Frame Height** and **Frame Width** to 425x240.

**Frame Rate:** 30 fps          **Pixel Aspect Ratio:** Square Pixels (1.0)
**Maximum Bitrate:** 500 Kbps   **Image Quality:** 50%   **Keyframe Interval:** 3 seconds

When you click **OK**, you'll be prompted to name your project preset. Type in "Video for Web." These project settings will then be permanently available as a preset under the WMV presets.

### Create a Web-ready MOV file

1   Go to **Share/Computer** and select the **QuickTime** output option with the **NTSC DV** setting.

2   Click the **Advanced** button.

3   On the **Export Setting** screen that opens, set the following options:

**On the Video tab:**
**Video Codec:** H.264          **Quality:** 65%
**Frame Width:** 320            **Frame Height:** 240

You may need to click on the chainlink button to un-constrain the proportions.
For widescreen video, set **Frame Height** and **Frame Width** to 425x240.

**Frame Rate:** 15 fps          **Field Type:** Progressive          **Aspect:** Square Pixels (1.0)
**Key frame** every 15 frames   **Limit Data Rate** to 550 Kbps

**On the Audio tab:**
**Audio Codec:** AAC

When you click **OK**, you'll be prompted to name your project preset. Type in "Video for Web." These project settings will then be permanently available as a preset under the MOV presets.

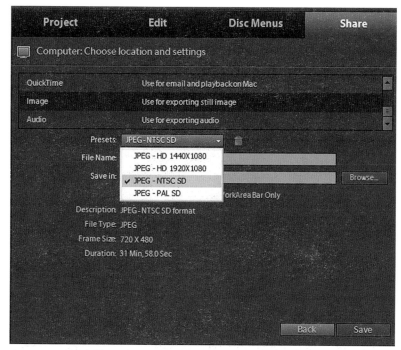

The option to Share an Image includes presets for a number of JPEGs stills.

## Output a still of your current video frame

The **Computer** destination in Premiere Elements includes the option to **Share** your video as an **Image**. This **Image** option includes presets for saving the current frame of your video as a **JPEG** or a segment of your video as an **Animated GIF** (at a variety of frame sizes).

The **JPEG** output option here makes a great alternative to the **Freeze Frame** option available within the program's editing interface (discussed on page 102 of **Chapter 8, Edit with Monitor Panel Tools**) since it includes more options for customizing the settings of your output, including the option to save it as a **JPEG** rather than a BMP file.

The one challenge with these presets is that they are all anamorphic. In other words, they all produce stills with non-square pixels. This is fine if you're outputting a still that you want to use in a video, since video frames are constructed of non-square pixels.

However, in many cases, you'll want to output a still that can be printed out or used on a Web page. And, if you were to use one of these anamorphic presets, your printed photo would appear distorted or stretched unnaturally tall or wide.

The sidebar on page 218 shows you how to create your own preset for outputting an image that uses square rather than non-square pixels.

## Create a custom JPEG output preset

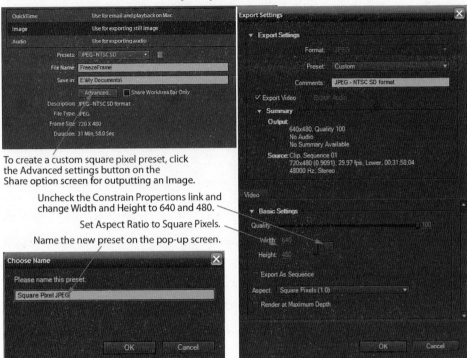

To create a custom square pixel preset, click the Advanced settings button on the Share option screen for outputting an Image.

Uncheck the Constrain Proportions link and change Width and Height to 640 and 480.

Set Aspect Ratio to Square Pixels.

Name the new preset on the pop-up screen.

The **Image** output presets included with Premiere Elements are designed to produce a still photo that can be used in a video. Because of this, these options will produce a still that is composed of anamorphic – or *non-square*, video pixels. This means that, if you use one of these stills on a Web site or in a print project, it will produce an oddly distorted picture.

For this reason, we recommend that, in addition to the pre-loaded presets, you create an additional, *square pixel* output preset for your general-purpose JPEG frame grabs.

1   Go to the **Share** tab and select the **Computer** destination option.

From the list of options that appear on the options page, select **Image**.

2   Set the **Preset** drop-down to **JPEG- NTSC SD.**

Click the **Advanced** button.

3   In the **Export Settings** options panel, in the **Video** section, set the **Aspect** drop-down to **Square Pixels (1.0)**.

Click the chainlink button to turn off **Constrain Proportions** and set the **Width** to 640 and the **Height** to 480.

Click **Okay.**

4   In the **Choose Name** screen, type the name "**Square Pixels**," then click **Okay** to save it.

The **Square Pixels** option will now be available in the Presets drop-down whenever you use Share to create a JPEG still of your current video frame.

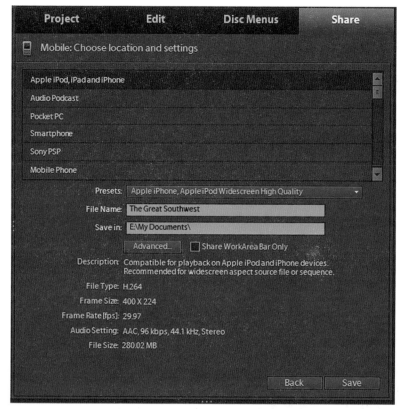

Output options to mobile devices include a variety of presets for many popular devices, including H.264/MPEG4s for both video and audio and WMVs for Smartphones.

## Output to a mobile phone or portable video player

Selecting the option to share to **Mobile Phones and Players** takes you to a screen on which all of the major mobile devices for viewing video – from iPods, iPads and Pocket PCs to Smartphones and even Sony PSPs. (You may need to scroll the list to see the entire listing.)

Whichever you choose, the program will recommend the optimal format for that device.

You can, however, select other options from the **Preset** drop-down menu or click the **Advanced** button for deeper settings. You'll find a detailed discussion of each file option in **Video output options** on page 220.

Type your file name in the space provided and click the **Browse** button to select the location on your computer in which you'd like to save your file.

You can also save directly to many devices connected to your computer.

To export only the segment of your project defined by the **Work Area Bar**, check the **Share Work Area Bar Only** option. (For more information, see **Output a segment of your video using the Work Area Bar** on page 80 of **Chapter 6, Edit Your Video in Timeline Mode**.)

When you've selected all of the appropriate output options, click the **Save** button in the lower right corner of the panel.

## Output to tape

Now that DVDs and BluRay discs have become so universal and popular, it's much less common to send completed projects back to tape. However, there's still no better way to archive your finished project in a high-quality, re-editable format than to send it back to the same device that created it in the first place.

Remember, miniDV and HDV camcorders and video editing programs speak the same language. This means that saving your finished project back to tape is a cheap and convenient way to store 13 gigabytes of high-quality, re-editable video data.

## Video output formats

The main video output formats available under the various **Share** tab destinations are **DV-AVI**s (Windows only), **MPEG**s, **WMV**s (Windows Media Video – available on Windows computers only), **FLV**s (Flash video), **MOV**s (Quicktime video – including **DV-MOV** files) and **MP4**s. You'll find at least one of these options offered at each of the **Share** output destinations.

Here's a brief discussion of the best uses for each:

**DV-AVI**s are the "purest" and highest quality standard definition video output format available on a Windows PC, though the files are considerably larger than the other options. (It's the file format that a miniDV camcorder produces when the video is captured to a PC.) This format is also your best output choice for creating an editable video output if, for example if you are outputting your project, or a segment of your project, for use as part of another video editing project, as discussed on page 215. **DV-AVI**s are the universal language of PC-based video editors, the perfect balance of compression and file size for working with on a computer. They are created by selecting **Share/Computer/AVI** with a DV preset. (This option is not available in the MacIntosh version of Premiere Elements. However, the **DV-MOV**, discussed below, is virtually identical.)

**DV-MOV**s are the MacIntosh equivalent of the **DV-AVI**s. This is the format that is created when miniDV footage is captured to a MacIntosh computer. Like the **DV-AVI** on a Windows machine, the **DV-MOV** file will load into a standard-definition Premiere Elements project without needing to be rendered. **DV-MOV**s are created by Premiere Elements when you select **Share/Computer/QuickTime** with a DV preset.

**MPEG**s are a high quality video delivery format that comes in a number of forms. This means that they play at nearly the quality of your original footage. (A form of **MPEG**, called a VOB file, is the format used to store the video on DVDs.) For standard definition video, you should think of **MPEG**s primarily as a delivery format rather than an editing or re-editing format. For high-definition video editing, however, a form of **MPEG** called the **M2T** is the ideal video source format, as discussed below.

**M2T** videos are high-definition video files. This is the format that is created when you capture video from an HDV camcorder or download video from an AVCHD camcorder, as discussed in **Chapter 3, Get Media into Your Project**. To output an **MTS** video from Premiere Elements, select **Share/Computer/MPEG** with the MPEG2 1440x1080 preset. This is the ideal format to output if you plan to use your output in another high-def project, as discussed on page 215.

**AVCHD** is an advanced format for outputting your video. Its H.264 codec delivers high-quality video in a highly-compressed file. To output an AVC file, select **Share/Computer/AVCHD**. At this output option you'll find presets for creating **M2T**s and **MP4**s in a variety of resolutions as well as video formatted for playback on Tivo, Vimeo and YouTube.

**Windows Media (WMVs), QuickTime (MOVs)** and **Adobe Flash Video (FLVs)** are generally considered to be Web formats. This is because they are highly compressed and often have reduced frame rates and frame sizes (most often 320x240 pixels – about one-fourth the size of a standard video frame) in order to produce the smallest, most efficient file sizes.

Currently, **WMVs** (Windows Media Video) are considered the Internet standard for web-based video. This is because Microsoft's ubiquitous presence means that virtually every computer in the world has the necessary software to play them.

**MOVs** (Apple's Quicktime format) are also fairly ubiquitous (though PC users must load the Quicktime player manually the first time they play one). Apple's efforts to continually improve the format means that often they can produce a higher quality video than **WMVs**.

**FLVs** (Flash video files) are gaining tremendous popularity on the internet, thanks to video sharing sites, like YouTube, which appreciate the fact that **FLVs** produce excellent video quality while using minimal Internet bandwith. The biggest challenge with **FLV** files is that they require a special player to view them – a player most people don't have on their computers. In order for **FLVs**, then, to be playable on your Web site, your Web page must have a Flash player embedded in it (as YouTube does).

**WMVs, MOVs** and **FLVs** can be created by selecting a **Share/Computer** option. However, these formats are also present in a number of other **Share** destination. **FLVs**, for instance, will automatically be your output for video shared to YouTube, while forms of **MOV** and **WMV** will be your automatic **Share** outputs for some portable devices.

These formats are available in various forms through each of the other **Share** destinations, including both the **Online** and **Mobile Phones and Players** destinations.

In fact, if you are having problems uploading directly to a **YouTube, Facebook** or **Photoshop.com** or if you're unhappy with the results using the **Share/Online** tools in Premiere Elements, you can manually produce your own Web videos and then manually upload them, as discussed on page 216.

## Understand non-square pixels

Pixels are the tiny blocks of color that make up your digital photos and video.

For reasons that date back to the early days of television, the vast majority of television video is made up of **non-square pixels**. This is true for PAL as well as NTSC video.

In standard NTSC video, these pixels are approximately 90% as wide as they are tall. Thus a 720x480 pixel video image becomes a 4:3 aspect ratio video (the equivalent of a 640x480 *square-pixel* video). A widescreen video is made up of the *same number of pixels* – however, because these pixels are 120% as wide as they are tall, a 720x480 pixel widescreen video has a 16:9 aspect ratio.

Many high-definition camcorders shoot their video in 1440x1080 *non-square* pixels. This produces exactly the same size video as a cam that shoots in 1920x1080 *square* pixels.

However, while it is also available to manually produce your own video files for your portable devices using the **Share/Computer/ AVCHD** destination, as described at the bottom of the facing page, the destinations listed under **Share/Mobile Phones and Players** are pre-configured to produce video and audio files that are optimized for the devices listed.

Some of the output options under **Share/Mobile Phones and Players** include presets for creating video files at various resolutions and quality levels. If you select the **iPod, iPad and iPhone** option, you will find presets ranging from **iPhone/iPod Low Quality** (which produces a 400x300 pixel video with a .34 Mbps bit rate) to **iPad Widescreen High Quality** (640x360 pixel video with a 1.1 Mbps bit rate).

**"Real World" System Requirements**

**Optimizing Windows Operating Systems**

**Recommended Computer Maintenance**

**Video File Conversion Tools**

**Video Capture Tools**

**Audio Editing Software**

**FTP Utilities**

**The DVD Burn Workaround**

**Premiere Elements Keyboard Shortcuts**

# An Appendix
## More things worth knowing

## Recommended "Real World" computer specs

The rule of thumb for figuring out the minimum computer specs to run a program is to take the minimums recommended by the manufacturer and double them.

That's certainly true in the case of Premiere Elements, for which Adobe vastly understates the power needed to run this program effectively.

Virtually any computer made in the last couple of years should run Premiere Elements just fine – although laptops, which tend to be built for portability rather than power, often cost about 50% more for the same power as a desktop equivalent. They also tend to have limited hard drive space and smaller monitors than desktops. So, if you do decide to edit on a laptop, be ready and willing to put down the extra cash for the necessary power and hardware.

Here are our recommended *minimum* specs for running Premiere Elements as you edit standard DV and HDV footage.

- A dual-core processor running at at least 2.6 ghz per core
- 2-4 gigabytes of RAM
- 128 mb video card, ideally ATI or nVidia technology
- 100 gigabytes of free hard drive (This allows plenty of room for captured footage and scratch disk space)
- An ASIO (Audio Stream Input/Output) supported sound card
- DVD burner
- 19" monitor set to at least a 1280x1024 display (dual-monitors are even better)
- IEEE-1394/FireWire/iLink connection

AVCHD video editing specs

AVCHD, a highly compressed high-definition format, requires considerably more power to work with successfully.

For that reason, we recommend these minimums for AVCHD video editing.

- A fast quad-core or i7 processor
- 4 gigabytes of RAM
- 128 mb video card, ideally ATI or nVidia technology
- A DVD or, better, BluRay DVD burner
- 19" monitor set to at least a 1280x1024 display
  (a 22" widescreen or dual 19" monitors are even better)
- IEEE-1394/FireWire/iLink connection

The addition of a second hard drive (either internal or external) – one dedicated to your video projects and source files – can give your workflow a tremendous boost.

Not only does it often make the process go more smoothly, since it keeps the video data flow and scratch disk files separate from your operating system's paging files, but it also reduces fragmentation of your video files.

If you install an internal second hard drive for video editing, make sure to set it up in your BIOS (the set-up that displays before the operating system launches, when you first start up your computer) as well as in your operating system.

And, whether you use an internal or external drive, make sure that the drive is formatted NTFS rather than FAT32 (which all drives are factory formatted as by default) in order to avoid FAT32's file size limitations.

Converting a drive from FAT32 to NTFS is easy and you won't lose any data already on the drive in the process. The instructions for doing so are available all over the Web, including on the Microsoft site.

## Features not included in the Mac version

Although the Mac and the Window versions of Premiere Elements function virtually identically, there are a number of features available on the PC that are not available on the Mac.

The Windows version includes 87 video effects and 23 audio effects. The Mac version includes 72 video effects and 19 audio effects. The following **Video Effects** are not included in the Mac version:

**Blur & Sharpen**: Anti-Alias, Ghosting

**Distort**: Bend, Lens Distortion

**Image Control**: Color Pass, Color Replace

**Keying**: Blue Screen Key, Green Screen Key, Chroma Key, RGB Difference Key

**Transform**: Camera View, Clip, Horizontal Hold, Vertical Hold

The following **Audio Effects** are not included in the Mac version:

**Denoiser, Dynamics, Pitch Shifter, Reverb**

The Windows version includes 107 video transitions. The Mac version includes 50 video transitions.

The following **Video Transitions** are not included in the Mac version:

**3D Motion**: Curtain, Doors, Fold-Up, Spin, Spin Away, Swing In, Swing Out, Tumble Away

**Dissolve**: Dither Dissolve, Non-Additive Dissolve, Random Invert

**Iris**: Iris Points, Iris Shapes, Iris Star

**Map**: Channel Map, Luminance Map

**Page Peel**: Center Peel, Peel Back, Roll Away

**Slide**: Band Slide, Center Merge, MultiSpin, Slash Slide, Sliding Bands, Sliding Boxes, Swap, Swirl

**Special Effect**: Direct, Displace, Image Mask, Take, Texturize, Three-D

**Stretch**: Cross Stretch, Funnel, Stretch, Stretch In, Stretch Over

**Wipe**: Band Wipe, Checker Wipe, CheckerBoard, Clock Wipe, Paint Splatter, Pinwheel, Radial Wipe, Random Blocks, Random Wipe, Spiral Boxes, Venetian Blinds, Wedge Wipe, Zig Zag Blocks

**Zoom**: Cross Zoom, Zoom, Zoom Boxes, Zoom Trails

## Optimize XP for video editing

XP is a pretty efficient operating system, and you may not have any problems running Premiere Elements on it without modification.

However, to squeeze the most juice out of your XP machine:

1   Right-click **My Computer** and select **Properties** to bring up your **System Properties** panel.

Under the **Advanced** tab, click the **Settings** button at **Performance**.

Under the **Visual Effects** tab, uncheck all except (to keep the XP look) "Use visual styles on windows and buttons."

Under the **Advanced** tab, make sure **Processor Scheduling** and **Memory Usage** are set to programs.

2   Click on **Virtual Memory.**

For the most part, XP does a very good job of allocating Virtual Memory, so checking **System Managed** will work fine.

Some people, however, recommend setting the VM manually. If you'd prefer, set both the **Minimum** and **Maximum** to 1½ times your RAM load. Then click **Set.**

3   Open **My Computer.**

Right-click on each of your hard drive(s) and choose **Properties.**

At the **Hard Drive Properties** window, uncheck both **Compress Drive to Save Space** and **Allow Indexing Service**.

(The Indexing Service, which logs every new file added to your drive, frequently interrupts intensive processes such as captures.)

You will need to reboot your system for these settings to take effect.

## Optimize Vista and Windows 7 for best performance

Most computers made in the past year can edit with Premiere Elements on an up-to-date version of Vista or Windows 7 without modification. However, if you'd like to squeeze more juice out of your Vista or Windows 7 system, there are some mostly aesthetic features you can shut down:

1   From **Start**, go to your **Control Panel**, then select **Performance Information and Tools**.

In the dialog box that opens, select **Indexing Options** in the left pane.

Click the **Modify** button in the **Indexing Options** dialog box and click the **Show All Locations** button at the bottom of the Indexed Locations dialog box. For best performance, turn off **Indexing** on all of your drives.

2   Click **Start**, right-click on **Computer**, and click **Properties**.

Click **Advanced System Settings**. Select the **Advanced** tab.

Under **Performance**, click **Settings**.

Uncheck these options:

- Fade or slide menus into view
- Fade or slide tooltips into view
- Fade out menu items after clicking
- Show shadows under menus
- Slide open combo boxes
- Slide taskbar buttons
- Use a background image for each folder type

Close the **Performance Options & System Properties** dialogs.

3   The **Windows Sidebar** provides instant access to gadgets. However, the **Sidebar** is one of Windows' top resource suckers. Turn it off and your computer will sigh in relief.

4   Turn off the **Aero** interface!

Right-click on your desktop, select **Properties** and then **Appearance**. Select the **Basic Look**.

It may not be quite as cool as Aero's semi-transparent windows, but it's well worth the trade-off in performance. And, in two days, you probably won't miss it anyway.

## Maintain your Windows computer

Your computer doesn't just *seem* to run slower as it ages, it often *does* run slower. This is due to the accumulation of data 'sludge' on your hard drive – temp files and bits and pieces of programs you've installed and/or removed from your system. Additionally, any time spent on the Internet loads your hard drive with cache files, cookies and, often, spyware.

The regimen below will help keep your computer running like new. Think of it as cleaning the dust bunnies out of your system.

And, at the very least, keep Windows updated and check the Apple site regularly to **ensure you have the latest version of Quicktime**!

Quicktime plays an important role in Premiere Elements' functions, and a surprising number of problems (such as video not displaying in the monitor while capturing) can be cured simply by loading the newest version.

**Do this weekly:**

1  Go to **Microsoft Update** and make sure Windows is updated. In fact, don't just check for priority updates, click on the **Custom** button and look for other updates (like RealTek drivers and updated hardware drivers) that may not update automatically. (In Vista and Windows 7, select the option to **Restore Hidden Updates**.)

   You may not need everything offered, but it certainly doesn't hurt to have them.

2  Make sure your **virus software** is updated. (If your virus software isn't set to run in the middle of the night, waking your computer from sleep for a virus scan, you also may want to do a regular virus scan.)

   And, every once in a while, go to the Web site for your virus software and make sure you have the latest *VERSION* of the anti-virus software. You may have the latest virus definitions added automatically – but, if you're still using last year's version of the software, you could still be vulnerable.

3  Install the excellent (and free!) **Spybot Search & Destroy** and **Spyware Blaster** to clear off and block spyware. (Update them before you use them, and regularly check their Web sites to make sure you're using the latest versions before you run them.)

   You can pick both up from the links on this page:
   http://savemybutt.com/downloads.php

4  Run the free, excellent, easy-to-use tool **Advanced SystemCare Free** to tune up your registry and clear off temp and other files that are just taking up space. This program also is available at:

   http://www.iobit.com/advancedwindowscareper.html

5  Run the **Defragmenter** on all of your hard drives.

6  And don't forget to back up your files (at least the **My Documents** folder) regularly!

   The one piece of hardware on your computer that absolutely *WILL* eventually fail is your hard drive. If you're lucky, you'll have replaced your computer before then. But if not – *please* remember to back up your files regularly.

**Do this monthly:**

1  Check your graphic's card's manufacturer's site, your sound card's manufacturer's site and, if applicable, the **RealTek** site to make sure your drivers and firmware are up to date. Also, double-check the Apple site to ensure you have the latest version of **Quicktime**.

2  Secunia offers a free (for personal use) application that will automatically keep all of your computer's software updated – or remind you when it needs to be done.

   To download it, go to **http://secunia.com/**

   From the **Products** menu, select **Personal Software Inspector (PSI)**.

3    Go to your web browser and clear the cache.

In Internet Explorer, you'll find the option for doing this right under the **Tools** drop-down.

Older versions and other browsers (including Firefox) keep them under **Tools** and in **Internet Options**.

You can leave the cookies – but do delete the **Temporary Internet Files**. Accumulate enough of them and they will slow down your entire computer system.

## Valuable free or low cost tools and utilities

### Windows video conversion tools

All video may  look the same and sound the same, but it actually comes in many flavors, formats and compression systems (codecs).

Premiere Elements, on Windows computers, is built around a DV-AVI workflow. (DV-AVIs are AVI files that use the DV codec.) This means that DV-AVIs flow easily through it and place the least strain on the program and, ultimately, your system. Not all AVIs use the DV codec, and many AVI videos (such as video from still cameras) can cause real problems for Premiere Elements.

**A good rule of thumb is that, whenever possible, use DV-AVIs as your video source files.** (On Macs, the ideal format is the DV Quicktime file.)

A number of free or low-cost programs will convert your files. Here are some Muvipix favorites.

Additionally, we have included in this list software for converting AVCHD files to more conventional HDV.

AVCHD are highly compressed files and can prove to be pretty challenging to work with on even the more powerful personal computers.

Converting AVCHD to HDV can make for a much less intensive high-definition video editing experience.

### Windows MovieMaker

If you've got a Windows-based computer, **Windows MovieMaker** is already on your system. Despite being a rather limited video editor, **MovieMaker** can handle a wider range of video formats than Premiere Elements (including, for instance, video from still cameras). It therefore makes an excellent tool for converting many video formats into more standardized DV-AVIs.

To convert a video into a DV-AVI with **MovieMaker**:

1    Import the video into a **MovieMaker** project and place it on the timeline.

2    From the **Main Menu** select **File/Save Movie File**.

A dialog box will open.

3    Select the option to save to **My Computer,** then click **Next**.

4    On the next option screen, name your new file and select/browse to a folder to put the file in.

Click **Next**.

5. On the next option screen, click the link that says **Show More Choices**.

   There will be three radio buttons to choose from.

6. Select **Other Settings** and, from the drop-down menu, select **DV-AVI**. Click **Make Movie**.

NOTE: **Windows Live MovieMaker**, the new, online version of **MovieMaker** included with Windows 7, will *not* output DV-AVIs.

To convert AVIs from still cameras to DV-AVIs for use in Premiere Elements, the best free alternative solution is **MPEG Streamclip**, as discussed below.

For converting MOVs to DV-AVIs, use **Super** or *Quicktime Pro*.

## MPEG Streamclip

A great tool for easily converting MPEGs and VOB files (DVD video files) to more Premiere Elements-friendly DV-AVIs.

1. Select the option to open your VOB or MPEG file(s) with **MPEG Streamclip** from its **File** menu.

2. Open the **AVI/DivX Exporter** window from **File/Export to AVI**.

3. Set **Compression** to the **Apple DV/DVPRO_NTSC** (or **DV PAL**, if appropriate) codec.

4. Set **Field Order** to **Lower Field First**.

5. Change the default sound settings from **MPEG Layer 3** to **Uncompressed**.

6. If you have widescreen footage click on **Options** at the top right.

   Leave the **Scan Mode** as is but change the **Aspect Ratio** from 4:3 to 16:9.

If you would like to save these settings, click on the **Presets** button at the bottom left of then panel, then click on the **New** button to name and save your preset. The next time you run **MPEG Streamclip**, you can go directly to the **Presets** button and load your saved settings.

7. Click on **Make AVI** and choose a folder and filename for your DV-AVI file.

**MPEG Streamclip** is free from http://www.squared5.com

## Super Video Converter

**Super** can convert almost any video format to almost any other video format. The latest version of the program is capable of outputting both PAL and NTSC DV files.

To use **Super** to convert virtually any video to a Premiere Elements-compatible DV file:

1. Set the **Output Container** drop-down menu to DV.

   Leave everything else at its default setting.

2. To output a PAL video, ensure that *Video Scale Size* is set to 720:576
   To output an NTSC video, ensure that **Video Scale Size** is set to 720:480

3. Drag the video you want to convert from your Windows Explorer panel to the area indicated, just below the **Output** specs.

   Click **Encode**.

Your video will be created with a .dv suffix and should not require rendering in a standard Premiere Elements DV project.

**Super** is free – although finding the link to the download on its messy Web site can be very challenging.

It's available from www.erightsoft.com/SUPER.html

### Quicktime Pro

**Quicktime Pro** is a great tool to own if your input sources tend to be MOVs (Quicktime) files. These files include video from still cameras and many MP4s.

Not only will it convert these files to DV-AVIs but the program also includes some basic video editing functions.

**Quicktime Pro** is available for $29 from www.apple.com.

### Premiere Elements

Premiere Elements, especially current versions, can often do an excellent job of converting video. You can use the program to convert video from DVDs, hard drive camcorders and even HDV and AVCHD sources into more manageable DV-AVIs – a process that's particularly effective if you're mixing video from several sources.

Converting everything to DV-AVIs before mixing them into a final project will allow the program to work much more efficiently and with much less likelihood of problems.

To use Premiere Elements to convert your video, open a project (ensuring that the project presets match your source video), import your video into the project and place it on the timeline.

Click the **Share** tab, select click the **Personal Computer** destination and select the **AVI** output option as described on page 215 of **Chapter 18, Share Your Movie**.

### Virtual Dub

**Virtual Dub** is a terrific tool that should be on everyone's computer.

Less a conversion tool than a video processor, it will make many AVIs (including Type 1 DV-AVIs) compatible with Premiere Elements as well as converting many other file types to more standard, more editable video.

Converting your video into editable DV-AVIs with **VirtualDub** is as easy as opening your file in the program and then selecting the option to **Save As**.

Your newly saved AVI will be perfectly compatible with Premiere Elements!

VirtualDub is available from www.virtualdub.org.

### Free Video Converter from KoyoteSoft

**Free Video Converter** will convert AVCHD video into more manageable HDV MPEG2 with virtually no loss of quality.

1    Open your AVCHD file in the **Free Video Convertor.**

2   Set the output bit rate to 25000kbs.

3   Output your file.

The output file will be 1920x1080 MPEG2.

One downside is that, when you install it, the program will automatically install a search tool to your browser toolbar – but this toolbar can easily be removed using Windows Add/Remove Programs.

The program is available from koyotesoft.com/indexEn.html

### Other AVCHD converters

**AVCHD UpShift**, from NewBlue, will convert AVCHD video to more standard HDV (a hi-def MPEG .m2t).

**AVCHD UpShift** sells for $49.95 and is available from www.newbluefx.com/avchd-upshift.html

Another excellent AVCHD convertor is **VoltaicHD**. The program costs $34.99 and is available from www.shedworx.com/voltaichd

A great program for converting AVCHD to standard-definition DV-AVI, is **Corel VideoStudio Pro**, one of the best PC-based programs for working with AVCHD video.

The program sells for $59.99 and is available from www.corel.com.

### Capture utilities

In the event that Premiere Elements won't capture your video no matter what you do, these free or low-cost tools will capture miniDV and HDV as perfectly compatible video files.

WinDV (free from windv.mourek.cz/) – A great capture utility with a simple interface.

HDVSplit (free from strony.aster.pl/paviko/hdvsplit.htm) – A great capture utility for HDV video.

Scenalyzer ($30 from www.scenalyzer.com) – A low-cost capture utility with some great extra features.

Windows MovieMaker – Video captured from a miniDV camcorder into MovieMaker is perfectly compatible with Premiere Elements.

Nero – Sometimes Nero's presence on your computer is the *reason* you can't capture from Premiere Elements. However, if you've got it on your computer, you can use it to do your capture also.

If all else fails, you can use the software that came with your camcorder to capture your video. However, if this software will not capture your video as a DV-AVI (or MPEG2 for high-definition video) or convert to one of those formats, we recommend you convert your captured video using the software above, before you bring it into a Premiere Elements project, for best program performance.

### Our favorite free audio utility

Audacity (audacity.sourceforge.net) is, hands down, the best *free* audio editing software you'll find anywhere. Easy to use, loaded with preset audio filters and yet extremely versatile.

**Audacity** can convert audio formats as well as adjust audio levels and "sweeten" your audio's sound. You can also record into it from a microphone or external audio device and edit audio with it. A real must-have freebie that you'll find yourself going to regularly!

### FTP software

FTP software uploads files from your computer to a web site and downloads files from a site to your computer. There are many great applications out there.

Here are a couple of personal favorites.

FileZilla Client is the current favorite FTP utility of a number of Muvipixers. Efficient, dependable and easy-to-use, sending files to a Web site with **FileZilla** is as simple as dragging and dropping.

**FileZilla Client** is available free from filezilla-project.org.

Easy FTP (free from www.download.com and other sources) – Completely free and nearly as intuitive as **FileZilla**.

### Manually output a high-quality video for a video sharing site

If you prefer to manually output your video and then upload it with one of these FTP tools rather than use Premiere Elements' direct-to-site tools for YouTube, Facebook and Photoshop.com, the Muvipix.com team has come up with these very effective output settings:

From the **Share** tab, choose **Computer** and then **QuickTime/MOV**. Choose the DV preset and as a starting point and then click the **Advanced** button.

In the **Advanced** options window, set your output to the following. (You may need to turn off the chain/Constrain Aspect Ratio toggle or order to set the Frame Height/Width :

**Video Tab**
Video Codec: H.264
Quality: 100
Frame Width/Height: 1280x720
(For standard def video set it to
640x480 or, for widescreen, 640x360)
Frame Rate: 29.97
Field Type: Progressive
Pixel Aspect Ratio: square
Render at Maximum Depth: checked

**Audio Tab**
Audio Code: AAC
Output Channels: Stereo
Sample Rate: 44100

## The "Burn Disc" workaround

In a perfect world, you could put together a project out of any media, click the **Share** tab and burn it to a disc.

Unfortunately, for a variety of reasons – some related to Premiere Elements, most related to operating system drivers or program conflicts, this sometimes doesn't go as smoothly as it should.

There are three main reasons for a problem burning a DVD or BluRay disc:

- Challenging source video (including photos that are larger than the recommended 1000x750 pixels in size);
- Interfacing issues with your disc burner (often the result of a program like Nero not sharing the burner with other programs);
- Lack of computer resources (namely lack of available scratch disk space on your hard drive). This workaround eliminates most Burn Disc problems. And when it doesn't eliminate them, it at least helps you isolate where the problems are occurring.

The simplest solution is to break the process down into its elements and then troubleshoot each element individually.

1   **Create a "pure" AVI project.** Click on the timeline panel and then go to **Share/Personal Computer/AVI** (or **MOV** on a Mac) to create a DV-AVI or DV-MOV of your entire project.

   If this works, do a **Save As** to save a copy of your project, delete all of the video except this newly created AVI, then place the AVI on the timeline in place of the deleted video (the DVD markers should still line up).

   If you find that you are unable to create an AVI or MOV from your project, it could be that your photos are too large or you lack the resources to render the files (as discussed in step 3, below).

   Ensure that, whenever possible, your photos are no larger than 1000x750 pixels in size, as discussed in **Work with photos** in **Chapter 3, Get Media into Your Project.**

2   **Burn to a folder** rather than directly to a disc.

   Select the **Burn to Folder** option, as we discuss in **Output to a DVD or BluRay Disc** in **Chapter 18**.

   This eliminates the possibility that other disc burning software is interfering with communication with your computer's burner.

   Once the disc files are created, you can use your computer's burner software to burn the VIDEO_TS folder and its contents to a DVD or BluRay disc.

   If this doesn't work, it could be that your computer lacks the necessary resources, as discussed below.

3   **Clear space on and defragment your hard drive**. A one-hour video can require up to 50 gigabytes of free, defragmented space on your hard drive to render and process (depending on your source files).

   Even a "pure" AVI project can require 20-30 gigabytes of space.

Clear off your computer and regularly defragment it, per **Maintain Your Computer**, earlier in this chapter, and you'll reduce the likelihood of this being an issue. Assuming you've got an adequately powered computer and an adequately large hard drive in the first place.

## Need some Basic Training?

Want some help with the basics of Premiere Elements?

Want some free hands-on training?

Check out my free tutorial series **Basic Training with Premiere Elements** at Muvipix.com.

This simple, eight-part series will show you how to set up a project, how to import media into it, basic editing moves, adding transitions and effects, how to create titles, how to add and customize your DVD and BluRay disc menu navigation markers and how to export your finished video.

And did I mention that it's free?

To see the series, just go to http://Muvipix.com and type "Basic Training" in the product search box.

And while you're there, why not drop by the Community forum and say hi! We'd love to have you become a part of our growing city.

Happy moviemaking!

Steve, Chuck, Ron and the whole Muvipix team

# Keyboard shortcuts for Premiere Elements

These key strokes and key combinations are great, quick ways to launch features or use the program's tools without having to poke around the interface.

In virtually every workspace the arrow keys (Down, Up, Left, Right) will move the selected object in that direction. Shift+Arrow will move it several steps in one nudge.

Many of these shortcuts are slightly different on a MacIntosh computer. Usually the **Command**(⌘) key is used in place of the **Ctrl** key – although a number of keyboard shortcuts may not work at all.

## Program Controls

| | | | |
|---|---|---|---|
| Ctrl O | Open project | Ctrl X | Cut |
| Ctrl W | Close project | Ctrl C | Copy |
| Ctrl S | Save project | Ctrl V | Paste |
| Ctrl Shift S | Save project as... | Tab | Close floating windows |
| Ctrl Alt S | Save a copy | Ctrl Q | Quit program |
| Ctrl Z | Undo | F1 | Help |
| Ctrl Shift Z | Redo | | |

## Import/Export

| | | | |
|---|---|---|---|
| F5 | Capture | Ctrl Shift M | Export Frame |
| Ctrl I | Add Media | Ctrl Alt Shift M | Export Audio |
| Ctrl M | Export Movie | Ctrl Shift H | Get properties for selection |

## Media and Trimming

| | | | |
|---|---|---|---|
| I | Set in point | Page Up | Go to previous edit point |
| O | Set out point | G | Clear all in/out points |
| Q | Go to in point | D | Clear selected in point |
| Page Down | Go to next edit point | F | Clear selected out point |
| W | Go to out point | Ctrl E | Edit original |
| | | Ctrl H | Rename |

## Play/Scrub Controls

| | | | |
|---|---|---|---|
| Space bar | Play/stop | Shift Right | Step forward five frames |
| J | Shuttle left | Home | Go to beginning of timeline |
| L | Shuttle right | End | Go to end of timeline |
| Shift J | Slow shuttle left | Q | Go to in point |
| Shift L | Slow shuttle right | W | Go to out point |
| K | Shuttle stop | Page Down | Go to next edit point |
| Arrow Left | One frame back | Page Up | Go to previous edit point |
| Arrow Right | One frame forward | Ctrl Alt Space | Play in point to out point with preroll/postroll |
| Shift Left | Step back five frames | | |

# Appendix

## Timeline Controls

| | | | |
|---|---|---|---|
| Enter | Render work area | V | Selection tool |
| Ctrl K | Razor cut at CTI | Alt [ | Set Work Area Bar In Point |
| + | Zoom in | | |
| - | Zoom out | Alt ] | Set Work Area Bar Out Point |
| \ | Zoom to work area | Ctrl Alt C | Copy attributes |
| Ctrl A | Select all | Ctrl Alt V | Paste Attributes |
| Ctrl Shift A | Deselect all | Ctrl Shift / | Duplicate |
| , (comma) | Insert | Shift * (Num pad) | Set next unnumbered marker |
| . (period) | Overlay | * (Num pad) | Set unnumbered marker |
| Ctrl Shift V | Insert Clip | Ctrl Shift Right | Go to next clip marker |
| Alt [video clip] | Unlink audio/video | Ctrl Shift Left | Go to previous clip marker |
| Ctrl G | Group | Ctrl Shift 0 | Clear current marker |
| Ctrl Shift G | Ungroup | Alt Shift 0 | Clear all clip markers |
| X | Time stretch | Ctrl Right | Go to next timeline marker |
| Del | Clear clip (non-ripple) | Ctrl Left | Go to previous timeline marker |
| Backspace | Ripple delete (fill gap) | Ctrl 0 | Clear current timeline marker |
| S | Toggle snap | Alt 0 | Clear all timeline markers |
| C | Razor tool | | |

## Title Window Controls

| | | | |
|---|---|---|---|
| Ctrl Shift L | Title type align left | Alt Shift Left | Decrease kerning five units |
| Ctrl Shift R | Title type align right | Alt Shift Right | Increase kerning five units |
| Ctrl Shift C | Title type align center | Alt Left | Decrease kerning one unit |
| Ctrl Shift T | Set title type tab | Alt Right | Increase kerning one unit |
| Ctrl Shift D | Position object bottom safe margin | Alt Shift Up | Decrease leading five units |
| | | Alt Shift Down | Increase leading five units |
| Ctrl Shift F | Position object left safe margin | Alt Up | Decrease leading one unit |
| Ctrl Shift O | Position object top safe margin | Alt Down | Increase leading one unit |
| Ctrl Alt Shift C | Insert copyright symbol | Ctrl Up | Decrease text size five points |
| Ctrl Alt Shift R | Insert registered symbol | Ctrl Down | Increase text size five points |
| Ctrl J | Open title templates | Shift Up | Decrease text size one point |
| Ctrl Alt ] | Select object above | Shift Down | Increase text size one point |
| Ctrl Alt [ | Select object below | | |
| Ctrl Shift ] | Bring object to front | | |
| Ctrl [ | Bring object forward | | |
| Ctrl Shift [ | Send object to back | | |
| Ctrl [ | Send object backward | | |

## Media Window

| | | | |
|---|---|---|---|
| Ctrl Delete | Delete selection with options | End | Move selection to last clip |
| Shift Down | Extend selection down | Page Down | Move selection page down |
| Shift Left | Extend selection left | Page Up | Move selection page up |
| Shift Up | Extend selection up | Right | Move selection right |
| Down | Move selection to next clip | Shift ] | Thumbnail size next |
| Up | Move selection to previous clip | Shift [ | Thumbnail size previous |
| Home | Move selection to first clip | Shift \ | Toggle view |

## Capture Monitor Panel

| | | | |
|---|---|---|---|
| F | Fast forward | Left | Step back |
| G | Get frame | Right | Step forward |
| R | Rewind | S | Stop |

## Properties Panel

| | |
|---|---|
| Backspace | Delete selected effect |

## Narration Panel

| | | | |
|---|---|---|---|
| Delete | Delete present narration clip | Space | Play present narration clip |
| Right Arrow | Go to next narration clip | G | Start/Stop recording |
| Left Arrow | Go to previous narration clip | | |

Note that Premiere Elements also allows you to modify any of these keyboard shortcuts and to create your own shortcuts for dozens of other tasks. You'll find the option to do so under the Edit drop-down menu.

# Index